African Socialism in Practice

The Tanzanian Experience

edited by
Andrew Coulson

Spokesman

To the workers and peasants of Tanzania

First published in 1979
Second Impression 1982

ISBN 0 85124 269 3
Cloth

ISBN 0 85124 270 7
Paper

Published by Spokesman
Bertrand Russell House, Gamble Street, Nottingham
with the Review of African Political Economy

Printed by the Russell Press Ltd., Nottingham

AFRICAN SOCIALISM IN PRACTICE
The Tanzanian Experience

Contents

Preface

The case studies in this book have been selected from a mass of writing about the political economy of Tanzania which followed President Nyerere's essays in the late 1960s, Issa Shivji's *Tanzania: the Silent Class Struggle* of 1970, and the *Mwongozo*, or TANU Guidelines, of 1971. They have been chosen because they combine theoretical ideas with empirical discussion of what actually took place in the rural areas, in the parastatals, and in education, and so illustrate the problems facing leaders who try to introduce socialism in Africa.

The book also contains the *Mwongozo*, hitherto not readily available in English, and three policy papers by the President of the United Republic of Tanzania, Mwalimu Julius K. Nyerere. We are indebted to him for permission to reproduce them.

The book would not have been published in its present form without the help of Lionel Cliffe and Doris Cliffe, and the encouragement of the editorial working group of the Review of African Political Economy. Professor D.T. Edwards of the Project Planning Centre for Developing Countries, University of Bradford, England, arranged assistance for typing the manuscript. Ken Fleet of Spokesman Books made quick decisions when they were most needed. But the most important acknowledgements must be to the peasants, the workers, the thinkers, and the students of Tanzania, without whom these case studies could not have been written.

Andrew Coulson,
Bradford, May 1979

INTRODUCTION

Andrew Coulson

Tanganyika became independent in December 1961. The Arusha Declaration which committed the country to 'Socialism and Self-Reliance' was passed by the ruling party, TANU (the Tanganyika African National Union), in February 1967. During the first five years of Independence there had been little to differentiate the policies of Nyerere's government from those of other countries that became independent around the same time. Foreign companies were given tax concessions to invest in import-substituting industries. Attempts were made to speed up agricultural development through the use of irrigation and settlement schemes. The infrastructure, especially of roads and airports, was improved but still outward-looking. There was a rapid expansion of secondary schools and university facilities. The economy still depended, however, on a few hundred foreign-owned plantations and estates producing about half of the country's export earnings, and on more than two million peasant families producing most of their own food and in addition selling cash crops — cotton, coffee, cashew nuts, pyrethrum or tobacco — destined for world markets.

Colonial institutions were Africanised without great changes in what they did or how they did it. Parliament, the law, the civil service with its hierarchies and General Orders, the education system, even colonial economic planning were taken over and only slowly changed. The 1965 Interim Constitution, prepared following the merger of Tanganyika and Zanzibar in 1964 to form the United Republic of Tanzania, did, however, formally create a one party state.[1] During this period the country followed a foreign policy that won it respect outside its borders. President Nyerere travelled widely, and the consistency of his stances, especially over issues of independence in eastern and southern Africa, plus his willingness to give up immediate economic gain in favour of what he thought was morally right, made him second only to Nkrumah as a spokesman for Africa.

By the end of 1966 hopes of quick economic progress were dashed. The First Five Year Plan which started in 1964 assumed a substantial inflow of foreign aid. But 1964 and 1965 saw disputes with the United States, West Germany and Britain and the expected aid did not come. Industrial development plans relied on western multinational companies, but most of them preferred to invest in Kenya rather than Tanzania, and to serve the East African market from there. Agricultural policy had combined a 'transformation approach', involving capital-intensive schemes, with an 'improvement approach' based on helping small peasant producers. But the settlement schemes were social as well as agricultural failures and lost a lot of money; the difficulty with helping small-scale farmers was that usually richer peasants benefitted. Marketing cooperatives often proved corrupt, inefficient and easily manipulated by these richer peasants. In 1964, the army rebelled because it wanted more pay and a faster replacement of British officers. Independent trade unions were suppressed because their leaders wanted a faster take-over of top jobs, and university students were expelled because they refused to forego any of their privileges. Wages had risen, but the numbers in wage employment dropped, while the number of school leavers wanting jobs was rising sharply.

Nyerere and TANU could still draw on a reservoir of mass affection. But it was clear that to retain it they would have to undertake new initiatives. Nyerere chose to confront all his potential opponents together with a series of policy statements.[2]

The most important of these were the Arusha Declaration and the two papers *Education for Self-Reliance* and *Socialism and Rural Development,* all of which were approved by the Party during 1967.

The Arusha Declaration (a better translation of the swahili would be Arusha Resolutions) was an explicit commitment of the Party to socialism. Its slogan was 'Socialism and Self-Reliance'. The latter term was interpreted as freedom to implement development projects without depending on aid from the government or from abroad. The word 'Socialism' was used in several senses. It was given a positive meaning of national control of the commanding heights of the economy. The Declaration in fact was immediately followed by the nationalization of the banks, insurance companies, most of the sisal estates, grain milling, and the Tanzanian assets of seven multinational corporations. In the following years much of the wholesale and import-export trades plus buildings worth more than 100,000/- shillings were also nationalised.

The term 'Socialism' was also used in an essentially negative way to mean the absence of certain features: of exploitation, corruption and class divisions in society. The need for commitment and honesty among public servants was enshrined in a 'leadership code' which when passed by the Party prevented 'leaders' (senior civil servants, managers of nationalised industries and Party officials) from having more than one source of income, owning property for rental, or having shares or directorships in private companies. The political leadership, including civil servants as well as the President himself, took salary cuts, and Ministers were no longer provided with cars for private use at public expense.

Finally, the moral aspects of socialism were stressed:

> Socialism is a way of life, and a socialist society cannot simply come into existence. A socialist society can only be built by those who believe in, and who themselves practice, the principles of socialism . . .[3]

The Arusha Declaration was particularly directed against the contradictions facing educated Tanzanians who now held senior government sponsored jobs. *Education for Self-Reliance* was aimed at those who were still undergoing education. It was designed to counter the elitist and arrogant attitudes of many Tanzanians in secondary education as well as the all-too-obvious inability of many primary school leavers to get salaried jobs in urban areas. The paper emphasised that most of those leaving primary school could not go on to secondary education, while those leaving secondary school could not all go to university. So primary school syllabuses were to be revised to include training in agricultural and craft skills that would be useful to the vast majority who would not go on with schooling or get jobs in towns. In a similar way secondary school teaching would no longer just be an academic preparation for university entrance. Schools were also to be organised much more as democratic communities. The students themselves were to plan investments in profitable 'self-reliance activities' and the use of any profits that might be made. They would also be more integrated into village life than in the past. Arrangements would be made for school students to work on their parents' farms at peak periods of the agricultural year, and the school and its students would have a say in other aspects of planning and work in the village.

The third and last Presidential paper of 1967, *Socialism and Rural Development* (a better translation of the Swahili *Ujamaa Vijijini* would be 'Socialism in Villages') attempted to confront the kulaks — peasant farmers who were getting rich in agriculture by employing hired labour. The word *ujamaa* implies the sort of co-operative living that took place in the traditional extended family. And so in 'ujamaa villages' there would be no exploitation and no laziness. All would work together and work hard for the benefit of all. The product would be divided according to work done, with special provision for the old, the sick, and others who could not work. Eventually, through hard work and through the advantages of large-scale operations, prosperity would be shared by all who worked instead of just being enjoyed by a few. Nyerere stressed that participation in such villages must be voluntary, and that some areas of the country would present special problems. Thus implicit in **Socialism and Rural Development** is a recognition that, at least for a time, the new ujamaa villages would be islands of socialism in a hostile capitalist sea.

The Arusha Declaration and the related papers created a popular response second only to that of Independence itself. All over the country youth marched in support of the Arusha Declaration, and in late 1967 the President himself joined them, demonstrating that he was not only closer to the masses but also physically fitter than most of his cabinet colleagues.

In the following five years the position was consolidated. The nationalised banks, industries, and even trade and buildings, did not collapse. On the contrary in most cases the take-overs were extremely smooth. The British banks withdrew their expatriate staff, but within three months it was clear that the new National Bank of Commerce would survive. In the nationalised industries deals were made with the old owners. In most cases compensation was agreed and paid, and 'management agreements' were signed under which the old owners continued to manage their factories, but for a fee. Syllabus changes were made in the schools, and virtually all schools started or re-started farms. Ujamaa villages were registered, slowly at first but then in increasing numbers. The official statistics showed 809 villages by 1969, 1,956 in 1970 and 5,556 in 1972. Research at the time (such as that of Von Freyhold in the first of our case studies) indicated that few of these followed all the ideals of the President's paper. In particular many peasants decided to group themselves into villages as a means of getting preferential access to services provided by the government. Nonetheless the figures show that important changes were taking place in the rural areas. And in the end the leadership code was never openly opposed by the educated Tanzanians. This was partly because it was very difficult to disagree with it publicly. Kambona, the one cabinet minister who tried, could never decide whether to oppose the Arusha Declaration for going too far or for not going far enough. But it was also because the Tanzanians affected began to realise that the opportunities for promotion opened up by the nationalisations and by the consequent establishment of new government institutions exceeded for most of them the losses they would suffer under the leadership code. The President was also able to move very cautiously in the direction of workers' self-management, and in 1971 the Party passed an even more revolutionary document — the *Mwongozo* or Party Guidelines, reprinted as Chapter 3 of this book.

There was a utopian element in the 1967 papers. It was most obvious in the educational paper, for there was no underlying mass support for **Education for Self-Reliance** while parents and teachers saw little real prosperity in the rural areas and while education was the one path available to the security of a regularly paid job. There was very little that the President (or the Cabinet) could do to ensure that the new ujamaa villages would, in fact, be more efficient than the peasant agriculture which surrounded them, or to ensure that they found means of cooperating effectively together and solved the problems of work discipline. Even the leadership code depended on having some leaders who were willing to enforce it on their friends, and the group at the top was so small and so close-knit that this was very diffficult. There was nothing in any of these papers to suggest that political power would pass to the exploited classes.

Thus what actually happened in Tanzania after the Arusha Declaration can only to a limited extent be understood from the theoretical ideas so logically laid out in the President's speeches and papers, and from the picture of slow, steady progress presented by Government reports. One object of the studies in this book is to enable some of what took place at a local level to be compared with the rhetoric of the President's writings. The 1967 papers are not included. They are readily available elsewhere, and instead four later policy papers are included in Part One in which the thinking is taken beyond that of 1967.

The Rational Choice makes the case for the inevitability of socialism by showing the impossibility of independent capitalist development:

> . . . Third World capitalism would have no choice except to cooperate with external capita-
> lism, as a very junior partner . . . Development through capitalism therefore means that we
> Third World nations have to meet conditions laid down by others — by capitalists of other
> countries. And if we agreed to their conditions we should have to continue to be guided by
> them or face the threat of new enterprises being run down, of money and skills being
> withdrawn, and of other economic sanctions being applied against us.

The assumption is that by nationalization, by strict control of the activities of the multinational corporations, by democracy at all levels, and (though this is not stated) by success in raising agricultural production, an independent development can be achieved.

The second paper, the 1968 essay *Freedom and Development,* was written when a number of political leaders were found forcing peasants into ujamaa villages. In condemning this Nyerere produced a very explicit definition of an ujamaa village:

> . . . a voluntary association of people who decide of their own free will to live together and
> work together for their common good. They, and no one else, will decide how much of their
> land they will cultivate together from the beginning, and how much they will cultivate
> individually. They, and no one else, will decide how to use the money they earn jointly —
> whether to buy an ox-plough, install water, or do something else. They, and no one else, will
> make all the decisions about their working and living arrangements.

Nyerere was at the time quite specific about the use of force:

> Ujamaa villages . . . cannot be created from outside, nor governed from outside. No one can
> be forced into an ujamaa village, and no official — at any level — can tell the members of an
> ujamaa village what they should do together, and what they should continue to do as
> individual farmers . . . For if these things happen — that is, if an outsider gives such instruc-
> tions and enforces them — then it will no longer be an ujamaa village!

He also makes it very clear that he expected ujamaa villages to begin, in many cases, very small and to grow slowly:

> . . . if a group of 20 people discuss the idea and only 7 decide to go ahead, then that ujamaa
> village will consist of 7 people at the beginning. If 15 decide to start, then it will begin with
> 15 members — others will join as they are ready. There is no other way forward, because . . .
> five who come in unwillingly can destroy the efforts of the 15 who want to work out a new
> pattern for themselves.

This paper merits special comparison with the studies in the second part of this book concerned with actual villages, and with the way in which villages were started in the years after 1969.

The third policy paper is the *Mwongozo,* or *Party Guidelines,* of 1971. Unlike the others, the *Mwongozo* is a Party document rather than a Presidential paper — it was not included in the selection of Nyerere's essays published in 1973. It was brought to a Party conference during a wave of apprehension that followed Idi Amin's coup in Uganda. That coup, and the invasion of Sekou Toure's Guinea by the Portuguese a few months before, showed the two dangers facing the Tanzanian revolution: subversion from within, or invasion by white armies from outside. Yet the Portuguese had been driven out of Guinea. The lessons to be learnt from events in Uganda and Guina was therefore that 'although imperialism is still strong, its ability to topple a revolutionary government greatly depends on the possibility of getting domestic counter-revolutionary puppets to help in thwarting the revolution'.

The conclusions from this concerned the Party and its relationships with the people. A more central role than in the past is given to the Party: 'The time has now come for the Party to take the reins and lead all the people's activities'. But then in important sections on 'Defense and Security' and 'Economics and Progress' the logic of **Freedom and Development** is extended, and it is made clear that the people (and not 'a few experts and leaders') must decide on their own plans and implement them: 'The basis of Tanzania's development is the people themselves'. The army must become a 'people's army . . . to enable the people to safeguard their independence'. And in calling attention to the need for 'the Party to supervise the conduct and bearing of the leaders', people were urged to resist commandism. Political education is required so that 'every Tanzanian understands . . . the importance . . . of safeguarding our policies, our independence, our economy and our culture'. And to ensure the defence of the rural areas 'a people's militia' would be raised. In discussing economic policies similar themes are stressed:

> For a people who have been slaves or who have been oppressed, exploited and humilitated by colonialism or capitalism, 'development' means 'liberation'. Any action that gives them more control of their *own* affairs is an action for development, even if it does not offer them more health or more bread.

The document concludes with short paragraphs on particular policies, stressing the need for saving, for extension of the internal economy, and for the proper use of the surpluses produced by the parastatals 'to ensure that they help further our policy of socialism and self-reliance'.

The *Mwongozo* became — briefly — a workers' charter. Several of its clauses were used against arrogant and oppressive managers. There were strikes, and when these were outlawed the workers locked the 'oppressive managers' out of their offices and then demonstrated that production could be raised without them. There could no longer be any doubt that there was an articulate working class in Tanzania, conscious of its strengths and weaknesses, and able to use a document like the *Mwongozo* to highlight its grievances. The climax was reached in July 1973 at the Mount Carmel rubber factory, where the owner was locked out, and the factory taken over by the workers. The Government intervened on the owner's side, and almost the entire workforce was sacked. Paradoxically, control was maintained by insisting that before any industrial action be started, the approval of the Party had to be obtained.[4]

The *Mwongozo* and *The Rational Choice* can be read alongside the case studies in the other parts of this book. The most recent studies of the villagisation process show the increasingly bureaucratic role of Party officials in the rural areas. Several studies show parastatals whose conduct had very little relation to socialism or self-reliance. The National Milling Corporation, for instance, whose automatic bakery cost at least twice as much as it should have done, as well as making the Dar es Salaam bread supply dependent on foreign suppliers of spare parts; or the Tanga Fertilizer Company whose plant, opened in 1972, uses 140,000 tons of imports to produce 100,000 tons of fertilizers, and has been the cause of higher fertilizer prices for Tanzanian farmers. Both these projects have involved transfers of surplus out of the country, while bringing very little benefit to the workers and peasants.

Other studies show the attempt to control the parastatals — such as the use of the General Superintendence Company to control transfer pricing by checking the values of goods being imported into Tanzania before they left foreign ports. Or the Tanzania Publishing House, which, faced with unfavourable working arrangements with Macmillans, successfully went its own way. The study of the National Agricultural and Food Corporation (NAFCO), on the other hand, illustrates the problems faced by Governments which try to control parastatals. There are also several studies of the tensions and the dependence associated with the continued reliance (despite the rhetoric) on foreign aid. These are seen in the study of rural water supply, of the Maasai project, of the Lushoto Integrated Development Project, and of the grain silos. On the evidence here the objectives of the *Mwongozo,* and of *The Rational Choice,* were only very partially achieved.

The fourth and last document is President Nyerere's survey of February 1977, *The Arusha Declaration Ten Years After.* It has attracted attention in the West for its willingness to admit that there have been difficulties, and that everything has not always proceeded as planned.

However, Nyerere does claim five achievements for the years 1967-1977:

1. A change of direction in national development, so that resources are directed towards the needs of the nation and its people, and a reversal of the trend towards a differentiated society, with a few rich and many poor.
2. Establishment of some of the attitudes which are necessary for the development of socialism, notably a general recognition that it is wrong for a few to be rich while the majority stay poor, and that one of the main aims of economic development should be the extension of basic public facilities to the masses.
3. Establishment of many of the institutions and strategies necessary for socialist advance.
4. Reasonably good progress in providing basic health, education, and transport facilities for all the people in the country.
5. A continuing national contribution to the freedom struggle in Southern Africa.

Later in the paper Nyerere recognises the failures in agricultural, and especially in industrial production, and admits that there were in some places excesses in the way in which villagization was implemented.

Parts 2, 3 and 4 of this book consist of case studies which illustrate many of these points. Fourteen case studies are too few to be fully representative, but those included are illustrative of many of the most important situations encountered since 1967.

The first case study in Part II, based on fieldwork carried out in 1971, describes the interaction between Government staff and rich and poor villagers in two ujamaa villages. In 1969 the Government decided to give priority in its spending to registered ujamaa villages. In the study here, two villages were eventually registered very close together. The first became a successful ujamaa village. But this site was opposed by some rich peasants (kulaks) who had permanent crops, shops and a bar near the other site, which they feared would be lost if only the first site was registered. In the end the second site was registered too, even though there was no effective communal work at that site, and despite the fact that it was against the government's own policy to register two villages so close together. This was possible because of the links between the government officials and the rich peasants.

The second study is of the rural water supply programme. It has an obvious link with the first study, because it was often the possibility of getting social services such as a clean and convenient water supply that persuaded peasants all over the country to re-group themselves into villages.

Much of the finance for rural water supplies came from Sweden. This project was seen as an unusually 'progressive' aid project. The money was a grant, and it did not have to be spent in Sweden. Moreover, at the time when the agreement was signed it had not been decided precisely which rural water supplies would be built. A procedure was built in which enabled the aid to be used to finance new schemes as and when they were planned.

The impact of this project is discussed in the study. It shows how the aid project supported the ideology of 'experts'. The experts insisted on 'technically' sound plans, and formal procedures. They controlled the whole process of creating a water scheme — the planning, the construction and even the maintenance afterwards. The technology and much of the equipment was imported. Self-help was not encouraged. If peasants came forward with ideas of how a water scheme could be improved, they were not taken seriously. Their role was limited to some ritualistic consultation (with the actual decisions made afterwards by the experts) and to a compulsory contribution of unskilled labour under the experts' supervision. In no sense were they creatively involved. The project was built *for* them *by* the experts.

But if promises of social service provision were the main way of encouraging the formation of villages in the years immediately after the Arusha Declaration, they were soon to be superseded by the use of force. The third study is of the way villagization was implemented in Dodoma Region in 1970 and 1971. At the time this attracted international attention, as the world press picked up the headline that the Dodoma peasants were flocking to join the new villages, and Heads of State came to visit the Tanzanian President at Chamwino Ujamaa Village. Frances Hill was doing fieldwork in Dodoma at the time, and her study shows how the whole venture was far from spontaneous. On the contrary it was the result of the application of a whole range of bureaucratic pressures — culminating with the rumour spread by the field staff 'that in any future famine only those in ujamaa villages would receive government food'. As Dodoma was in the middle of a long famine this was a serious threat, and so the Gogo — and in particular the poor Gogo without large reserves of cash or cattle — 'decided to become socialists'.

The fourth and fifth studies (Chapters 8 & 9) are of the compulsory villagization that was widespread by 1974. The fourth is actually by a District Development Director, the civil servant responsible for implementing the villagization in Shinyanga District. The fifth is by two sociologists who worked in Iringa Region not long after the people had moved.

In October 1973 the TANU Biennial Conference had ruled that living in villages should be compulsory in all parts of the country by the end of 1976. The main population movements took place in 1974 and 1975. Most of the arguments used to justify it were concerned with social services: i.e. that unless the people lived in villages the Government could not supply them with water supplies, roads, schools, dispensaries, or agricultural advice.

Such a quick change could not be achieved uniformly over whole Districts in such a short time without the use, or the threat, of force. Experience in Dodoma, Kigoma, and elsewhere in previous years showed what had to be done. Occasionally the 'fire weapon' (burning of houses) was used, and with this threat hanging over them the majority of peasants decided to move first and argue later. Mwapachu's paper is remarkably frank about this. It is also indicative of the perceptions of those who were involved. In support of what happened, he draws on writers of the 'modernization' school who, like many of the bureaucrats involved in the villagization, regard peasants as primitive and backward, to be dragged, whether they like or not, into the twentieth century. (A view which fails, among other things, to explain how irrigation furrows on Mount Kilimanjaro came to be built centuries ago without any outside help, or how so many ordinary peasant farmers came to grow coffee). The Iringa study shows some bitter reactions to the way in which villagization was carried out, and the considerable short-term disruption that was involved, while leaving the long-term question of the success or failure of the 'operation' open.

The peasants have, however, been subject to ideological confusion. Although the President tried to draw a distinction between 'ujamaa villages' (voluntary and based on communal work) and 'development villages' (compulsory but not necessarily involving communal work) the distinction was not always clear to the villagers or even to the officials implementing the villagization. As a result the idea of ujamaa itself was debased.

The sixth study, by a Maasai, is of the various Government-inspired attempts to bring 'development' to the vast grasslands of Maasailand. These included a 'Maasai Project', financed by the United States Agency for Internal Development (AID) to bring about compulsory living in villages, and a programme of 'ujamaa ranches' financed by the World Bank. These programmes were not coordinated. Nor did they get to the heart of the problem, which was that the Maasai had evolved a relatively effective means of ecological control in a harsh environment, so were loath to change this system until they saw clear advantages in doing so. The 'experts' were not only technically incompetent but totally failed to understand this fact about the Maasai social system. The provision of dips and watering points simply led to devastation of the environment around these points. The 'livestock villages' strengthened the Maasai with the most cattle, and indeed it was hard to see how real change could take place until the power of the large stock-owners was ended. 'Experts' from outside, committed to technical rather than political solutions, were simply blundering around without any possibility of success.

The British tended to romanticise the Maasai. Nyerere and TANU have if anything gone to the opposite extreme, saying that the Maasai have to be 'taught a lesson', 'brought into the twentieth century', etc. There is still basically no difference between this and the treatment of other peasantries, as in the villagization or in the rural water supply programme. It is the same paternalism. As Parkipuny concludes:

> Livestock production can be the basis for a thriving economy . . . The crucial condition for this is development of the productive forces in the interest of and by the broad mass of the producers themselves . . . The people should not be made to sit back and let the government do whatever it wants. Since the well-being of the people must be the purpose of development, they must take control of the situation by creating their own socialist institutions of local management of the process of production without being overpowered by the uniformity requirements of the centre.

He earlier makes it clear that even this will only be possible as part of a bigger national programme (including industrialisation) and once the internal contradictions in societies such as the Maasai have been confronted.

The last of the rural studies is also concerned with the institutions that have been created in Tanzania after the Arusha Declaration. It is a study of the relationships of one particular institution, the Lushoto Integrated Rural Development Project, to the peasants and to the different arms of the local bureaucracy. LIDEP was set up with money from West Germany, but it was responsible to Dar es Salaam rather than to the regional bureaucrats. Moreover it was very slow to promote its counterpart Tanzanian staff. In the end the local bureaucrats did get control of the Project, and in particular of its biggest component, the vegetable marketing section. But in the process the institution became a capitalist profit-making body:

> Peasants have no value in such an institution. The value is in the vegetable products from which UAC (the Usambara Agricultural Corporation — the parastatal body which succeeded LIDEP — Ed.), draws profits to pay for its increasing running costs and the salaries for the ever increasing bureaucracy. LIDEP's Central Marketing was but one of many institutions started with good intentions, but in the course of development the means to reach the ends became the ends themselves.

And so Matango concludes in words very close to Parkipuny's:

> These agencies cannot be imposed on the people in the rural areas but must grow among the rural populations. In other words the peasants will have to start their own cooperative or ujamaa enterprises whose organisations are peasant based. Then the peasants can command and direct development in the way they feel fit and use the agency as a tool of their own hands.

The studies in Part III are concerned with industrial or parastatal development. Chapter II is about a project to build grain silos, financed by Swedish aid, even though economic analysis showed that it was cheaper to store grain in sacks in conventional warehouses. This was pointed out by economists in both the donor and recipient bureaucracies, and the study highlights many of the problems faced by economists and administrators when they have to deal with foreign-aided projects.

The second study in this section is of an automated bakery built in Dar es Salaam with Canadian 'assistance'. The machinery cost twice as much as it need have cost, and ten much smaller bakeries whose combined output would have equalled that of the automated bakery would have employed four times as many workers and produced bread at no extra cost. In trying to understand why the automated bakery was built, it is suggested that in part it was the desire of the management of the National Milling Corporation to control bread production in the capital. It was easier for them to think of doing this with one large bakery (even if it had expatriate management for a period) than with ten small ones scattered over the city.

Chapter 13 deals with a fertiliser factory, the biggest manufacturing industry in Tanzania, which depends entirely on imported inputs, cost Tanzania vastly more in foreign exchange than it was planned to cost, and produces high-cost fertilisers so lowering the profitability of Tanzanian agriculture. It is a study of a partnership between a multinational company (Kloeckner Industries of West Germany) and the National Development Corporation (NDC), the Government holding company responsible for industrial investments. Kloeckner supplied the plant on a 'turn-key' basis (i.e. they designed the plant, chose the machinery, built the factory and sold it ready to start operating). They then signed a management agreement to operate it for the first few years. Many agreements of this sort were signed in the years immediately after the Arusha Declaration, and (as in this case) they nearly all worked out for the benefit of the multinationals who supplied the technology and the experts, and badly for Tanzania.

There is also a study of transfer pricing — the practice by which multinationals take money out of one country into another without ever revealing it as profits. They do this by adjusting the prices used in transactions between their subsidiaries in various countries. Given the nationalisations, strict controls on the export of foreign exchange, and relatively high rates of taxation it is not surprising to discover that transfer pricing was being used to take money out of Tanzania by several well-known companies.

Part III concludes with an important study of a parastatal holding company — not the most famous one, NDC, but the less well known but almost equally important National Agricultural and Food Corporation (NAFCO). It was through holding companies such as these that the civil service was supposed to control the activities of state-owned farms and industries. (It was never clear how the *Party* could implement the directive of the *Mwongozo* to control the use of the surplus). In this paper Packard discusses the management systems that were used, and shows that the action of the holding company was 'administrative', like that of a government ministry, rather than business-oriented as one would expect in a holding company concerned to maximise the profits from the group as a whole. He traces this to the ambiguity and lack of clear weighting of objectives in the directives under which these holding companies were supposed to operate. Thus in practice they tended to be more concerned with procedures and with establishing the largest possible number of subsidiaries, than with economic viability or with discovering whether there was some other way in which the desired aims could be met. For example they never considered whether small farmer production of milk or sugar (which would not have been controlled by NAFCO) could have replaced estate production, which would have been controlled by NAFCO, and which they consequently tried to expand as fast as possible. This conclusion resembles that of the bakery study (Chapter 12), and it obviously encouraged multinationals to propose large-scale, capital-intensive partnership projects, which were not particularly efficient or even profitable but which enabled the parastatals to control hitherto untouched sections of the economy.

The two studies in the last Section cover two very different aspects of Tanzanian education policy. Marjorie Mbilinyi's paper starts with a theoretical statement of the way in which education relates to a social formation such as that in Tanzania. It has the function of creating and transmitting ideology, as well as contributing to the reproduction and expansion of the means of production. In an underdeveloped capitalist social formation, such as the Tanzanian, where most of the surplus is produced by peasant farmers but appropriated by the state, it is likely that there will be highly significant contradictions between educational theory and its application in practice.

With this background, Mbilinyi discusses the educational reforms since 1967. This part of the paper can be compared with sections of *The Arusha Declaration Ten Years After* which cover some of the same ground. The greatest achievements have been in raising the numbers in primary education (especially in connection with the drive for Universal Primary Education by the end of 1977), in adult literacy campaigns (in which 5 million people registered, and 3.8 million persevered long enough to sit for a test), in school building by self-help, in achieving significant levels of agricultural and craft production from 'self-reliance' activities in schools, and in saving running costs by getting school-children to perform many of the maintenances and cleaning tasks in schools that were previously done by wage labour.

But contradictions remain. Mbilinyi draws attention to the hierarchical and authoritarian organisation of schools: to the continuing role of examinations, to the regular use of the cane, and expulsions from secondary schools. She also points to the success of the rich in manipulating the system to ensure that their children have a much greater chance of proceeding to secondary school than children of the poor, and to the failure to make manual work more than a chore. Finally she points to some of the consequences of having educational planning and investment financed from foreign aid from capitalist sources such as the World Bank.

> Underlying (the resulting) struggles is the fundamental contradiction between capital and peasant labour, which at the level of the social formation itself becomes the struggle between the state and peasant labour . . . The skills and knowledge necessary for peasant production are acquired at the site of production, the peasant household, whereas the ideological preparation to fit into a state-managed production system organised on a village basis is being shifted to the school.

She concludes:

> The ideas of *Mwongozo*, of *Decentralisation*, of *Musoma* (Universal Primary Education — ed.) and *Education for Self-Reliance* have contributed to growing struggles by workers and peasants and students for control over state instruments like schools, and production and distribution enterprises . . . The consequences of such struggles will partly depend upon adequate organisation and direction, which relate struggles in one level to struggles in all levels of the social formation, and correctly situates conceptually the social formation within the context of worldwide capitalism.

The last study illustrates many different facets of neo-colonialism. It is a study of the Tanzania Publishing House, set up by Macmillans in the late 1960s to produce mainly educational books, especially in Swahili. It is partly a study of ideology: several of the expatriate managers employed by Macmillans had little sympathy for Nyerere's ideas, and this affected their choice of books to publish. But the more conventional aspects of neo-colonialism are also covered in this study: the desire to make quick profits and the lack of incentive to develop the productive forces inside Tanzania. However, in describing this particular enterprise, the author is also reminding us that the alternative to nationalization was often a blimpish, bumbling inefficiency. He shows how from the start some Tanzanians realised the dangers, and how, in a short time after the Macmillan influence ended, Tanzanians were able to take over and run this firm without outside help.

There is a unity in all these studies in that they all deal with aspects of the bureaucracy at work in the post-Arusha situation. In fact they show the bureaucrats increasing their power. In the first study, the bureaucrats eventually ally themselves with the richer peasants. In the studies concerned with villagization, and in the Maasai study, they disregard *Freedom and Development* and use force. In no less than six of the studies they use foreign aid more to expand their own spheres of influence than to achieve any sort of self-reliance. There are two studies of management agreements with foreign multinational corporations, and two of attempts by the civil service to limit the excesses of the multinationals.

There is no doubt that the role of bureaucracy is a key theme in any study of the period. Its expansion can be seen in expenditure figures: government recurrent expenditure (which is closely related to numbers of staff in post) rose at 20% per annum compound interest over the period. It can also be seen by listing the new institutions that were founded: companies to run industries taken over; new partnerships with the multinations; the 23 companies of the decentralised State Trading Corporation; District Development Corporations (such as the Usambara Development Corporation in Chapter 10) to run small ventures in the Districts; new parts of the Civil Service set up for various reasons as independent corporations. The 1975 issue of the Parastatal Telephone Directory listed no less than 140 such organisations.

In 1972 the administration of Government was decentralised. The detailed plans for this were worked out over a period of two years by McKinsey's, a prestigeous firm of management consultants based in New York and London. The word decentralisation does not fully describe what took place. What in fact happened was that elected local governments were replaced by locally-based arms of the central bureaucracy. Teams of highly paid civil servants were posted by the centre to each region, and one of their main tasks was to prepare regional budgets which had to be approved at the centre and were funded entirely by centrally raised taxation. While undoubtedly the old regional administrations were inefficient and could not have been left as they were, clearly these moves reduced democratic involvement and increased the power of the centre at the regional level.

There was a parallel reform of the Party bureaucracy. This involved giving administrative status to the salaried party officials and raising their salaries. In particular their status vis-a-vis that of the elected representatives was raised. This was particularly true at the lowest levels, the ward and the division. The ward executive officer was suddenly in receipt of a salary higher than a primary school teacher, while a divisional executive officer received the salary of a headmaster. These officials were appointed by the regional authorities, and their loyalty was to them. The villagers soon realised that the officials had much more influence than (say) the chairman of an ujamaa village, who was elected but did not have such close links to government. It is very doubtful if the villagization 'operations' could have been carried through without this expansion of the local arms of the central bureaucracy.

It should now be clear why writers like Shivji, Mapolu, or Tschannerl (in the second study) are re-writing the nationalist histories in terms of class analysis, and in particular analysing post-independence government actions in terms of a 'bureaucratic bourgeoisie'.[5]

Their analysis runs something like this. Independence was won by TANU, a party led by sections of the petty bourgeoisie. The Independence cabinet was made up of school teachers, civil servants, trade unionists and cooperative officials, joined by one Asian businessman and one white farmer. But the trade union leaders were not in any sense members of the working class. A real working class leadership had been overthrown many years before, and trade unions had been allowed to re-establish themselves only when they could produce an educated leadership and learn the conventions of 'collective bargaining'. In a similar way, the cooperative leadership were not peasants, or even farmers in a normal sense of the word. They were salaried officials who had been schooled (often in England) in the traditions of the British cooperative movement. In fact the colonial government had found it convenient to allow the establishment of cooperative unions as a way of taking produce marketing away from the Asian commercial class.

Peasants on their own could obstruct colonial development plans that they did not like. Workers could strike. But neither class could make a successful bid for state power. But once all these groups were co-ordinated by the petty bourgeoisie they were irresistable, and the British soon came to realise that the best thing for them was to hand over power as quickly as possible.

Many British civil servants stayed on after Independence and they were encouraged in their task of handing over their institutions to suitably educated Tanzanians. In this way the British institutions — the civil service, the schools, the law, the co-operatives, the trade unions, even the Christian missions — survived the departure of the British. (An interesting comparison is with Mozambique, where apparently the institutions are not being preserved in the same way — FRELIMO was perhaps fortunate to take over only after a war of liberation).

A new leadership in the trade unions (many of the old leaders were in the Cabinet) pressed for a much faster take-over of expatriate jobs. The implications of their demands was that education should be downgraded as the necessary qualification for executive or managerial posts. The TANU leadership was not prepared to tolerate this, and a series of strikes followed. By 1964 the union leaders had lost the power struggle, and the trade unions were absorbed into the bureaucracy. Education thus remained more or less the only path to a top job.

A similar situation arose in the rural areas when immediately after Independence the Tanu Youth League tried to persuade the Government to nationalise sisal estates. They were told instead to go and start new sisal production schemes of their own. Spontaneous settlement schemes sprang up all over the country, but particularly in the sisal areas. At one time there were as many as 400 schemes. But the schemes had hardly started when the sisal price began to fall — from £103 per ton in 1960/62 to £70 per ton in 1967. Foreign advisers were called in, and they recommended that settlement schemes needed to be 'planned'. The result was a capital cost of Shs.3,000,000/- per settlement scheme, only enough money in the First Five Year Plan for 75 schemes, and the loss of many millions of shillings when the settlement schemes failed to produce. Part of the blame for this was put on 'the ungrateful peasants' who were told that they had little to contribute towards increased agricultural production. Change could only be brought about by 'experts', and rural projects and planning came more and more to reflect their role.

The effect of the Arusha Declaration was to concentrate even more power into the hands of the ruling section of the petty bourgeoisie, for they now had a direct stake in the industrial production process. They already controlled agricultural surpluses through the cooperative marketing system and much of the foreign and internal trade, and they proceeded to expand this control through decentralisation and villagization, as discussed above. By insisting on higher education as the only path to a top job, and by making maximum use of both private and government secondary schools, they were able to ensure that most of their children got into the upper salaried grades.

From the time of the Arusha Declaration, Shivji calls the ruling section of the petty bourgeoisie a 'bureaucratic bourgeoisie'. In this he includes the cabinet, the top civil servants and industrial leaders, top party officials, top army officers: in other words a relatively small group of people who take the decisions in present day Tanzania.

In Shivji's analysis the bureaucratic bourgeoisie is a dependent class. Internally it does not control agricultural production, which is still largely carried out by small-scale peasant producers (the villagization may be interpreted as a first step towards control and organisation of this production). Moreover, most of the cash crops (coffee, cotton, sisal, cashew nuts, tea, etc.) are still destined for the capitalist centres, so that in relation to the peasants the bureaucratic bourgeoisie are mer- chants, with the typical merchant dilemma of whether to increase their surplus by raising their profit margins (i.e. by giving lower prices to the farmers, which may discourage production) or by raising farm prices (which means lower margins, which is no good to them if production does not rise). In fact agricultural production has not risen greatly since 1966, and the terms of trade have worsened, so that the cost of running the bureaucracy has consumed a larger and larger share of the surplus produced by the peasants.

The bureaucratic bourgeoisie is also dependent on the leaders of international capitalism, what Shivji calls the 'metropolitan bourgeoisie'. It depends on them for the running of most of its industries — the management agreements have not significantly lessened the dependence, as the industrial studies in this collection show. It depends on them for markets. And increasingly, and counter to the rhetoric of the Arusha Declaration, it depends on them for aid.

By the mid 1970s, 55% of the Government development budget came from aid, and 85% of the Ministry of Agriculture's part of that budget. Tanzania had become one of the largest recipients of World Bank aid in Africa. The Chinese, the Swedes, the West Germans and the Americans had major bilateral aid programmes, and nearly every other possible bilateral donor had a small programme. Without this aid it is hard to see how Tanzania could have weathered the crisis of agricultural production and the resulting balance of payments deficits of the 1970s.

Six of the case studies explore this aid and collectively show that the bureaucratic bourgeoisie, while dependent on the aid, were also able to use it to increase their power and influence locally. They also suggest that although the aid may have cemented a coalition between the bureaucratic bourgeoisie and international capital, it did little to expand the forces of production. It has even been suggested that the World Bank was consciously using Tanzania to experiment with new forms of cooperation between finance capital and the neo-colonial state. The United States certainly gave support to Tanzania in 1972 to prevent the British Govern- ment blocking a World Bank loan to Tanzania.

It is of course too soon to make a historical judgement on the contemporary Tanzanian state. Moreover a history of Tanzania written entirely in terms of class struggle, such as Shivji's, fails to do justice to the role of the President. For Nyerere is not simply a prisoner of the Tanzania ruling class; he is also a philosopher and, most fundamentally, a creator of ideology.

The studies in this book raise many questions about how this ideology is created and used. It can be seen, for example, that by no means everything Nyerere says or writes is eventually accepted by the Tanzanian ruling class. Some elements are accepted for a time and then ignored: such as the prohibition on the use of force in *Freedom and Development,* or the rights of workers to expose irresponsible managers in the *Mwongozo.* But — to use the *Mwongozo* as an illustration again — the ideology can be used (and it was used for a short time) by the oppressed classes. It is probably because of the economic difficulties of starting communal cultivation that the peasantry have never managed to use the ideology of *Freedom and Develop- ment* in the same way that the workers used the *Mwongozo* to protect themselves from bureaucrats who wanted to push them around.

But when Nyerere claims, in *The Arusha Declaration Ten Years After,* that at least some socialist attitudes are beginning to be taken for granted, one wonders whether he is talking about socialism in the sense of power being held by the oppressed classes, or whether he is just concerned with the use of power by the state. Even in *The Rational Choice,* probably Nyerere's most explicit direct defence of socialism, the strongest arguments are negative — capitalism cannot bring development, so socialism is the only alternative. But is socialism the only alternative? Many actions of the Tanzanian state, the aid agencies (especially the World Bank), and even the multinational corporations themselves, suggest that Tanzania may in fact be pioneering a third alternative, a variety of state capitalism.

Meanwhile Nyerere's analysis survives on the printed page, and it continues to influence the Tanzanian ruling class. But there is no possibility of socialism in Tanzania until the working class and especially the peasants are able to use those writings and other relevant ideological statements to organise and expand production, and to protect their own interests vis-à-vis those of other classes.

NOTES

1. For general introductions to this period, see I. Kimambo and A. Temu (eds), *A History of Tanzania,* (East African Publishing House and Heinemann Educational Books, Nairobi and London, 1969); J. Saul and L. Cliffe (eds), *Socialism in Tanzania,* 2 Volumes, (East African Publishing House, Nairobi, 1972 and 1973); R. Cranford Pratt, *The Critical Phase in Tanzania 1945-1968: Nyerere and the Emergence of a Socialist Strategy,* (Cambridge University Press, Cambridge, 1976).
2. See Pratt, *op.cit.,* Chapter 8. Nyerere's 1967 papers are collected together in his *Essays on Socialism* (Oxford University Press, Dar es Salaam and London, 1968).
3. Nyerere, *Essays on Socialism, op.cit.,* p.17.
4. Pascal Mihyo 'The Struggle for Workers' Control in Tanzania', *Review of African Political Economy,* No.4 (1975); see also Issa Shivji, *Class Struggles in Tanzania,* (Heinemann, London and Tanzania Publishing House, Dar es Salaam, 1975), Chapter 13.
5. Shivji, *op.cit;* H. Mapolu, (ed.), *Workers and Management,* (Tanzania Publishing House, Dar es Salaam, 1976).

Part I

POLICY DOCUMENTS

CHAPTER 1

The Rational Choice*

Julius Nyerere

My job today is to give a starting point for discussion and thought. And my subject is an examination of the alternative economic and social systems which are open to Third World countries. In order to keep this discussion within reasonable bounds I must make certain assumptions. It is important that these should be clear before I begin: for if the assumptions are not shared, then much of what I say will be irrelevant. Fortunately, my assumptions are not very controversial — at least within Africa.

THE ASSUMPTIONS

My first assumption is that any discussion about the appropriate economic and social organization must, for the time being at least, be concluded within each nation state, and the decision must be made exclusively by the people of that nation. Thus, it is the people of Tanzania as a whole, or the Sudan as a whole, who will decide the path for their country. Tanzania cannot decide for the Sudan, nor vice versa — and I hope that nothing I say today will be understood to imply otherwise! The fact that, for example, Zanzibar within the United Republic of Tanzania, and the Southern Provinces within Sudan, have autonomy in certain matters means that in these respects the smaller units will be the unit of choice rather than the nation as a whole.

Secondly, I take it to be axiomatic that all the peoples of the Third World desire to govern themselves, and want their country to be completely independent from external control. This does not rule out the possibility of political or economic links between two or more countries; nor does it exclude a possible voluntary merger of sovereignties, provided that these things are agreed upon after discussions based on the equality of all participants.

Thirdly, I shall assume that, to everyone in the Third World, the present degree of poverty, and the general lack of economic development, is completely unacceptable. We have to increase our production of wealth so that we may increase the level of our collective and individual consumption.

My fourth and final assumption is that our struggles for independence were national struggles, involving the rights of all the inhabitants. We were not aiming to replace our alien rulers by local privileged elites, but to create societies which ensure human dignity and self-respect for all. The concomitant of that is that every individual has the right to the maximum economic and political freedom which is compatible with equal freedom for all others; and that neither well-fed slavery nor the necessity to beg for subsistence are acceptable human conditions.

I have said that these assumptions are not very controversial within Africa. It is

*Text of a speech delivered on behalf of President Nyerere in Khartoum, January 1973.

equally true that they do not represent the present situation. They represent aspirations rather than facts. That is obvious from an examination of world affairs, or from the briefest visit to any of our rural areas — or even to those urban areas where our unskilled labourers live. Yet because these stated assumptions are also a list of our fundamental aspirations, they must be the basis for our choice of policies. If a policy militates against the achievement of these conditions, then its acceptability must be questioned. Even more, if a social and economic system is incompatible with these goals, then it must be rejected.

THE CHOICE

In the modern world there are two basic systems of economic and social organization — capitalism and socialism. There are variations within these broad classifications, like welfare capitalism or humanistic socialism; but the broad distinction between the two systems remains, and our first choice has to be between them.

Remnants of feudalism and of primitive communalism do, of course, still exist in the world; but neither of these are viable systems when challenged by the organised technology of the twentieth century. Sometimes, as in Japan, these old systems influence the organisation of capitalism for a while; but the influences are subordinate to the logic of the later organisation, and will eventually be completely eradicated. For in the last resort anything which detracts from the profit of an individual capitalist enterprise will be abandoned by that enterprise; and anything which militates against the efficiency of the capitalist system will be uprooted.

Primitive communalism is equally doomed. The movement the first enamel pot, or factory woven cloth, is imported into a self-sufficient communal society, the economic and social structure of that society receives its death blow. Afterwards it is merely a question of time, and of whether the members of that community will be participants or victims in the new economic order.

Thus the choice for new nations lies effectively between socialism and capitalism. It is not a completely free choice, for all of us inherited certain patterns of trade, and have been to a greater or lesser extent indoctrinated by the value systems of our colonial master. Further, the great powers continue to regard us as being within the sphere of influence of one or other of them — which usually demonstrates its displeasure if we refuse to conform to the expected pattern of behaviour. But ultimately, if we so determine, and if we are prepared to overcome our recent past and the difficulties which others may place in our way, we can move towards the growth of one system or the other within our society.

Yet having said that, I now propose to argue that there is no real choice. In practice Third World nations cannot become developed capitalist societies without surrendering the reality of their freedom and without accepting a degree of inequality between their citizens which would deny the moral validity of our independence struggle. I will argue that our present poverty and national weakness make socialism the only rational choice for us.

CAPITALISM AND INDEPENDENCE

Under a capitalist system the purpose of production and distribution is the making of profit for those who own the means of production and exchange. The need for goods is subsidiary to the profit involved in making them. Therefore the owner of the machines and equipment used in production — that is, he who provides the money for these things — is the one who determines whether there shall be any

production, and of what kind, and in what quantity. Neither the men who provide
the labour for the production, nor the men who need the goods which could be
produced, have any say in these decisions. Under capitalism, money is King. He
who owns wealth owns also power. He has power over all the workers who he can
employ or not, and power over the governments which he can paralyse by withholding vital production, or sabotage by the manipulation of men and machines.

That has always been the essence of capitalism. But there is a further relevant
fact in these decades of the twentieth century. That is that this power is now
concentrated in very few hands. For whereas one hundred years ago a quite small
amount of money sufficed to establish an industrial or commercial enterprise,
modern technology now precludes this in all important areas of production. Thus,
for example, Henry Ford could begin his manufacture of cars in a bicycle repair
shop, and build up his capacity bit by bit. But now, in the 1970s, anyone who
decides to begin making vehicles must be prepared to make a multi-million dollar
investment before the first one rolls off the assembly line. Mass production techniques make small units uneconomic — they go bankrupt in an attempt to compete
with the giants, or else sell out to a larger business. Therefore, instead of having
a very large number of small capitalists, we have a very small number of large
capitalists. 'Small men' exist; but they initiate an insignificant proportion of the
total wealth produced, and usually confine their attention to the luxury trades.

This development is part of the dynamic of capitalism — for capitalism is very
dynamic. It is a fighting system. Each capitalist enterprise survives by successfully
fighting other capitalist enterprises. And the capitalist system as a whole survives by
expansion, that is, by extending its area of operations and in the process eradicating
all restraints upon it, and all weaker systems of society. Consider now what this
means for the new nations of the Third World.

According to capitalist theory, if we choose capitalism our citizens would be free
to establish capitalist enterprises, and these Tanzanian or Sudanese capitalists would
compete — that is, would fight — all other capitalist enterprises, including the
foreign ones. In practice, however, two questions immediately arise. First, where
in our lands are those citizens who have sufficient capital to establish modern
industries; and second, how would our infant industries fight other capitalist
enterprises?

I believe the answer to these questions is clear in all Third World countries. For
Tanzania is no exception in not having within its borders the kind of wealth which
is necessary to establish modern industrial units. As a general rule no individual, or
group of individuals, from within any of our nations, has the capacity to establish
even a large modern textile mill, much less to operate a diamond mine, put up a
steel mill, or run a large-scale commercial enterprise. That amount of money and
that kind of expertise, just do not exist. Certainly, the most which could be done
by Tanzanians is the establishment of little workshops, which either assemble
imported components, or which undertake simple processing of locally produced
crops. Our citizens can establish small retail shops; wholesaling on any economic
scale is likely to demand more resources than they have.

When Britain experienced its industrial revolution at the end of the eighteenth
century, that was enough. It is not enough now! How could these little Tanzanian
capitalists compete with ICI, Ford, Nippon Enterprises, and the other big multinational corporations — or even with Walls Food Products? The answer is simple:
they could not! The best they could do would be to become agents of these international capitalist concerns. And this would not bring progress in the attack on

our underdevelopment; for the result would not be modern factories producing necessities, but local agents importing and processing those things — and only those things — which were profitable to both the local agents and the overseas enterprise.

In fact, Third World capitalism would have no choice except to cooperate with external capitalism, as a very junior partner. Otherwise it would be strangled at birth. You cannot develop capitalism in our countries without foreign capitalists, their money and their management expertise. And these foreign capitalists will invest in Third World countries only if, when, and to the extent that, they are convinced that to do so would be more profitable to them than any other investment. Development through capitalism therefore means that we Third World nations have to meet conditions laid down by others — by capitalists of other countries. And if we agree to their conditions we should have to continue to be guided by them or face the threat of the new enterprises being run down, of money and skills being withdrawn, and of other economic sanctions being applied to us.

In fact, a reliance upon capitalist development means that we give to others the power to make vital decisions about our economy. The kind of economic production we shall undertake; the location of factories, offices and stores; the amount of employment available in any area; and even the kind of taxation system we adopt; all these matters will be determined by outsiders.

It is claimed that this would be a temporary phenomenon, as foreign capitalist investment in a Third World country would be a catalyst for local capitalist enterprise. To some extent this is true; small local businesses may grow up in the shadow of a major, foreign-owned factory. But all such businesses would have the purpose of providing services to the workers of the big industry, or of making small components for it. They would therefore be absolutely dependent upon it, flourishing when it expanded and collapsing if it closed down. Local businesses would thus be the puppets, not the enemies of the foreign enterprise — the subsidiaries, not the competitors. They would be forced to identify themselves with all demands made by the foreign capitalists. The loss of real national self-determination would therefore be increased — not decreased; for the foreign owners would have secured a local political base to back up their economic power.

This is very easy to understand. If the Government, for example, proposed to lay down new minimum wages, or to raise revenue from a tariff on goods of interest to the factory, the big employers may say — politely or otherwise — that in such a case they will close their factory. They can point out that this will not only result in a loss of livelihood for all those directly employed; it will also force into bankruptcy a number of ancillary units. Of course, the independent government can still go ahead with its proposals; but it will then have to deal with the consequences — and they are not likely to be pleasant for either that government or the people it wishes to serve.

Nor is this all. Foreign policy questions will also be affected by reliance upon foreign capitalists for economic development. It is true that American, British, or Japanese capitalists have no patriotic loyalty to their country of origin. But they do have loyalty to their largest investments — and these are unlikely to be inside any one under-developed country! Therefore, a poor nation's quarrel with one of the imperialist countries about, for example, its support for Zionist expansionism, or for South Africa, Rhodesia, or Portuguese colonialism, can easily lead to the contraction and eventual closing of established enterprises.

What I am saying is that, given the present inequalities between nations, capitalist development is incompatible with full national independence for Third World countries. For such development will be foreign owned, and foreign controlled; local capitalists will be subsidiary, and will remain subsidiary. There can be no question about this — the foreign domination is permanent, not temporary. It is the big enterprise which will make the large profits and have large monies available for the next investment. The small ones will remain small — or be bought out! For confirmation of this fact, and its meaning, it is only necessary to look at what has happened within the major capitalist countries. One sees that medium size enterprises gobble up small ones, and are themselves gobbled up by large ones. Finally, the giants fight among themselves for ultimate supremacy. In the end the rich governments of the big capitalist countries find their own freedom of action is restricted by the economic power of the capitalist giants. Even if they are elected to fight capitalism, they find it necessary to ensure the raw materials, and the profitability, of the big corporations, or face mass unemployment and major economic crises.

The fact that a number of competing big capitalist institutions may invest in a particular developing country — perhaps from different foreign bases — does not invalidate this simplified analysis. As a general rule the meaning is that the poor country has given several hostages to fortune instead of one. In theory it can endeavour to play one enterprise off against another; but in practice it is much more likely to discover that its economic destiny has been determined by enterprise conflicts which originate outside its own borders, and about which it knows nothing! A 'take-over bid', or a rationalisation scheme, or a new cartel arrangement, can undo years of local negotiation, and the independent government may well hear about the prospect only if one giant or the other hopes to use it in order to get better terms for its own shareholders!

CAPITALISM AND THE NATURE OF SOCIETY

This inevitable loss of real national freedom is, however, only one of those results of capitalism which I believe to be incompatible with the national purposes of all Third World governments. For capitalism does not only imply a fight between capitalists, with the developing nations' capitalists inevitably being worsted. It also involves a permanent fight between capitalists on one side and workers on the other. This is a very important matter for us, coming as most of the African Third World countries do out of primitive communalism into the modern world. For it means a new factor of national division at a time when all of us are still fighting to overcome the divisive forces of tribalism, religion and race. It also means that the fruits of independence will be denied to the mass of the people who worked for it, or in whose name it was demanded.

There is no escaping this effect of capitalism. For the purpose of capitalist enterprise is the making of profit. To do this, the capitalist must keep his costs of production as low as possible, and get the maximum return from the sale of the products. In other words, he must pay the lowest wages for which he can get workers, and charge the maximum price at which he can sell the goods produced. A permanent conflict of interest between the workers and the employer inevitably follows. The former want to get high wages so as to live decently — and perhaps buy some of the goods they work to produce. The latter needs to pay low wages so as to maximise his profit, that is, the return on the money he has invested.

Thus capitalism automatically brings with it the development of two classes of people: a small group whose ownership of the means of production brings them wealth, power and privilege; and a very much larger group whose work provides that wealth and privilege. The one benefits by exploiting the other, and a failure in the attempt to exploit leads to a breakdown of the whole system with a consequent end to all production! The exploitation of the masses is, in fact, the basis on which capitalism has won the accolade for having solved the problem of production. There is no other basis on which it can operate. For if the workers ever succeeded in obtaining the full benefits of their industry, then the capitalist would receive no profit and would close down the enterprise!

What this means for the masses of the people in the Third World countries should be obvious. Their conditions of employment, and their return from employment, will be just sufficient to maintain the labour supply. Further, if the nation is dependent upon capitalist investment for all its desired economic expansion, the workers will have to be prevented from organising themselves to fight for their rights. For an effective trade union struggle might lead the employer to argue once again that his factory has become uneconomic. The resultant threat of a close down may well prompt the government to intervene on the side of the employers in order to safeguard the economic growth rate and its own miserably small, but vital, tax revenue.

Development through capitalism is thus basically incompatible with the fourth aspiration I listed — that of human dignity and self-respect for all, with equal freedom for all inhabitants of the society. For capitalism means that the masses will work, and a few people — who may not labour at all — will benefit from that work. The few will sit down to a banquet, and the masses will eat whatever is left over.

This has a further implication. With a capitalist system the production of goods, measured statistically, may well go up considerably; if it happens to possess certain mineral resources, the Third World country may even find itself high on the list of 'successful states' as regards the growth rate of its gross national product. But the mass of the people, who produce the goods which are measured, will be without sufficient money to buy the things they need for a decent life. Their demand will exist, but it will not be effective. Consequently, the production of basic necessities — decent houses, food, and nice clothes — will be limited; such production would be less profitable to the capitalist investor than the provision of 'luxury goods'. It was no accident, for example, that one of the early post-independence investments in Tanzania was a drive-in cinema. Much more profit could be made from using cement that way than in producing workers' houses!

For on top of everything else, the choice of capitalism as the road to development means a particular kind of production, and a particular kind of social organisation. Rural water supplies will have a low priority, regardless of the fact that they are needed for the health of the people. The importation, and perhaps even the production, of air conditioners, of private cars, and of other 'consumer durables' will have a high priority. The former brings no profit; the latter do. To see the real meaning of this we can once again look at the developed capitalist societies. Then we can see the malnutrition among the people of the Appalachian mountains and of Harlem contrasted with the gadgetry of suburban America; or in Britain we can see the problem of homelessness while colour television sets are produced endlessly; and in the same societies we can observe the small resources devoted to things like education and health for the people as compared with those spent to satisfy the inessential desires of the minority.

THE ALTERNATIVE OF SOCIALISM

To argue, as I have been doing, that capitalism is incompatible with the aspirations of the Third World does not mean that the alternative of socialism is an easy one, nor that success under it is automatic. But socialism can be compatible with our aspirations; by adopting socialist policies it is possible for us to maintain our independence and develop towards human dignity for all our people.

The vital point is that the basis of socialist organisation is the meeting of people's needs, not the making of profit. The decision to devote the nation's resources to the production of one thing rather than another is made in the light of what is needed, not what is most profitable. Furthermore, such decisions are made by the people through their responsible institutions — their own government, their own industrial corporations, their own commercial institutions. They are not made by a small group of capitalists, either local or foreign — and the question of foreign domination through economic ownership is thus excluded. Further the workers of the nation can receive — directly or indirectly — the full fruits of their industry; there is no group of private owners which constantly appropriates a large proportion of the wealth produced.

None of this means that great inequalities within the society, or the exploitation of groups, or even the seizure of power and privilege by a small minority, is automatically ruled out in a society which opts for socialism. Looking around the world we can see so-called socialist countries where all these happen. But my point is that such things mark a failure to implement socialism; they are not inherent in it in the way they are inherent in capitalism.

The major argument used against socialism for the developing world is, in fact, that it will not work, and that all socialist states are poor states because of their socialism. Without speaking for as long again as I have already spoken — which I do not propose to do — it is not possible to refute this argument in any detail. There are, however, three very fundamental points which I would ask you to consider in this respect.

The first is that to measure a country's wealth by its gross national product is to measure things, not satisfactions. An increase in the sale of heroin, in a country where this is legal, would be recorded as an increase in its national wealth; if human well-being was the unit of measurement, such an increase of sales would be a negative factor. Similarly, the spread of good health through the eradication of endemic diseases may, or may not, be recorded as an increase in statistical national wealth; it is certainly better for the people if it has happened!

My second point is that a successful harlot, or a favoured slave, may be better off materially than a woman who refuses to sell her body, or a man to sell his freedom. We do not regard the condition of the harlot or slave as being consequently enviable — unless, of course, we are starving, and even then we recognise the possible amelioration in our circumstances as being uncertain and insecure.

Thirdly, I do not accept that the so-called unworkability of socialism has been proved. Capitalism has been developing for about two centuries. The first national commitment to socialism was made in 1917, by a backward and feudal nation devastated by war, which has subsequently suffered greatly from further civil and international conflict. Even so, few people would deny the material transformation which has been effected in the USSR during the past fifty-five years. And in fact, despite the major criticisms which can be made of all the socialist countries, it is difficult to argue that their peoples are worse off than the late capitalist starters — countries like Greece, or Spain, or Turkey, for example. On the contrary, they are clearly better off in the vital matters of health, education, and the security of their food and shelter. Whether or not they have the same number of television sets seems to me to be much less important!

CONCLUSION

It cannot be denied that many difficulties face a Third World country which chooses the socialist alternative of development. Not least among these are its own past, the dynamism of capitalist initiative techniques, and the gambler instinct which every human being seems to possess, so that we all hope we shall be among the privileged not the exploited! But I believe that we can choose the socialist path, and that by so doing we can develop ourselves in freedom, and towards those conditions which allow dignity and self-respect for every one of our citizens.

I believe that this prospect must be pursued, with vigour and determination. We shall not create socialist societies overnight; because we have to start from where we are, we shall have to make compromises with capitalist money and skill, and we shall have to take risks in our development. But I am convinced that Third World countries have the power to transform themselves, over time, into socialist societies in which their peoples can live in harmony and cooperation as they work together for their common benefit.

CHAPTER 2

Freedom and Development*

Julius Nyerere

Freedom and development are as completely linked together as are chickens and eggs! Without chickens you get no eggs; and without eggs you soon have no chickens. Similarly, without freedom you get no development, and without development you very soon lose your freedom.

FREEDOM DEPENDS ON DEVELOPMENT

For what do we mean when we talk of freedom? First, there is national freedom; that is, the ability of the citizens of Tanzania to determine their own future, and to govern themselves without interference from non-Tanzanians. Second, there is freedom from hunger, disease, and poverty. And third, there is personal freedom for the individual; that is, his right to live in dignity and equality with all others, his right to freedom of speech, freedom to participate in the making of all decisions which affect his life, and freedom from arbitrary arrest because he happens to annoy someone in authority — and so on. All these things are aspects of freedom, and the citizens of Tanzania cannot be said to be truly free until all of them are assured.

Yet it is obvious that these things depend on economic and social development. To the extent that our country remains poor, and its people illiterate and without understanding or strength, then our national freedom can be endangered by any foreign power which is better equipped. This is not simply a question of military armaments — although if these are necessary they have to be paid for out of the wealth of the community. It is a question of consciousness among all the people of the nation that they are free men who have something to defend, whether the appropriate means of defence be by force of arms or by more subtle methods.

Equally obvious is the fact that freedom from hunger, sickness and poverty depends upon an increase in the wealth and the knowledge available in the community: for a group of people can only consume and use the wealth they have already produced. And even personal freedom becomes more real if it is buttressed by development. A man can defend his rights effectively only when he understands what they are, and knows how to use the constitutional machinery which exists for the defence of those rights — and knowledge of this kind is part of development.

For the truth is that development means the development of **people.** Roads, buildings, the increases of crop output, and other things of this nature, are not development: they are only tools of development. A new road extends a man's freedom only if he travels upon it. An increase in the number of school buildings is development only if those buildings can be, and are being, used to develop the minds and the understanding of people. An increase in the output of wheat, maize,

*Paper presented to the TANU National Executive Committee, October, 1968.

or beans, is only development if it leads to the better nutrition of people. An expansion of the cotton, coffee, or sisal crop is only development if these things can be sold, and the money used for other things which improve the health, comfort, and understanding of the people. Development which is not development of people may be of interest to historians in the year 3,000; it is irrelevant to the kind of future which is created. Thus, for example, the pyramids of Egypt, and the Roman roads of Europe, were material developments which still excite our amazement. But because they were only buildings, and the people of those times were not developed, the empires, and the cultures, of which they were a part have long ago collapsed. The Egyptian culture of those days — with all the knowledge and wisdom which it possessed — was quickly overthrown by foreign invasion, because it was a culture of a few; the masses were slaves who simply suffered because of the demands of this material development, and did not benefit from it. Equally, when the Roman Empire was attacked, and its legionnaires retreated to their homeland, the fine roads and buildings were left to rot because they were irrelevant to the people of the occupied areas. Further, it is doubtful whether either the Egyptian pyramids, or the Roman roads have made the slightest difference to the histories of the countries concerned, or the lives of their peoples.

Development brings freedom, provided it is development *of people.* But people cannot be developed; they can only develop themselves. For while it is possible for an outsider to build a man's house, an outsider cannot give the man pride and self-confidence in himself as a human being. Those things a man has to create in himself by his own actions. He develops himself by what he does; he develops himself by making his own decisions, by increasing his understanding of what he is doing, and why; by increasing his own knowledge and ability, and by his own full participation — as an equal — in the life of the community he lives in. Thus, for example, a man is developing himself when he grows, or earns, enough to provide decent conditions for himself and his family; he is not being developed if someone gives him these things. A man is developing himself when he improves his education — whatever he learns about; he is not being developed if he simply carries out orders from someone better educated than himself without understanding why those orders have been given. A man develops himself by joining in free discussion of a new venture, and participating in the subsequent decision; he is not being developed if he is herded like an animal into the new venture. Development to a man can, in fact, only be affected by that man; development of the people can only be affected *by the people.*

Finally, if development is to increase people's freedom, it must be development for the people. It must serve them, and their interests. Every proposal must be judged by the criterion of whether it serves the purpose of development — and the purpose of development is the people. Yet if a proposal contributes to the development of people, and if it is being carried out by the people of their own free will, it will automatically be for the people's interests, provided three conditions are fulfilled. First, if the people understand their own needs; second, if they understand how these needs can be met; and third, if they have the freedom to make their own decisions, and to carry them into effect.

DEVELOPMENT DEPENDS UPON FREEDOM

If the purpose of development is the greater freedom and well-being of the people, it cannot result from force. For the proverb tells the truth in this matter: you can drive a donkey to water, but you cannot make it drink. By orders, or even by slavery, you can build pyramids and magnificent roads, you can achieve expanded acreages of cultivation, and increases in the quantity of goods produced in your factories. All these things, and many more, can be achieved through the use of force; but none of them result in the development of people. Force, and deceitful promises, can in fact, only achieve short-term material goals. They cannot bring strength to a nation or a community, and they cannot provide a basis for the freedom of the people, or security for any individual or group of persons.

There is only one way in which you can cause people to undertake their own development. That is by education and friendship. Through these means — and no other — people can be helped to understand both their own needs, and the things which they can do to satisfy these needs. This is the kind of leadership which TANU and Government officials should be giving the people; this is the way in which we can bring development to Tanzania. But, although we must give this leadership, the decisions must come from the people themselves, and they themselves must carry out the programmes they have decided upon.

There are thus two factors which are essential in the development of people. The first is leadership through education, and the second is democracy in decision-making. For leadership does not mean shouting at people; it does not mean abusing individuals or groups of people you disagree with; even less does it mean ordering people to do this or that. Leadership means talking and discussing with the people, explaining and persuading. It means making constructive suggestions, and working with the people to show by actions what it is that you are urging them to do. It means being one of the people, and recognising your equality with them.

In particular, at this stage in our history we should not be trying to blame particular groups or individuals for things which are not to our liking, or not to the liking of the people. The exploiters, who are now apparently so beloved by our leaders that they spend all their time talking about them, are a negligible factor in our development now. Those few who remain can most effectively be dealt with by constructive development work on the part of the people and their leaders; it is certainly absurd that we leaders should spend all our time abusing exploiters — especially as some of us do not understand the work which is being done by some of the individuals we abuse. Instead we should be providing creative and positive leadership. We should have taken the trouble to understand the development policies our Party is trying to pursue, and we should be explaining these policies to the people. When we have convinced the people that TANU's policies are good and sound, then we should be working with them to create a society in which exploiters will find no opportunities for their evil doing.

But giving leadership does not mean usurping the role of the people. The people must make the decisions about their own future through democratic procedures. Leadership cannot replace democracy; it must be part of democracy. If the decision relates to national affairs, then the people make it through the National Executive Committee, and Parliament, and through the National Conference of TANU. If it is a decision about district affairs, the people make it through the District Committee and District Council. If it is a question of purely local interests — for example whether to undertake a particular self-help scheme — then the people directly concerned must make the decision following a free debate. There is no other way in which real development can take place. For just as real freedom for the people requires development, so real development of the people requires freedom.

TWO ESSENTIALS OF DEMOCRACY

There are, however, two essential elements of democracy without which it cannot work. First, is that everyone must be allowed to speak freely, and everyone must be listened to. It does not matter how unpopular a man's ideas, or how mistaken the majority think him. It does not make any difference whether he is liked or disliked for his personal qualities. Every Tanzanian, every member of a community, every member of a District Council, every Member of Parliament, and so on, must have the freedom to speak without fear of intimidation — either inside or outside the meeting place. The minority in any debate must have the right to speak without fear of persecution; it must be defeated in argument, not by threat of force. The debates leading to a decision must be free debates. And even after a decision has been made, free discussion about it should be allowed to continue. For the minority must know that if it has a good case, and if it argues properly and correctly, it will be able to convert the majority. Similarly, the majority must be willing to maintain the argument until the minority has been convinced of the correctness of the decision which has been made. Free debate must continue. It is an essential element of personal freedom.

But the necessity for continued freedom in discussion must not be allowed to prevent decisions from being made. There comes a point where action must follow discussion, or else we shall do nothing but talk. When there has been adequate discussion of a question, and every point of view has been expressed, then the decision must be reached, and the majority must be allowed to prevail. For just as the minority on any question have a right to be heard, so the majority have the right to be obeyed. Once a decision is reached, it must be accepted as the decision of all. And everyone — including those who were in opposition — have to cooperate in carrying out that decision. Thus, for example, once a law has been passed it must be obeyed by everyone, including those who spoke against it and have not been convinced by the arguments put forward in its support. More than that, once a law has been passed, it must be actively supported by everyone. It should not be merely a matter of acquiescence. It is not enough that a citizen should himself refrain from stealing; he must cooperate with the police in upholding the law, and must give over to the police those who transgress it.

For democratic decision-making must be followed by discipline in carrying out the decisions. The minority must be allowed to campaign for a change in the law or the decision. But until they have succeeded in getting majority support for a change, they must obey the law or the rule which has been laid down. Without this kind of discipline no development of any kind is possible.

DISCIPLINE MUST FOLLOW DECISION

Discipline must exist in every aspect of our lives. And it must be willingly accepted discipline. For it is an essential part of both freedom and development. The greater freedom which comes from working together, and achieving things by cooperation which none of us could achieve alone, is only possible if there is disciplined acceptance of joint decisions. And this involves the acceptance of lawfully constituted authority. It means that if we work in a factory, we have to accept the discipline of that factory. Whether the factory is privately or publicly owned makes no difference; its rules must be adhered to, and the people who are in charge of particular operations must be obeyed. Similarly, in hospitals, schools, offices, and so on. If the doctor orders certain treatment for the patient, it must be carried out by the nurse without argument, and without carelessness. If the matron lays down rules designed to ensure the smooth operation of the hospital, every nurse must obey these rules. If there are difficulties, representations can be made, but in the meantime the hospital discipline must be maintained or the person must accept dismissal. The same thing is true in our villages and rural communities. Once a community has democratically decided upon a particular self-help scheme, every-one must cooperate in carrying out that decision, or pay the penalty which the village agrees upon.

Yet provided decisions are made after free and friendly discussion, and by majority will, the essential discipline should be freely accepted, and should in fact, be largely self-discipline. For if our people want freedom for themselves, and if they want development, then they will accept the need for disciplined action. Indeed, the acceptance of community discipline is only a problem in Tanzania when our people do not understand the implications of the changes which we have already effected in our lives. In traditional society we had discipline — often very severe. It was accepted by everyone, and everyone cooperated in imposing it. Our problem now comes not from the discipline itself, but from a lack of understanding about the machinery which is necessary for discipline in a modern state, and from a failure to realise that different kinds of discipline are needed in the organisation of a modern society. Thus, for example, theft was dealt with directly by the com-munity when each village looked after its own peace and security. Now it is essen-tial that suspected thieves should be handed over to the police, and not mishandled by the people themselves. Or again, the simple rules of an isolated village are not enough for the running of a modern factory. In the village it rarely mattered whether a man carried out his task at daybreak or at noon; in a factory hundreds of other people can be made idle just because one man does not do his job at the right time.

These new kinds of discipline must be accepted by our people, and by all our leaders. And if anyone is unwilling to accept his responsibilities in this matter, then he must accept the penalties of his failure. If he disobeys the law, then the courts must punish him. If he fails to observe discipline in his work, then he must be dismissed. For we have to accept that the people in authority in Tanzania now are the agents of the people of Tanzania. If they do their job badly, or if they fail to respect the humanity of every human being, then the Government will replace them, or at an election the people will replace them. But in the meantime they must be upheld while they are carrying out the law, or issuing orders which are in conformity with the law. We must ourselves stop abusing people who are trying to ensure discipline; we must stop calling a man an *mkoloni* (colonialist) when he demands strict observance of the rules in an office, a factory, a hospital, a school, or any other institution.

If we are to live our lives in peace and harmony, and if we are to achieve our ambitions of improving the conditions under which we live, we must have both freedom and discipline. For freedom without discipline is anarchy: discipline without freedom is tyranny.

Discipline, however, must be a means of implementing decisions. Only in the very limited sense of orderly debate is discipline involved in the making of decisions. And discipline is not another word for force. A meeting must be disciplined if every member is to have an opportunity to be heard, but a disciplined meeting is not one where everyone automatically says 'yes' to whatever is suggested. A disciplined meeting is one where the rules which have been accepted as fair are observed by everyone — for example, where every member speaks through the chairman, and where each person is allowed to make his point without being shouted down or abused. For discipline allows the orderly conduct of affairs; it is the means by which decisions are implemented — not the way they are made.

UJAMAA VILLAGES

It is particularly important that we should now understand the connection between freedom, development, and discipline, because our national policy of creating socialist villages throughout the rural areas depends upon it. For we have known for a very long time that development had to go on in the rural areas, and that this required cooperative activities by the people. Ever since 1959, therefore, TANU has encouraged people to go in groups to farm in the rural areas, and our TANU Government has initiated settlement schemes of many kinds. But we can now see that we have committed many mistakes, and it is important that we should learn the right lessons from them.

When we tried to promote rural development in the past, we sometimes spent huge sums of money on establishing a settlement, and supplying it with modern equipment, and social services, as well as often providing it with a management hierarchy. In other cases, we just encouraged young men to leave the towns for a particular rural area and then left them to their own devices. We did these things because we recognised that the land is important to our economic future, but we acted on the assumption that there was a short cut to development in these rural areas. All too often, therefore, we persuaded people to go to new settlements by promising them that they could quickly grow rich there, or that Government would give them services and equipment which they could not hope to receive either in the towns or in their traditional farming places. In very few cases was any ideology involved; we thought and talked in terms of greatly increased output, and of things being provided for the settlers.

What we were doing, in fact, was thinking of development in terms of things, and not of people. Further, we thought in terms of monetary investment in order to achieve the increases in output we were aiming at. In effect, we said that capital equipment, or other forms of investment, would lead to increased output, and this would lead to a transformation in the lives of the people involved. The people were secondary; the first priority was the output. As a result, there have been very many cases where heavy capital investment has resulted in no increase in output — where the investment has been wasted. And in most of the officially sponsored or supported schemes, the majority of the people who went to settle lost their enthusiasm, and either left the scheme altogether, or failed to carry out the orders of the outsiders who were put in charge — and who were not themselves involved in the success or failure of the project.

It is important, therefore, to realise that the policy of *Ujamaa Vijijini* is not intended to be merely a revival of the old settlement schemes under another name. The ujamaa village is a new conception, based on the post-Arusha Declaration understanding that what we need to develop is people, not things, and that people can only develop themselves. The policy is, in fact, the result of learning from the failures which we have had, and from the successes of those small groups which began and grew on a different basis.

Ujamaa villages are intended to be socialist organisations created by the people, and governed by those who live and work in them. They cannot be created from outside, nor governed from outside. No one can be forced into an ujamaa village, and no official — at any level — can go and tell the members of an ujamaa village what they should do together, and what they should continue to do as individual farmers. No official of the Government or Party can go to an ujamaa village and tell the members what they must grow. No non-member of the village can go and tell the members to use a tractor, or not to use a tractor. For if these things happen — that is, if an outsider gives such instructions and enforces them — then it will no longer be an ujamaa village!

An ujamaa village is a voluntary association of people who decide of their own free will to live together and work together for their common good. They, and no one else, will decide how much of their land they will cultivate together from the beginning, and how much they will cultivate individually. They, and no one else, will decide how to use the money they earn jointly — whether to buy an ox-plough, install water, or do something else. They, and no one else, will make all the decisions about their working and living arrangements.

It is important that these things should be thoroughly understood. It is also important that the people should not be persuaded to start an ujamaa village by promises of the things which will be given to them if they do so. A group of people must decide to start an ujamaa village because they have understood that only through this method can they live and develop in dignity and freedom, receiving the full benefits of their cooperative endeavour. They must understand that there will be difficulties, and that the sheer coming together will not bring them prosperity. They must understand that coming together enables their work to be more productive in the long run, but is not a replacement for that work.

Unless the purpose and socialist ideology of an ujamaa village is understood by the members from the beginning — at least to some extent — it will not survive the early difficulties. For no one can guarantee that there will not be a crop failure in the first or second year — there might be a drought, or floods. And the greater self-discipline which is necessary when working in a community will only be forthcoming if the people understand what they are doing and why. Yet if the purposes, and the potential, are understood and accepted, then the members of an ujamaa village will be able to surmount such difficulties, and use them to strengthen their organisation and determination. The difficulties will help to speed up their development to socialism. But the people have to realise that ujamaa living does not cause miracles; it only allows them to improve their own lives.

The fact that people cannot be forced into ujamaa villages, nor told how to run them, does not mean that Government and TANU have just to sit back and hope that people will be inspired to create them on their own. To get ujamaa villages established and to help them to succeed, education and leadership are required. These are the things which TANU has to provide. It is our job to explain what an ujamaa village is, and to keep explaining it until the people understand. But the decision to start must be made by the people themselves — and it must be made by each individual. For if a group of 20 people discuss the idea and only 7 decide to go ahead, then that ujamaa village will consist of 7 people at the beginning. If 15 decide to start, then it will begin with 15 members — others will join as they are ready. There is no other way forward, because by joining a man has committed himself to a particular kind of life, and five who come in unwillingly can destroy the efforts of the 15 who want to work out a new pattern for themselves.

The decision to join with others in creating an ujamaa village is an individual one. But once that decision is made, then normal democratic rules will apply to all members. Thus, for example, the 15 people will sit down together and discuss

whether to cultivate all their crops together, or whether to begin by jointly cultivating only the cash crops, leaving food crops for individual activity. If they can,
they will talk until they agree; but if they cannot come to a unanimous agreement
before it is time for work to begin, then they will decide by majority rule. Once this
decision has been taken for the forthcoming season, all the members have to accept
the discipline of the work which has been made necessary by the majority decision
— even if they voted against it. While working hard the minority can continue to try
to persuade the other members to make a change next year, but their talk must not
lead to a reduction in the effort they make in carrying out the majority decision.

In fact, once an ujamaa village is created, it is a democracy at work. For it
provides an example of free discussion among equals, leading to their own decision-
making; it shows that when discussion has to give way to action, then the majority
will prevails; and it demonstrates the need for discipline by all members in the
implementation of the decisions which the group has made. And in this very process, the people will have begun to develop themselves as dignified and confident
human beings, in a way which is impossible if they simply take orders from someone else. The fact that the orders of an 'expert' may have led to greater output of
a crop if they were fully carried out, does not affect this issue. By debating this
matter and then deciding for themselves, the people will be doing real development
of themselves. Achieving greater output will come later as they learn from their
own experience, and as they are convinved that it would be a good idea to try a
new method. Progress may appear to be slower in the sense that statistics of crop
output will not increase very fast at the beginning. We should remember, however, that those people who marched hundreds of miles in support of the Arusha
Declaration did not break speed records. They plodded steadily on until they
reached their objective, suiting both their speed, and their hours of walking, to
what they felt they could maintain.

Yet Government and TANU leaders can and should help these ujamaa villages
and their members. Leaders should help people to understand the arguments for
and against different methods of organisation. We should help a group which
decides to start by making sure that they can get adequate land in a convenient
parcel. We should help to explain the advantages of working a communal farm, and
how the problems can be overcome. We should make sure that the members have
agricultural and other advice available to them when they are making their decisions.

Further, Government and Party leaders must make sure that ujamaa villages
get priority in service to back up their own efforts and their own decisions. For
example, if the members of an ujamaa village decide that they have a priority need
for water, and that they can dig the ditches and buy the pipes but not the pump,
then Government and Party should help them by providing a pump rather than
laying on water to some other area. But there must be no question of Government
assistance replacing the efforts of the members of an ujamaa village. Advice must
be given, but the decisions must be those of the members themselves; help must be
given when possible, but it must be help for something the people are already doing
for themselves. These villages must start, and must grow, on the basis of self-
reliance. For self-reliance is the means by which people develop.

TANZANIA IS ALL THE PEOPLE

By developing the people of Tanzania, we are developing Tanzania. For Tanzania is
the people; and the people means everyone *(Tanzania ni ya Watanzania; na, Watanzania ni wote)*. No one person has the right to say, 'I am the People'. No Tanzanian

has the right to say 'I know what is good for Tanzania and the others must do it'.

All Tanzanians have to make the decisions for Tanzania; all have to work together, and all of us have to accept the discipline we impose upon ourselves. It must be joint discipline — applying to us all equally. But in accepting this discipline we must remain free men, implementing our own decisions. The group involved in any particular decision, and any particular discipline, will vary. Some decisions are national, and the discipline is that of law which we must all obey. Some decisions affect only those who live in a particular town or district, and the discipline is that of by-laws. Some decisions arise out of our own free decision to participate in a particular group — to work in a factory, to live in an ujamaa village, etc.; and the discipline then applies to us because of our membership of that group. But all of us are Tanzanians. Together we are the people. Our development is our affair; and it is the development of ourselves as people that we must dedicate ourselves to.

CHAPTER 3

TANU Guidelines on Guarding, Consolidating and Advancing the Revolution of Tanzania, and of Africa (Mwongozo)*

We have been oppressed a great deal, we have been exploited a great deal and we have been disregarded a great deal. It is our weakness that has led to our being oppressed, exploited and disregarded. Now we want a revolution . . .

(Arusha Declaration)

INTRODUCTION

1. Today our African continent is a hot-bed of the liberation struggle. This struggle is between those who have for centuries been exploiting Africa's natural resources and using the people of this continent as their tools and as their slaves, and the people of Africa who have, after realising their weakness and exploitation, decided to engage in the struggle to liberate themselves. It is both a bitter and continuing struggle: at times it is a silent one, occasionally it explodes like gunpowder, at other times the successes and gains achieved by the people slip away.

This has been the history of Africa since 1960 when many African states obtained flag independence. Since that year many legitimate African governments have been forcefully toppled and new governments established. Recently, sudden changes have been brought about by force in Uganda, where puppet Amin and a group of fellow soldiers have rebelled against the government of the revolutionary UPC led by President Obote.

The majority of the armed forces do not accept the rebellion and many of them, particularly senior officers, have been killed by the puppets. It is obvious that those who hail the rebellion are those who opposed the UPC policy of bringing about unity and socialism and eradicating tribalism and exploitation.

This is why our Party has the duty to spell out the aims of the Tanzanian and the African revolution, and to identify the enemies of this revolution, in order to set out policies and strategies which will enable us to safeguard, consolidate and further our revolution.

2. Revolutions are quick social changes, changes which wrest from the minority the power they exploited for their own benefit (and that of external exploiters) and put it in the hands of the majority so that they can promote their own well-being. The opposite of a revolution is a counter-revolution: that is, quick and sudden changes which wrest power from the majority and hand it over to the minority with the aim of stopping the progress of the masses.

3. The greatest aim of the African revolution is to liberate the African. This liberation is not sent from heaven, it is achieved by combating exploitation, colonialism and imperialism. Nor is liberation brought by specialists or experts. We who are being humiliated, exploited and oppressed are the experts of this liberation. There

*Adopted by the TANU National Executive Committee, January, 1971.

is no nation in the world which can teach the Africans how to liberate themselves. The duty of liberating ourselves lies with us, and the necessary expertise will be obtained during the struggle itself.

4. Furthermore, the present situation in Africa shows that there is no people in any African state which has achieved the stage of total liberation. Africa is still a continent of people suffering from the weakness inherent in being exploited and humiliated. That is why revolutionary political parties in independent African countries, such as TANU, are still in fact Liberation Movements.

5. The African revolution, whose aim is the true liberation of the African, is in conflict with policies of exploitation, colonialism, neo-colonialism and imperialism. The object of colonialism, neo-colonialism and imperialism is to ensure that Africa's wealth is used for the benefit of the capitalists of Europe and America, instead of benefiting the African countries themselves. Therefore, participating in the African revolution is participating in the struggle against colonialism and imperialism.

6. The imperialist countries which have been exploiting and oppressing Africa for centuries are those in Western Europe, particularly Britain, France, Portugal, Belgium and Spain. These countries are the ones really confronting the African people on the question of liberating Africa. Different attempts to distort the progress of the African revolution stem from the plots of European imperialists who are bent on maintaining and continuing their old exploitation.

7. For Tanzania it must be understood that the imperialist enemies we are confronting are British imperialism, Portuguese colonialism, the racism and apartheid of South Africa and Rhodesia. For historical, geographical and political reasons these imperialists will be ready to attack us whenever they have an opportunity.

8. The Portuguese invasion of the Republic of Guinea is a big lesson for us. Guinea was invaded by the Portuguese imperialists firstly because of its policy of equality and its opposition to exploitation, and secondly because of its genuine stand in supporting the freedom fighters in Guinea Bissau and Africa. For similar reasons the imperialists may attempt to attack Tanzania one day. But Guinea has also taught us that when the people and the army stand solidly together, no imperialist will be able to subvert their independence.

9. The lesson we draw from Uganda is one of treachery and counter-revolution. It shows that, instead of invading the country to overthrow the revolutionary government, imperialism prefers to use local puppets to overthrow the legitimate government and replace it with a government of 'frontmen' or puppets. Such a government will allow the imperialists to exploit national wealth in partnership with the local bourgeoisie.

The people must learn from the events in Uganda and those in Guinea that, although imperialism is still strong, its ability to topple a revolutionary government greatly depends on the possibility of getting domestic counter-revolutionary puppets to help in thwarting the revolution.

10. We Tanzanians value our national independence because it is from that point that our liberation, and our aspirations for a liberation struggle in conjunction with other African people, begin. For this reason, we have the duty to take all necessary steps to enable us to guard our independence in order to further our revolution and thus make Tanzania a true example of the African revolution.

POLITICS
The Party

11. The responsibility of the party is to lead the masses, and their various

institutions, in the effort to safeguard national independence and to advance the liberation of the African. The duty of a socialist party is to guide all activities of the masses. The Government, parastatals, national organisations, etc, are instruments for implementing the Party's policies. Our short history of independence reveals problems that may arise when a Party does not guide its instruments. The time has now come for the Party to take the reins and lead all the people's activities.

12. The first task of the leadership is to spell out the national goal. This is understood and the party has already fulfilled this duty. Our aim is to build Socialism in Tanzania. But to attain this objective the Party must offer policies and guidelines concerning different aspects of the people's activities. The Party has already given guidelines on socialism in rural areas, education for self-reliance, etc. There is still the need to clarify the Party's policies on other matters, such as housing, workers, money and loan policies, etc.

13. But the charting of objectives and policies does not by itself constitute good leadership. Leadership also means organising the people. It is the Party which decides on the structure of government, various institutions, the army, etc. In addition, the Party should provide guidelines on work methods and attitudes, and decision-making.

The truth is that we have not only inherited a colonial governmental structure but have also adopted colonial working habits and leadership methods. For example, we have inherited in the government, industries and other institutions the habit in which one man gives the orders and the rest just obey them. If you do not involve the people in work plans, the result is to make them feel a national institution is not theirs, and consequently workers adopt the habits of hired employees. The Party has a duty to emphasise its leadership on the issue.

14. In addition to organising the people, leadership involves supervising the implementation of the Party's policy. Ways must be found to ensure that the Party actively supervises the activities and the running of its implementing agencies. Leadership also entails reviewing the results of implementation. It is the Party's duty to ensure that it assesses the effects of the policy implementation undertaken by its agencies. This is the only way to establish whether people participate in devising solutions to their problems in offices, institutions, the army, villages, industries, etc.

15. Together with the issue of involving the people in solving their problems, there is also the question of the habits of leaders in their work and in day-to-day life.

There must be a deliberate effort to build equality between the leaders and those they lead. For a Tanzanian leader it must be forbidden to be arrogant, extravagant, contemptuous and oppressive. The Tanzanian leader has to be a person who respects people, scorns ostentation and who is not a tyrant. He should epitomise heroism, bravery, and be a champion of justice and equality.

Similarly, the Party has the responsibility to fight the vindictiveness of some of its agents. Such actions do not promote socialism but drive a wedge between the Party and the Government on the one side and the people on the other.

16. There are presently some leaders who do not fulfil these conditions. They disregard and cleverly avoid the leadership code. The time has come for the Party to supervise the conduct and the bearing of the leaders.

Foreign Policy

17. Our foreign policy is one of non-alignment. We are ready to cooperate in a

friendly manner with any country that wishes us well, be it from the East or West. The second important aspect of our foreign policy is to strengthen relations with, and cooperate in supporting, genuine liberation movements in Africa. We have said earlier that our own Party is still a Liberation Movement.

At the moment in Africa the liberation movements are in the vanguard of the struggle against colonialism and imperialism. By strengthening our cooperation, in the knowledge that their war is our war, we shall double our strength in bringing about the total liberation of Africa. The Party must take the necessary steps to establish this revolutionary relationship with revolutionary movements of Africa, Asia and Latin America.

Similarly it is our duty to establish fraternal and revolutionary relations with those American citizens fighting for justice and human equality.

18. In addition, we have the obligation to strengthen cooperation and solidarity with revolutionary African countries because all of us are in the same boat and our destination is one. With unity and cooperation, our enemies will not be able to destroy us one by one as is now their habit.

19. At the United Nations and other international organisations, there is need to stress cooperation with all friendly, socialist and revolutionary countries in Africa, Asia, and Latin America.

Uganda and the EAC

20. We value the political and economic benefits derived from the cooperation that exists among the partner states of the East African Community. Therefore, the present situation created by the puppet Amin in subverting the legitimate Government of the UPC greatly disturbs us, because it has given rise to difficulties in cooperation and in running the activities of the Community.

If the situation continues as it is, it may make the progress and the activities of the Community extremely difficult to maintain, and will weaken East African cooperation. The Party supports the Government's stand on Uganda and the East African Community. Although it is for the people of Uganda to decide on matters relating to Uganda's liberation, it is the duty of the Tanzanian people to support the efforts of their Ugandan brothers to liberate themselves.

DEFENCE AND SECURITY

And for the defence of our nation, it is necessary for us to be on guard against internal stooges who could be used by external enemies who aim to destroy us.
(Arusha Declaration)

21. The basis of Tanzania's development is the people themselves — every Tanzanian — in particular each patriot and each socialist. Tanzania's defence and security depend on Tanzanians themselves — every Tanzanian, in particular each patriot, each socialist.

22. Had our Party been forced to wage a liberation war, every TANU member would have been a solider, either in the army or wherever he was. A TANU member would have been a soldier and a soldier a TANU member. It is not only the Party which would have been a Liberation Army — fist and shield of the Liberation Movement.

23. Our Party was not forced to fight a liberation war. It was a Liberation Movement without a Liberation Army. But since 1964 we have been building the

Tanzania People's Defence Forces. And just as TANU is still a Liberation Movement, the Tanzania People's Defence Force is the Liberation Army of the people of Tanzania.

TANU's relations with the TPDF should be those of a People's Party and a People's Army. It is up to TANU to ensure that the people's army is the army for both the liberation and the defence of the people. It is TANU's responsibility to ensure that the army's main task in peace-time is to enable the people to safeguard their independence and their policy of socialism and self-reliance.

24. The National Executive Committee stresses the implementation of the Arusha Declaration and particularly the need to arouse political consciousness so that every Tanzanian understands our national environment and the importance of safeguarding the security and the lives of the people, and of safeguarding our policies, our independence, our economy and our culture.

25. Political education must make the people aware of our national enemies and the strategies they employ to subvert our policies, our independence, our economy and our culture. To enable the people to confront the enemy, it is necessary to make them aware of the enemy's strength in all spheres, such as their army, their commercial enterprise, their life and habits, and the way these conflict with our convictions and aspirations.

26. In order that they may be able to oppose our enemies, the people must know that it is they who are the nation's shield. This means that defence and security matters must be placed in the hands of the people themselves. We do not have the means to establish large permanent armies to guard the whole country. Our army must be the people's army, used in teaching the people how to defend themselves in their localities and to enable them to report on matters of national security. Therefore it is imperative to start training a militia for the whole country. Since the militia will spread through the country, in cooperation with the regular army, they will have the duty to defend our territorial borders, our air space and to expose traitors and enemies, all in cooperation with our regular army.

The Party leads the Army

27. The registration of the militia and the army must be scrutinised very carefully, and supervised by the Party. Ensuring cooperation between the army and the militia, and providing for political education to both, must be a prime responsibility of the Party. The Party must establish a sub-committee of the Central Committee to look into defence and security.

ECONOMICS AND PROGRESS

The development of a country is brought about by people.
            (Arusha Declaration)

Progress of the People

28. For a people who have been slaves or have been oppressed, exploited and humiliated by colonialism or capitalism, 'development' means 'liberation'. Any action that gives them more control of their own affairs is an action for development, even if it does not offer them better health or more bread. Any action that reduces their say in determining their own affairs or running their own lives is not development and retards them even if the action brings them a little better health and a little more bread.

To us development means both the elimination of oppression, exploitation, enslavement and humiliation, and the promotion of our independence and human dignity. Therefore, in considering the development of our nation and in preparing development plans, our main emphasis at all times should be the development of people and not of things. If development is to benefit the people, the people must participate in considering, planning and implementing their development plans.

The duty of our Party is not to urge the people to implement plans which have been decided upon by a few experts and leaders. The duty of our Party is to ensure that the leaders and experts implement the plans that have been agreed upon by the people themselves. When the people's decision requires information which is only available to the leaders and the experts, it will be the duty of leaders and experts to make such information available to the people. But it is not correct for leaders and experts to usurp the people's right to decide on an issue just because they have the expertise.

29. In order that the people shall be enthusiastic in the defence of their country, it is of first importance for the TANU Government to place a lot of emphasis on improving their conditions.

The inherited economic structure which has kept many people out of the economic main stream must be replaced immediately by programmes designed to boost the development expenditure and to spread investment to all districts. The Regional Development Fund has helped to arouse economic activities and has thus brought visible benefits to the people. It will be beneficial to increase allocations to the fund and to give this expenditure special priority when approaching Government finances. The Party must stress the participation of people in the various nation-building projects.

Savings

30. It is also the Party's duty to educate the people on the importance of saving through national institutions such as the Savings Bank and the National Bank of Commerce, instead of just hoarding their money.

National Economy

31. In consolidating the people's development, there is now a need to build and promote the internal economy. Although this was touched upon in the Second Five-Year Development Plan, its implementation has not been stressed, and therefore results have not been seen. The things that are produced in this country must also be protected from unnecessary foreign competition.

Foreign Trade

32. In our external trade, we must avoid using our foreign reserves in buying items that do not help our economy. The Government and its Corporations must be an example — a thing that is not now being done. Our importing agencies must be given guidelines appropriate to our policy of socialism and self-reliance, and the guidelines must be adhered to. It is the duty of every Tanzanian, and particularly a leader, to remember that shortage of foreign exchange weakens our economy and endangers our national independence.

Parastatal Institutions

33. The conduct and activities of the parastatals must be looked into to ensure

that they help further our policy of socialism and self-reliance. The activities of the parastatals should be a source of satisfaction and not discontent. The Party must ensure that the parastatals do not spend money extravagently on items which do not contribute to the development of the national economy as a whole.

Surpluses

34. The Government must supervise and guide the expenditure of surpluses accruing from the economic activities of the parastatals.

35. We have been oppressed a great deal we have been exploited a great deal and we have been disregarded a great deal. It is out weakness that has led to our being oppressed, exploited and disregarded. Now we want a revolution — a revolution which brings to an end our weakness. so that we are never again exploited, oppressed, or humiliated.

(Arusha Declaration)

CHAPTER 4

The Arusha Declaration Ten Years After*

Julius K. Nyerere

The Arusha Declaration was passed by TANU in January, 1967. It explained the meaning of Socialism and Self-Reliance, and their relevance to Tanzania. At the same time TANU adopted the Arusha Resolution, and instructed the Government and other public institutions of mainland Tanzania to implement policies which would make Tanzania into a socialist and self-reliant nation.

Action began within twenty-four hours of the publication of the Declaration and Resolution. On 6th February, 1967, all private commercial banks were nationalised; on each of the succeeding four days further steps were taken to bring the economy of the country into the ownership and control of the people. Since that exciting week, never a month has passed without further endeavours by TANU, Government, public institutions, or individual groups of the people themselves, to translate into a reality the principles and policies outlined in these basic Party documents.

But I am a very poor prophet. In 1956 I was asked how long it would take Tanganyika to become Independent. I thought 10 to 12 years. We became independent 6 years later! In 1967 a group of the youth who were marching in support of the Arusha Declaration asked me how long it would take Tanzania to become socialist. I though 30 years. I was wrong again: I am now sure that it will take us much longer!

Ten years after the Arusha Declaration Tanzania is certainly neither socialist, nor self-reliant. The nature of exploitation has changed, but it has not been altogether eliminated. There are still great inequalities between citizens. Our democracy is imperfect. A life of poverty is still the experience of the majority of our citizens. Too many of our people still suffer from the indignities of preventable disease and ignorance, and the aged and disabled do not all live in decency or even security, despite the clear statement in the Declaration that they have a right to support. Further, our nation is still economically dependent upon the vagaries of the weather, and upon economic and political decisions taken by other peoples without our participation or consent. And this latter is not a reciprocal situation; Tanzania is still a dependent nation, not an interdependent one.

We have not reached our goal; it is not even in sight. But that is neither surprising, nor alarming. No country in the world is yet fully socialist, although many committed themselves to this philosophy decades before Tanzania even became independent. Few other developing countries, and those only the biggest, are fully self-reliant. What matters is that in the last ten years we in Tanzania have taken some very important steps towards our goal, despite adverse climatic and international conditions.

First and foremost, we in Tanzania have stopped, and reversed, a national drift

*A Report to the TANU Executive Committee, January, 1977.

towards the growth of a class society, based on ever-increasing inequality and the exploitation of the majority for the benefit of a few. We have changed the direction of our national development, so that our national resources are now being deliberately directed towards the needs of this nation and its people.

Secondly, we have established some of the attitudes which are necessary to the development of socialism. There is now a general recognition that it is wrong for some people to live in luxury while others are destitute. The argument now is not on the principle, but on how, and how fast, we can move from our inheritance of great inequalities to a position where differences of income are slight and depend entirely upon service to society. Cooperation for common benefit rather than the relentless pursuit of individual advancement, is now the more generally approved social behaviour, even in the modern sector of our society. A person is therefore beginning — only beginning — to be judged for what he contributes rather than by what he acquires. And we are learning to take pride in the extension of basic public facilities to the mass of our people, rather than in grandiose public buildings or the evidence of personal prosperity for a few. Our National Ethic, in other words, is beginning to be a socialist ethic — that is, a concern for the well-being of all rather than a pride in material goods for their own sake.

Thirdly, we have established many of the institutions, and worked out many of the strategies, for socialist advance. These are by no means complete, or perfect; a very great deal remains to be done. But in 1977 we are not starting from the beginning as we were in 1967; the public financial, productive, and social organisations which are necessary to serve the people's needs do mostly exist. We have even gained some experience, although it has been too often the experience which comes from making mistakes.

Fourthly, we have made reasonably good progress towards providing basic health, education, and transportation facilities for all the people of this country. Staff training has been multiplied, and by a combined effort from the people organised in TANU, and the Government, many new dispensaries, schools, community centres, and water supplies, have been created. Connected with these things has been the movement of virtually our entire people into villages, so that they can work together to provide, and get together to use, the public facilities which are essential to an improved standard of living for all.

And fifthly; we have, as a nation, continued to make some contribution to the freedom struggle in Africa, and therefore to strengthening our own freedom. Individuals and groups all over the country have made voluntary financial contributions to the struggles being waged by our brothers and sisters to the south of Tanzania. As a nation we have been active politically, and diplomatically, in support of freedom in Southern Africa. And we have provided training places and rear bases when it has become necessary for the political freedom struggle to be converted into a war of liberation.

The measure of our success is that these fundamental achievements are generally taken for granted. We are now much more conscious of the difficulties in our daily lives than of fundamental exploitation. And that is as it should be.

Daily difficulties certainly exist. The absence of luxury goods in our shops affects only a small number of people. But the intermittent shortage of simple goods, and even of necessities, is a continuing problem for some people — especially in the more remote villages. Further, crops are not always collected, or paid for, as soon as they are harvested, with consequent loss or hardship to hardworking peasants. Work is delayed and people are frustrated by poor bus services or the absence of sufficient transportation for their goods. There are numerous regulations covering what appear to the individual to be simple transactions; these are always unpopular, sometimes unnecessary, and very often badly administered. And on top of all this, a few people have found their standard of living actually reduced over the past ten years.

Today such difficulties and frustrations make us forget where we came from, and even make a reminder seem like an irrelevant impertinence. It is quite true that when our shops were full of a large variety of goods, the vast majority of people had no money to buy them. It is quite true that ten years ago most people walked to work because they could not afford the bus fare, and that they did not complain about their children not going to secondary school because they had not even gone to primary school! But people have now developed a little; they have higher expectations of life. No longer does a man or woman think of life as an endless round of hard physical labour, enlivened only by marriage and birth and the fellowship of community. For here also we have achieved fundamental success. Our people are now more conscious of their potential as human beings, and of the possibilities of human life. So they reject the argument that because they did not resent the limited boundaries of their lives when they were mentally asleep, therefore they should not complain when the expectations of awareness are frustrated. They see that this argument is too often used as an excuse.

But a reminder is still necessary. Our current difficulties, and our failures, must not be allowed to hide our greatest achievement. It is one which usually goes unrecognised inside Tanzania, although many people outside — from their own bitter experience, or from observation — are aware of it. For we are like a man who does not get smallpox because he has got himself vaccinated. His arm is sore and he feels sick for a while; if he has never seen what smallpox does to people he may feel very unhappy during that period, and wish that he had never agreed to the vaccination.

There are some evils which Tanzania was too undeveloped to suffer from up to the time of independence. Among these were: the destitution which comes from landlessness when there is no other form of livelihood available; private usury; and literal starvation in the midst of plenty. In countries like India millions of people experienced these evils — and indeed still experience them because it is very difficult for a poor country to eradicate them once they are established. But all these things are liable to come from economic development, if it is not pursued along socialist lines.

We in Tanzania do not now have, and we shall not have in the future unless we abandon socialist policies, many problems for individuals and the society which afflict even the wealthiest of capitalist nations. Our people do not suffer from the tyranny of landlords who control their land and therefore their means of livelihood. They do not find it impossible to obtain or build a house because individuals own all the houses, and all the land, and charge what they like. Our workers are not grossly exploited by employers, and forced to work hard for a paltry wage or see their children die from lack of food or shelter. With a few exceptions which come from lack of understanding and which we have not yet managed to control, our land and natural resources are not destroyed to make private profit for a few.

Further, because of our socialist policies, there are not growing inequalities between our citizens, with the already rich growing richer and the poor getting poorer. On the contrary, we have been — and still are — gradually reducing economic and therefore social inequalities among our people.

And although our nation is not by any means economically independent, we are not becoming more dependent on others as time goes on and development increases. As a result of our socialist policies, it is the people of this country — not foreigners — who determine what kind of factories and farms shall be established in Tanzania. This means that we can gradually increase our control over the Tanzanian economy; we are not being bound tighter and tighter into an international capitalist structure which we can never hope to control, or even influence.

All these evils, and many others which we are now spared, would have happened in Tanzania had we not adopted the Arusha Declaration. Indeed, the first signs of them could be seen before 1967, despite certain socialist measures which had been taken before that time. Thus, for example, immediately after independence, some citizens of African descent who had previously been denied bank loans or credit, suddenly found them easy to get. They were the political leaders, and the newly promoted civil servants. They were able, and indeed were encouraged by the private banks and financial institutions to borrow money to buy or build large houses, which they could then rent at a profit. Sometimes they were even getting public money for such purposes. On the strength of that, they could get more credit in order to build more houses, and get more profit. Again; in the rural areas, a few individuals who had better education or were believed to be 'leaders of opinion' were getting a private claim over large areas of land, and employing others to work for them. Individuals, and again mostly political or NUTA or co-op leaders, were acquiring buses, or taxis, from which they reaped a profit by employing others to run them on their behalf. Capitalism was beginning. And it was beginning with the leadership. Certainly it was a mean and unproductive kind of capitalism which was beginning in Tanzania, but it was capitalism all the same.

Fortunately, these things, this 'creation of an African middle class', had not gone very far. Our leaders had begun to think that individual riches were part of the prerequistes of leadership; but they had not begun actually to become rich. So the Arusha Resolution came in time; it was passed after a long argument about its effect on individuals, but it was passed. For our leaders had been elected by the people from among themselves; they were not a separate group. And they realised that the only way they could really serve their country and their fellow citizens was as set out in the Arusha Declaration.

OUR ACHIEVEMENTS UNDER THE ARUSHA DECLARATION
Public Ownership of the means of Production and Exchange

The nationalisation of existing industries and services, which took place immediately after the Arusha Declaration, was more important for what it enabled us to do later than for its own sake. For you can only nationalise what exists, and there was very little industrial development in Tanzania. Even so, the nationalisation exercise was fundamental to what followed. And it has meant a reduction in the outflow of Tanzania's wealth in the form of interest and profits.

It is impossible to assess the total amount of money which would have been sent out of Tanzania over the past 10 years if we had not taken over the major means of production and exchange in 1967. Looking at the National Bank of Commerce alone, its total net profits retained in Tanzania from 1967-1976 amounted to Shs. 557.3 million. This is after paying full compensation to the private banks out of which the NBC was formed, and therefore gives some indication of the money which would probably have gone out of Tanzania during the period from this source alone.

It can therefore be said, without hesitation, that one result of the Arusha Declaration, from which we are now benefiting, is that such wealth as we do produce in Tanzania is available for use in Tanzania. A *mrija* (reed), through which our little wealth was being sucked, has been cut.

Even more important, however, is that by taking the productive and distributive sectors of our economy into public hands, we have been able to decide for ourselves what we want to build, and determine our own priorities. We have therefore been able to use our limited resources (either of our own, or from overseas borrowing) to create industries which will serve the needs of our people. Obviously we made some mistakes; there were one or two occasions when we fell into the trap of being 'modern' at all costs, and invested in large capital-intensive factories when a number of small labour-intensive plants could have given the same service at lower financial cost and with less use of external technical expertise.

A few mistakes apart, however, we have made advances in industrialisation. In the last ten years we have started a large number of small and cottage industries, either in urban industrial estates, or in the villages of Tanzania. We have also started factories manufacturing such varied goods as farm implements, tyres, fertilisers, radios, batteries and bicycles, as well as cement works, printing plants, etc. All these and many other industrial enterprises produce goods needed by the people of Tanzania. We have also expanded some of the factories we took over in 1967 — as for example the shoe and tobacco factories. More industrial plants are currently under construction.

Apart from those mentioned, we have given particular emphasis to the expansion of enterprises which use our own raw materials. For example, in 1967 hardly any of our cotton was made into cloth in Tanzania; by 1975 we had 8 textile mills, capable of producing over 84 million square metres of cloth. Sisal rope production has greatly expanded. Still further expansion of these industries is planned or in process; a new textile mill is to be built in Musoma, and the Mwanza Mill is now being expanded. The expansion of the *Urafiki* (Friendship) Textile Mill has been completed. A sisal carpet factory is being constructed in Kilosa; new cement works are planned for Tanga and Mbeya; several different factories are being planned for Morogoro; and so on. In all these cases our dual aim is to be able to meet the mass needs of our own people by production within Tanzania and also to convert our raw materials into manufactured goods before exporting them. By that means we shall increase our foreign exchange earnings, because the value added by the manufacturing processes will accrue to Tanzania, and be paid in the form of wages and investible surplus to Tanzanians.

The industrial expansion over the last ten years is certainly small in comparison with our needs, but it is nothing to be ashamed of. Once again it is good to remember where we come from. The value of our industrial production has trebled over the decade, and industry now accounts for about 10 per cent of our national income instead of 8.0 per cent in 1966. This is in a much more expanded economy. The number of people who earn their living in industry is now about 2½ times as great as it was in 1967.

Few, if any, of these new factories would have been started in Tanzania had we relied upon private investment for industrial expansion. Even had there been an increase in foreign private investment and a consequent growth in the monetary value of Tanzanian industrial production, it is quite certain that the new factories would not have been directed at making goods needed by Tanzanians or at maximising the value of Tanzania's primary products. For such activities in a poor country are not very profitable in money terms.

It is true that had we tried indiscriminately to attract foreign capital, factories might have been started to produce other things. For example, in some new states Transnational Corporations have established factories which produce some of the components for complicated manufactured goods. These components are then exported and assembled in Europe, together with different parts made in other poor countries. The major effect of this so-called industrial development is to make certain important sectors of the national economy become dependent upon a capitalist Transnational Corporation. As such institutions have the sole objective of maximising their total international profit, regardless of the interests of any of the individual states in which they operate, that kind of 'development' is not really national development at all. It can make the industrial growth statistics look very good, but in the end the country can be worse off as far as its independence and people's welfare are concerned. Some countries have such urgent unemployment problems, and so little land, that it is difficult for them not to adopt this strategy. But Tanzania has no such need to increase its economic dependence on foreign capitalists. And we have avoided any danger of doing so by insisting that, in all large or important activities, foreign capital shall operate in this country as a minority partner, and therefore under public control.

Equality

Human equality and dignity is fundamental to socialism, as the Arusha Declaration makes very clear. And although we still have a long way to go, we have made very commendable progress towards equality since 1967.

There are three aspects to the development of greater equality within a nation. One is differentials in personal incomes. The second is different degrees of access to public services, and the extent to which taxation-supported activities serve the interests of the people as a whole rather than those of a small minority. And the third is participation in decision-making.

In some ways the second aspect of equality — that is the communal aspect — is more important than the first in a poor country when market forces are prevented from operating freely by decisions of the democratically elected Government. For provided that everyone is assured of minimum food, clothing, and shelter, a great advance towards equality has been made if such things as education, health services, clean water, agricultural advice, and transport are equally available to everyone — or even if their availability is made less unequal.

And the third aspect of equality, that is the power to participate in decision-making, is absolutely fundamental. Unless every person plays an effective part in his own government, rather than always being the recipient of decisions made by others, there can be no equality in human dignity and status. Nor is there likely to be very much progress in economic equality. In all these aspects of equality we have made some advance.

Education

In order to train Tanzanians for the middle and senior posts in the administration and the economy of the country, it was necessary immediately after independence to emphasise the creation of secondary and post-secondary educational facilities. In the last ten years, we have been able to turn our attention more to basic education for everyone, although secondary, and higher education (especially teacher-training) has continued to be expanded. In 1974 TANU even took the bold step of opting for universal primary education for all our children by the end of 1977, despite the current intense economic difficulties.

A tremendous jump in the number of children attending primary school has been the result. In 1967 there were about 825,000 pupils in Tanzanian primary schools. In 1975, the comparable figure was 1,532,000 pupils, and the numbers will continue to rise rapidly for some years to come. Thus, in 1976, there was a still further increase in the school population as 665,621 children entered school for the first time, compared with a total of 187,537 who entered standard I in 1967.

Great advances have been made in adult education — especially the extension of literacy. Thus, during the five years of the illiteracy eradication campaign, over 5 million people registered themselves in literacy classes, and of these some 3.8 million sat for the literacy test conducted in August 1975. All the people who persisted with their classes deserve our congratulations, because it is not easy for adults to learn these skills for the first time at the end of a day's work. Further, 1.9 million people passed the literacy test at the 3rd or 4th level, which means that they can read, write, and do simple sums with ease. We should salute their achievement — and must make certain that they can obtain reading materials of the kind which interests them and from which they can learn more.

For equally important with the fact of learning is what people learn. Since the publication of *Education for Self-Reliance* in 1967, our teaching at all levels has become increasingly appropriate to the needs of our people and of Tanzanian society taken as a whole. In the primary schools, and in special post-primary groups, there has been new emphasis given to technical and agricultural training, and the pupils no longer spend most of their time preparing for secondary school education which the majority of them will never receive. The literacy campaign also was designed to pass on other knowledge while people were learning to read and write; thus books were about better husbandry methods for crops important in the locality, or about good health and child-care requirements, etc. The secondary schools are also giving increased emphasis to technical and scientific subjects, with most schools now specialising in either agriculture, science or technology. Such changes in curriculum and syllabus can only be a gain, both to the individuals who find their knowledge more useful in their lives, and to the country whose stock of practical skills is increased.

Such rapid educational expansion does, however, put a great strain on the teachers and educational administrators. They have accepted the challenge, and are overcoming it; they have done very well, and have worked hard for many extra hours without any extra pay. They have earned the respect, and deserve the thanks, of the whole community.

But the expansion also costs a lot of money! Our people cannot finance UPE nor larger numbers of secondary schools through taxation or any other way if we continue to support the schools and school-children in the manner of the past. The 'Self-Reliance' of institutions has thus become vital to the Tanzania educational system. We have made a beginning on this, although we need to go much further. It is estimated that in the school year 1974/75 economic activities in our schools produced goods to the value of over Shs. 7.7 million. These activities include the growing of different crops — mostly food which was consumed by the schools — and the raising of chicken and livestock, all of which were used to provide food in one way or another. In addition, many schools made bricks, furniture, or clothes, either for their own use or for sale. These self-reliance activities are still small and often ill-organised; but they are being accepted as part of the normal educational system.

One other important education development which is relevant to the growth of socialist attitudes was the changed method of entry to University. Now all students finish their education at the end of secondary school. Only those who have been working in our villages or factories are eligible to go to University, and their admission depends upon character references given by their work-mates as well as upon academic qualifications.

It has been necessary to make some temporary exceptions to this rule. Women students and students for the Engineering Faculty are all allowed to enter directly after completing their National Service. This is intended as a temporary compensation for the social and education disadvantages suffered by Tanzanian women in the past, and in order to ensure that expensive technical and scientific equipment, and teaching capacity, at the University is fully used during the transition to the new system. But in time the same rules will apply to all. And it is interesting to see from reports of the first year under the new system that the more mature students in fact get better results on average, even in technical and scientific subjects, than did the students who were accepted straight from school. This is not surprising; a mature student has greater understanding of what he wants to do at University.

Health

We were slower in changing the direction of our health service towards meeting the needs of the people in the rural areas. But the new emphasis began in 1972, and has gathered speed since then. Thus, for example, in 1967 there were only 42 rural health centres in operation; in 1976 there were 152, with many more under construction. And there were 610 more maternal and child-care clinics in 1976 than were operating ten years before. There was also a 200% increase in the number of Rural Medical Aids and a 270% increase in the number of Medical Assistants at work in the country. As these provide most of the medical service in the village dispensaries and health centres, it is obvious that we are directing our care to where the majority of the people live rather than spending all our resources on big urban hospitals.

Preventive medicine is part of the work of the health centres, clinics, and dispensaries. It has been receiving greater emphasis, for it is obviously better to prevent someone from getting ill than try to cure them afterwards. For this purpose, mass education campaigns — *Mtu ni Afya* (Man is Health), and *Chakula ni Uhai* (Food is Life) — have been conducted throughout the country so that people understand what they can do to help themselves. The digging of latrines, and general cleanliness are of even greater importance now that people are living in villages than they were before. But this kind of educational work has to go on continually, as has vaccination and innoculation against preventable diseases like tuberculosis, measles and polio. The response of the people in all these matters has been generally good; many of the new village dispensaries, etc. are being built at least partly on a self-help basis.

So we have not made a bad beginning in the extension of basic health care to the people. And the results are just beginning to show in the statistics; it is now estimated that in Tanzania the expectation of life at birth is something like 47 years as against 35-40 years in 1961; the infant mortality rate has gone down from 161 per thousand in 1967 to about 152 per thousand now. Yet although these figures show an improvement, they also show how far we still have to go. The expectation of life in Europe is over 70 years and the European infant mortality rate is about 20 per thousand! So we must continue our efforts, and even increase them.

Clean water is one vital factor in improved health and living standards, and it is estimated that about 3 million people in the rural areas now have this available reasonably near at hand. That means that about 10 million people do not! They are still using dirty water, and often walking distances to get it. Further, few of them will have the time or resources to boil their water and let it cool before drinking it. The consequences to health do not need elaboration.

A lot of work is being done on extending clean water supplies, which is now a high priority for the Party and the government — as well as for the people directly affected! Something like Shs. 100 million has been spent in each of the last 5 years on rural water supplies, and the self-help efforts of the people are now beginning to be marshalled in support of the work. However, we are not doing enough to train village people to maintain their own pumps and pipes; too often these break down after a short while, sometimes leaving the people worse off than before, because for the sake of cleanliness their well has been sealed up when the pump was installed. The resistance by our water engineers to the use of windmills continues to be absolute but quite impossible to understand! It is a kind of mental block.

Personal Incomes

Although it is true that equal access to basic public services is at the core of socialist equality, the relationship between different personal incomes is also important — especially in social terms. In this also we have made great progress.

It is now probably true to say that in Tanzania no able-bodied person lives on an unearned income; such incomes have been reduced almost to nothing by the combined effect of all government policies. In 1967 the top salary in the public sector of the economy was 29 times as much as the minimum wage. After direct tax is taken into account the proportion was 20:1. In other words, a person earning the minimum wage had to work for 20 years in order to receive the amount which the highest paid public employee received in one year. By the end of 1976 this degree of inequality had been greatly reduced. After direct tax was deducted, the highest paid employee in the public sector took home 9 times as much as the minimum wage earner did. To any objective observer this differential will still seem very great, but our achievement so far is even greater. At independence the top incomes were about 50 times as great as the lowest incomes, even after direct tax was deducted. Tanzanian senior officials in government and parastatal organisations should receive full credit for the spirit with which they have accepted this worsening of their economic position; for in recent years they have suffered from a real reduction in income as well as a reduction relative to other workers. This country is fortunate in their patriotism, and their commitment to our socialist policies. Those armchair revolutionaries who denounce these young men are talking like idiots. Not all young nations have been so well served by their educated leaders.

In the last ten years we have also corrected the tendency for urban average incomes to grow much faster than those in the rural areas. Although reliable statistics are non-existent in this area, it appears that since 1967 the hard working peasant (especially in areas with a good cash crop) has improved his lot faster than an equally hard working wage-earner in the towns. The increasing cost of buying building materials for a house, and paying cash for all food, is one factor in this change; another is the deliberate bias in the tax structure in favour of the peasants in the rural areas .

Yet one problem which still makes life in the rural areas less attractive to the young is that the peasant's income does not come in the form of a regular cash payment. He never knows how much he will get until he has sold the harvest, and even then he may not get the money straight away. For many months in a year the peasant may therefore be without any cash, even to buy little necessities like soap or cloth. For those who grow crops like tobacco, or coffee, this is mostly a problem of organisation. They get good money if they use proper methods of husbandry, but it all comes together as one or two payments in a year. And many of them spend it all at once. Therefore a further extension of the Banking system into these areas, combined with education about the use of a Bank Account to make deposits and draw out at need, will help. But for farmers whose land cannot grow the best paying crops, this is not so much of an answer, for their cash income is very small even considered on an annual basis. They need further help to earn cash, either through the establishment of village industries or the introduction of new crops. Both these things are being attempted, although they will take time to bring results. But in the meantime, when people work on ujamaa farms they may consider distributing the income earned on a regular monthly basis rather than all at once when payment is made for the crop sold.

These various movements towards greater equality of incomes within the country have not happened by accident. They are the result of deliberate government policies to that end. Among these are the incomes policies, the pricing policies — both to the producers and consumers — and the taxation structure.

Democracy

The administrative decentralisation which was introduced in 1972 had two objectives. One was to speed up decision-making, and the other was to give local people greater control over events in their own District and Region, as well as greater access to the implementors of development decisions. Decision-making has been speeded up; Districts and Regions can now act in many matters without waiting to refer everything to Dar es Salaam. It is, however, still difficult to say how far the decentralisation has increased the people's democratic control over the district and regional administration. It appears that this varies considerably from place to place, dependent in part upon the personalities of the leaders and officials concerned, and to a larger extent upon the political consciousness and democratic forcefulness of the people themselves.

Villagisation has already helped to give the people more effective power, and as the villages become more settled their power should grow still more. For the villagisation exercise is now virtually complete. There are some 7,684 villages in Tanzania, with a population of about 1,700 people to a village. Village Councils and elected Village Committees now exist almost everywhere in accordance with the Act of 1975. This means that the people in a village can determine the development of their own place, and within the framework of our national policies draw up their own rules for living and working together. They will also be able to participate more effectively in District and Regional decision-making by regular discussions with their representatives on these bodies.

Thus it is truer now than ever before that the people can determine their own rate of progress towards socialism and the human dignity which comes from economic sufficiency. But they have to use these democratic powers. If they do not use them — if they sit back and wait for someone to tell them what to do — then others will take over effective power. For decisions have to be made, and work has to be done. Just as water fills up the low places near a river, so within a theoretically democratic structure small tyrants will fill up a gap left by low political consciousness and apathy. During the next decade continued political education will remain necessary if we are to reach the objective of democratic practice.

Agriculture as the basis of development

Since the Arusha Declaration was passed, we have talked a very great deal about rural development and the expansion of agriculture as the basis for Tanzania's future. And we have spent large sums of money on rural development — some of it from friends abroad. Thus, for example, whereas in 1967 something like Shs. 45 million was spent on agricultural development, the figure has been around Shs. 400 million in each of the past two years!

Also in support of agricultural expansion, the government has subsidised the sale of fertiliser (the consumption of which has more than doubled in the last five years); made credits available to cooperatives and ujamaa villages through the Rural Development Bank; helped with the planning of irrigation; and provided training in the use of animal-drawn implements, etc. Not enough has been done, and sometimes the efforts have been misapplied, or too late in arrival But some attempt has been made.

However, the truth is that the agricultural results have been very disappointing. Modern methods have not spread very quickly or very widely; the majority of our traditional crops are still being grown by the same methods as our forefathers used. Irrigation, and even the building of small dams, is talked about more than done. People still think in terms of getting a tractor for their farms — even when they are small — rather than learning how to use oxen-ploughs; or they concentrate on saving for a lorry when their real need is a number of small carts to move seeds and crops from the shamba to the collecting point or village store. Towards agriculture, and agricultural methods, even our attitudes have not changed as much as they need to do.

Of course our total agricultural output has increased over the past ten years. In some crops the expansion has been very creditable when allowance is made for the recent years of bad weather. But in food production, for example, the increase in output has not kept pace with the increase in the population. It is true that when the weather is good we have been generally self-sufficient in food. The large imports of grain in 1974/75 were unusual. But the explanation for our normal self-sufficiency is not our agricultural efficiency. We are a peasant country. And if peasants have land they will at least produce the food they need. This they have been doing. Our urban population is very small. Therefore the surplus we need to feed this population is also very small. If the weather is good the peasant can produce this surplus. But our agricultural productivity is too low to produce a surplus that can feed a larger urban population or maintain strategic reserves.

Looking back it is possible to see many contributory factors to this lack of sufficient agricultural growth. Government has been too slow in changing the prices offered to the farmers, so that at times they were not recompensed for their effort on food crops or for the increased costs of production following inflation. This has now changed; the new prices should enable an active farmer to get a reasonable return for his effort if the rains do not fall. Also, difficulties with transportation, and inefficient service from the cooperative societies have been discouraging. But the real failure seems to have been a lack of political leadership and technical understanding at the village and district level. Despite the call in *Politics is Agriculture* for all political leaders to learn the basics of good husbandry in their areas, and to join with the peasants in production, we have continued to shout at the peasants, and exhort them to produce more, without doing much to help them or to work with them in a relationship of mutual respect. Many of our leaders know nothing about agriculture; what is more, they don't want to learn!

As regards forestry, our progress has also been smaller than it should have been; but it would be wrong to say that we have done badly. 16,500 hectares of new forest have been planted with soft woods during the past nine years, and 3,200 hectares with hard wood. Also some villages have begun to plant their own trees, either in areas set apart for that purpose, or along village roads, between their shamba, or along ridges. This is a very good development and should be encouraged. Every village should plant trees for future building needs, and for furniture etc., as well as for firewood.

We must, however, pay more attention to guarding the river sources and banks, and to protecting the mountain sides. There has been a tendency for some villages to be quite ruthless in cutting down trees in such areas; by doing so they are — for their own immediate profit — destroying the land on which we all depend. For indiscriminate tree-felling leads to soil erosion and turns fertile valleys into areas without surface water. Regulations on these matters must be immediately enforced; at the same time educational work must be undertaken to help the people understand what they have been doing and how they can benefit economically from proper land conservation and use.

The one thing which cannot be said about the past ten years is that the peasants of Tanzania have failed to work. They have worked hard. But they have worked without sufficient knowledge and understanding of improved husbandry; they have also been badly hit by drought following successive years of poor rains. More effort on small-scale irrigation and the building of dams could at least reduce the loss imposed by rain shortage. And we must also stress the importance of planting, weeding and harvesting at the right times, as well as proper spacing; for these do not cost anything but can result in a greatly increased harvest.

Further, we must apply more widely the knowledge and the seeds which have been developed by scientists in our research institutions. For very good research work is being done. New seeds have recently been developed for the grain crops as well as for the cash crops — to which research used to be restricted. Seeds for some very good varieties of maize and millets are now in use in the country; we must plant them in appropriate areas. At present there is too great a tendency to cultivate maize even where sorghum and the very nutritious millets would give more assured and better harvests. In agriculture there has been plenty of *juhudi* (enthusiasm). The emphasis should now be on *maarifa* (productivity).

One other tradition to which we must return is the storage of grains in the villages. Traditional storage methods could often be made very effective if minor changes were made to keep out vermin. And village food stocks would provide additional security for the people against future disasters, including a breakdown of communications, and would save the peasants' cash income for other things. It will, however, still be necessary for us to build up national stores of food in different parts of the country — about which we have been remiss in the past.

Village workshops for the manufacture and repair of simple agricultural implements must be developed. The manufacture of furniture, clothes, and bricks for
improved housing can also be done in the villages. This work is just beginning, with
the support of SIDO and the Rural Development Bank. We must do more.

Political Education and Leadership

When moving a country from embryonic capitalism and capitalist attitudes towards
the growth of socialism, few things are of more long term importance than political
education. In this respect Tanzania has been very active indeed. Political education
has been introduced in schools, colleges, and other educational institutions; it has
been given emphasis in the National Service, and the TPDF. Very large numbers of
Political Education Seminars have been run in Government and Parastatals, especially
for senior personnel who can influence or affect decisions. The English language
newspaper has been nationalised so that we could rely upon it to report news
accurately, and to analyse events from a Tanzanian and socialist viewpoint
although in practice it has not been infallible on either count! And the radio has
been used as an educational medium, for it reaches further and more quickly into
our villages than any other form of communication.

All these things are important, for all our people need to understand our goals,
and the policies to which we are committed. Political education must be continued,
and intensified; it is the only way we shall be able to see clearly through the current
difficulties to the purpose of our activities and the needs of the future.

But although formal political education is important, people learn just as much
if not more from observing the behaviour, the attitudes, and the expectations, of
avowed socialists, and especially socialist leaders. The Leadership Code (and its
later extension to all Party members) was therefore one of the most crucial aspects
of the Arusha Resolution. For it has ensured that those who aspire to lead, or to
take an active part in, our movement towards socialism have been forced to share
the problems of the mass of the people. And we have been quite successful in
observing the Code. When the Central Committee of TANU investigated a series of
allegations that it was being broken, most of them were found to be based on
misunderstandings, and the Leadership Code Enforcement Commission which was
established after that time has not found many major breaches of the Code. But
observing — or rather, not breaking — the Leadership Code is not enough. We have
to be believing socialists. Party leaders have been known to break the Code as soon
as they cease to be leaders. This shows that they just wanted to hold office; they
were not believers in Ujamaa .

And another tendency which has grown up, and which has to be fought, is for
TANU leaders to expect payment for their services to the Party and the people.
There have even been suggestions that all Ten Cell leaders should receive 'subsistence',
— although no one has said who should pay this subsistence! It is of course necessary
that people who devote their whole time to political work, and who are not on
pension, should receive enough money to live on and to work properly. But our
Party grew on the basis of its members' commitment and willingness to contribute
their time and energy to the things they believed in. It must not become an organisation of mercenaries. Our commitment can best be judged by the amount of
voluntary and unpaid service we render both to the Party and to the general public.

But in general it can be asserted that through political education of all kinds —

that is, through teaching, action and example — great changes in attitudes have taken place in Tanzania. Government and leaders are beginning to be judged by how they live up to socialist ethics. People's complaints are now about the remaining inequalities, and about inefficiency in the execution of socialist policies; we have much less special pleading for high salaries or privileges for particular sections of the community.

Indeed, we have reached the stage where our greatest danger is a new one. The thing which could now do most to undermine our socialist development would be failure in the battles against corruption, against theft and loss of public money and goods, and other abuse of public office, or against slackness in fulfilling the duties for which people are being paid. All these evils breed cynicism among the mass of the people when they are committed by those entrusted with responsibility. The person who steals from the public, who allows public property to be destroyed, who gives or accepts bribes, or who fails to carry out his job as quickly and efficiently as possible, is now a very dangerous enemy of socialism in Tanzania. They are more dangerous than the honest man who keeps a private shop. We must wage unremitting war against such people.

The Freedom Struggle

The struggle for political freedom in Africa has advanced since 1967. Mozambique, Angola and Guinea-Bissau are now independent sovereign states, and members of the Organisation of African Unity. The struggle for majority rule in Zimbabwe, and for the independence of Namibia, is also further forward now than ten years ago. All these are achievements of the peoples of those countries themselves; no one else has fought their battles for them. But it has been Tanzania's duty, and privilege, to support these Freedom Movements in the past. We have fulfilled that duty; we are continuing to do so today; and we shall not change our policy. Nor shall we flinch from giving full political and diplomatic support to the anti-apartheid struggle. Rather, we shall continue with our efforts to isolate South Africa culturally, economically and politically; we shall continue to give what help we can to the South African victims of racist brutality. And in defence of the territorial integrity of our newly independent neighbouring state, we shall not hesitate, if requested, to render military support.

In the fight for economic independence, cooperation with other Third World countries has increased since February 1967, although difficulties have not been absent. The signing of the East African Treaty of Cooperation in December 1967 was a matter for rejoicing, in Tanzania and elsewhere in Africa; it seemed to take African economic unity a stage further forward. Unfortunately, political developments in Uganda, and a number of unilateral transgressions of the Treaty by Kenya, have put the Community in jeopardy. The Government is working to overcome the current difficulties and to get agreement on Treaty revisions which will enable all partner states to work together. Cooperation in East Africa is needed by the whole continent; it has been, and can again be, a valuable weapon in the fight for greater economic development and freedom. But I must confess, with very great sadness, that the hope of reviving the East African Community is now a very slight one. We tried; but it appears that we shall be defeated. Our colleagues neither had, nor have, the desire for real cooperation. There is still a long way to travel before Africa is liberated.

Cooperation with other developing countries has increased. With Zambia, Tanzania's communications links have been multiplied since 1967. The road to the border has been realigned and macadamised; it is now one of the best and strongest roads in the country — which is helpful to the people in Southern Tanzania as well as to our neighbour. The jointly-owned oil pipeline has helped Zambia to withstand the Smith regime's counter-attack against free Africa through that front line state. And the Uhuru Railway, also jointly owned by Zambia and Tanzania, was opened in 1976 although construction only began in 1970. For this very important inter-African link we are greatly indebted to the Government and People of China, who made us an interest-free loan and provided all the technicians and engineers needed for this major undertaking. The Railway has already provided greater economic security to Zambia — and therefore greater security for the freedom of this country; it provides an opportunity for an almost limitless expansion of trade between our two countries; and it also opens up large areas of Tanzania for economic development.

New trading opportunities have been created also by the independence of Mozambique, and our links are being fostered by a Joint Tanzania/Mozambique Economic Commission. A similar joint commission exists between Tanzania and India, for we have realised that some of the manufactured goods we used to buy from the developed world can be obtained more cheaply from India. This kind of reorientation of trade is an advantage to the Third World as a whole as well as to ourselves, for it makes the poor countries less dependent on the rich states.

And with China, Tanzania's economic links are constantly being strengthened. There has been something of a fall in the number of Chinese goods sold in this country now that the Commodity Credit connected with the railway has been exhausted; but this merely enables a re-arrangement of our trade and other links on a more permanent basis. The jointly owned Tanzania-Chinese Shipping Line is operational. We still have a number of Chinese doctors and other technicians helping us — and setting a first class example of socialist dedication as they do so. And cooperation between our two countries for the development of Tanzanian iron and coal is now being worked out. Another cause for satisfaction is the cooperation between Tanzania and Cuba which has been established in many fields.

Tanzania has also been working on a multilateral basis with other Third World countries in dealing with the developed world. The 'Group of 44' which negotiated the Agreement with the European Economic Community was able to obtain better terms for all of us than any poor country could have obtained on its own. And in the 'Group of 77' (which really involves more undeveloped countries than that) Tanzania has been able to work in unity with other exploited nations to fight for a New International Economic Order. As a result, this demand is no longer a dream; it is now a matter of world politics. Cooperation among the poor has forced the developed nations to listen to what we say. In time it will lead to greater achievements.

OUR MISTAKES AND FAILURES

Self-Reliance

In the Arusha Declaration there is a whole section attacking the outlook that 'money is the basis of development. Without it there can be no development'. Yet this attitude is still prevalent in Tanzania today. The Minister for Finance, and his officials, are still attacked as if they were deliberately frustrating legitimate demands of other Ministries and of Regions. Plans based on the use of money — sometimes large amounts — are still announced as if they were realities; with the Minister being blamed when he says there is no money.

Yet it is as true now as it was in 1967 that the calf can only suck the amount of milk which its mother cow produces! The total amount of goods — whether expressed in the form of money or not — which we can consume and invest is limited by the amount of wealth which we produce. External aid — of which we have received a great deal in recent years — is by its nature temporary and un-reliable. It must not become the basis of development; our plans should not rely upon it. Money is not the foundation of Tanzania's development; if we wait for money in order to develop our country then there will be hardly any development, for we have very little money.

Yet even the money we do have, and do allocate for development, is treated very casually. Plans are still being drawn up by Ministries on the basis of buying services or goods which we could create by voluntary effort — or do without. Ministries and Regions still issue cheques in excess of their budgetary allowance on the assumption that no government can refuse to honour its own cheques, and apparently without realising that the result must be either inflation (that is, a fall in the value of money) or that other projects will never be started at all. Further, our public institutions, our Districts, and our ujamaa villages, often seem to worry very little about repaying the debts they incur. For example, since 1972 debts to the value of over Shs. 70 million have not been repaid on the due date to the Rural Development Bank. As its loan portfolio is Shs. 350.7 million, that means that something in the region of 20 per cent of the loans made are not being repaid! On that basis the TRDB will soon be able to make no new loans at all, for all its capital will have been exhausted. In addition, it is noticeable that some villages are taking loans from the banks without the banks making sure that the projects are properly supervised, and that the villages will be able to repay those loans. Yet these banks are lending public money; the money they make available comes from taxes, or from overseas loans which have to be repaid either by the bank or from taxation. Such practices as failure to repay loans, or properly supervise plans which are financed by loans, are a further reflection of our failure to understand that money represents goods, and that if we waste money, or fail to repay the loans we have had, then other plans will have to be left undone.

At the root ot this whole problem is our failure to understand, and to apply to our own activities, the concept of 'Self-Reliance'. We are still thinking that big schemes, and 'orthodox' methods will solve our problems. We do not approach a problem by asking how we can solve it by our efforts, with the resources which we have in front of us. This applies from the village level to the Ministries; but the latter are most responsible. For when villages have a problem they ask for advice. And they are rarely shown how they can solve it within the village without outside assistance, or even given the training which would enable them to do so afterwards. Indeed, local initiatives are often scorned, as not being 'modern' enough. When the people build a dispensary with traditional materials they are told it is not hygenic; they are rarely if ever shown how a few alterations and special care from day to day could make it satisfactory .

The fact is that we are still thinking in terms of 'international standards' instead of what we can afford and what we can do ourselves. And we think of getting external assistance for simple projects, instead of reserving this for the really major projects which we could not undertake without it — like the Uhuru Railway, or the Kidatu Hydro-electric scheme. Villages buy tractors — or are sometimes given them through the Regional Development Fund — when they have not yet mastered the disciplines of working together with oxen-ploughs, and have no idea of mechanical maintenance. Doors, window-frames, beds and chairs, are not manufactured by village carpenters because the modern tools which would produce a sophisticated product are not available. And so on.

The same attitudes prevail about housing. Not very long ago it was estimated that to build an improved traditional house — that is one with a permanent roof, insect-proofed wood-work, and a thin cement floor — cost about Shs. 7,000/-; a smaller cement block house costs at least Shs. 18,000/- to construct. Yet although we know that most of our people cannot afford the mortgage or rental costs of the cement house, we persist in promoting its construction. Obviously it is more comfortable, and lasts longer. It is a case of the best being the enemy of the good. For most people the only effective choice is between an improved and an un-improved traditional house — they cannot afford the cement house. So if we do not help them to build an improved house of traditional materials, or of burnt bricks and tiles if they have a little more money, then we shall not be doing anything to help them live in a decent house.

We must become more practical in these matters — in Dodoma as well as else-where. It is no use expecting the National Housing Corporation to supply all the houses we need; it does not have the resources, and people's failure to pay the inevitably high rents of NHC-type houses has reduced its capacity still further. In fact since 1967, the NHC has constructed only 11,036 new houses for rent, and the rate of construction is going down. Instead we should concentrate on the develop-ment of Site-and-Service projects so that people can build for themselves houses which are appropriate to their income, and which can be gradually improved over time. A beginning has been made; the Housing Bank now makes loans of between one and five thousand shillings so that people can build improved traditional houses; and the Ministry Building Research Unit is investigating cheaper but still good modern housing methods. The Site-and-Service policy is also getting slowly off the ground; since 1972 about 9,000 new sites have been prepared, although most of these were in Dar es Salaam. Development in Dodoma must be based on this system. The new capital will never be built if we wait until the CDA has the capital resources to build modern housing for all expected inhabitants. And when the CDA does build, or when people can afford more modern type houses, they must use burnt brick and tiles, not cement and *bati* (corrugated iron).

The present widespread addiction to cement and tin roofs is a kind of mental paralysis. A *bati* roof is nothing compared with one of tiles. But those afflicted with this mental attitude will not agree. Cement is basically earth; but it is called 'European soil'. Therefore people refuse to build a house of burnt bricks and tiles; they insist on waiting for a tin roof and 'European soil'. If we want to progress more rapidly in the future we must overcome at least some of these mental blocks!

The developments mentioned as regards the financing of our new housing may be taken as a sign that we are now beginning to adapt our thinking to our capacity. And there are other examples of what can be — and is being — done by villagers working together in cooperatives or informal groups. Knives and other tools are being made by traditional blacksmiths in some villages while they wait for teaching about how to build a more modern furnace. Villages are making burnt bricks with which to replace their temporary school building; in other places people are working a communal *shamba,* in order to buy *bati* for the dispensary roof with the cotton or other cash crop they produce; and so on.

This kind of development should be encouraged. For a lot depends on leadership. Villagers have to be helped to understand what they can do for themselves to meet the needs they recognise. And they must be given training so as to upgrade their traditional skills in order that they can provide goods for their own use and for the market.

It is imperative that we should make more deliberate effort in these matters. Whenever any problem is being tackled, or any new development is being proposed, our first question must be: What can we, in this village, or district, or region, or nation, do to solve this problem by ourselves! And if the considered answer must be 'not everything', then the second question should be: How much can we do without seeking for financial help from outside the village, district region or nation? And always the further question must be asked: Are we doing this in the most economical, efficient, and appropriate manner, in the light of our circumstances?

A poor nation does not develop on the basis of money. It cannot be independent if it depends upon external help.

Production

Over the last ten years we have done quite well in spreading basic social services to more and more people in the rural areas. More remains to be done; but we shall only be able to do it if we produce more wealth. And we have not been doing very well on that front.

Measured in constant prices, our National Income has increased at a lower speed since 1967 than the rate at which is was increasing before. Thus, from 1964 to 1967, Tanzania's National Income rose by an average of 6.4 per cent per year. Between 1967 and 1975, it rose by an average of only 4.2 per cent a year. Even excluding the drought years when a fall in production was beyond our control, the average rate of increase was only 4.6 per cent a year. As the population is increasing by about 2.8 per cent every year, this means only a negligible real improvement in the per capita standard of living. The improved living standards of the majority of Tanzanians comes from better distribution of what we do produce, more than from an increase in the amount of production.

It is true that the last ten years have been very difficult ones economically. For example, the terms of trade between our imports and exports have been moving against us almost throughout the period, which means that the goods we produce for sale abroad have less value in terms of the kind of things we need to import. But we must not use that — or the drought years — as an excuse to cover up our own failures. These we must analyse and examine in order to do better in the coming decade.

The problem has not been a failure to make investments in new factories or farms. In the four years 1967-1970 Shs. 1,155 million was invested in new productive facilities by the parastatals alone, and the amount of directly productive investment increased steadily, even if slowly, for the next five years. By the financial year 1975/76 it became possible to put more emphasis on this, rather than on infrastructural investments: in that year the Development Budget allocated almost Shs. 890 million for directly productive national investments (investments made in the Regions would be additional) and in the current year the allocation has been further increased. Although these more recent investments will not yet be showing results, it is obvious that we should by now be receiving the benefit of the investments made in the first half of the post-Arusha Declaration decade.

But we are not using our investments as efficiently as we should. Almost all our industrial plants are running well below capacity; sometimes less than 50 per cent of what could be produced with existing machinery is actually being manufactured and put on to the market! Even the Tanzania Breweries was only using 68 per cent of its capacity in 1975; Tegry Plastics ran at 46 per cent capacity; and the Mara Milk Plant at less than 30 per cent capacity. Further, the Wazo Hill cement works is certainly not producing anything like the amount of cement it could do if it were working properly, and the textile mills could probably do better also. In 1975 at least, Bora Shoes were not only producing a much lower quantity than their machinery justified, but they were also producing shoes of low quality. However, in this case some improvement has been shown during the last year.

Certainly our parastatals are not producing sufficient surplus to finance new investment. In the eight years from 1967-74, only about 20 per cent of new productive investment was financed from the resources of the existing publicly owned corporations. They were not, in more common terms, making sufficient profit. For profit is necessary whether an enterprise is privately or publicly owned. Public ownership affects what happens to the profits, not the necessity for them. Taken as a whole, over eight years the profit of our parastatals as a percentage of sales was only an average of 6.5 per cent a year. In 1975 even the Breweries' pre-tax profit was only just over Shs. 4 million on gross sales valued at Shs. 535.5 million — and they certainly have no sales problems!

The fact is that we have been, and still are, grossly inefficient in our factories and workshops. Profits are not the only test which demonstrates this. For example, the value of output per worker in our industrial enterprises actually fell from an average of Shs. 18,870 in 1967 to an average of Shs. 16,540 in 1974 — by which time money was of much less value. A fall in the productivity per man-hour in the construction industry is also noticeable, and the expansion of our agricultural production is not keeping pace with the population increase.

Not every failure is the direct fault of the individual firm. The basic problem at the Mara Milk Plant, for example is that not enough milk is produced by the peasants in the area; and one of the problems of other firms is sometimes interruptions in the supply of vital imported raw materials — although often this itself is an indication of failure to make orders in time. Again, the frequent electricity and water supply failures in Dar es Salaam and Mwanza during 1974-76 did adversely affect production. And those hold-ups arose because Government was too slow in undertaking the basic infrastructural works, which then fell behind schedule once construction had started.

But problems external to the firm are not sufficient to account for the extent of our inefficiencies. Rather, there are many contributory factors, each of which has to be examined in relation to each enterprise.

Management and Administration costs are often much too high in relation to output. In every parastatal we have a whole series of managers for different functions, and a General Manager on top. Each manager has a secretary, an office of his own, and often a car. These facilities are sometimes justifiable when the managers are efficient at their jobs and active, for they can multiply the efficiency and profitability of the manager many times over. But this is not always the case. We employ some 'Sales Managers' who sit in their offices and wait for customers to search them out, without making any attempt to find out what needs the factory could be fulfilling and is not, or what change in their product could make it more useful to their customers, etc. We employ some 'Production Managers' who do not order spare parts or the necessary raw materials on time, or having done so just sit and complain instead of going after them if the goods are not delivered. We have 'Maintenance Managers' in our transport enterprises who apparently find it acceptable to have as many as 40 per cent of their vehicles off the road at any one time waiting for repairs or service!

Some of these failures are the result of inexperience or lack of confidence among the young people holding such posts. Where this is the case, more training may help, as would greater contact with older managers in other enterprises who can be consulted informally about serious problems. For it is true that our managerial cadre is very much younger, very much less experienced, and has less opportunity to learn by observing others, than people in comparable positions in older countries. Such people must be given the opportunity and the time to learn and to improve. But if they do not learn quickly, and if they do not improve, then they must be replaced, or even just relieved of their job; it is better to have a vacancy than a person who is taking pay for doing nothing.

But it is not only faults at management level which account for our low output; indeed, many of our managers are working extremely hard and for long hours every day. But some of the workers in our plants, offices, shops, and so on, have not yet realised that when the rights of the worker are more respected, so his duties increase. For we have virtually eliminated the discipline of fear; it is quite hard for a manager or employer to dismiss a worker, or even suspend or fine him for dereliction of duty. But in Tanzania is it not unusual for a manager to be locked out by the workers! For we have not everywhere succeeded in establishing the discipline which comes from understanding one's responsibilities, and having a commitment to a cooperative increase in production. Although attitudes have now greatly improved, in many places TANU and NUTA branches are still better at protecting the workers in the particular plant than they are at protecting the workers and peasants of Tanzania as a whole from bad workmanship or slackness.

It is essential that we should tighten up on industrial discipline. Slackness at work, and failure to give a hard day's effort in return for wages paid, is a form of exploitation; it is an exploitation of the other members of the society. And slackness has undoubtedly increased since the Arusha Declaration was passed. Both managers and workers are affected by this tendency, and each group is too ready to blame the other. The fact is that all of us must correct our own slackness, and expose the slackness of others to the light of day. Managers must involve their workers in this task; they must be willing to accept criticism and must give it. The same applies to more junior grades of workers; a messenger who does not deliver a letter quickly may cause the loss of an order or delay delivery of goods so that the work of a whole factory is held up; carelessness with a machine — whether it is a lathe or a bus — may cost thousands of shillings of the people's money. TANU branches should be more active in the struggle against such attitudes and actions. Defending slackness and negligence is not socialism; on the contrary, it is very stupid.

Every parastatal must examine its own record on efficiency and try to find ways in which costs can. be cut, or output increased with existing resources. In some places this work has already started; the NDC is involved in a complex cost-cutting and quality-improvement exercise covering all its subsidiaries. But this work is urgent and must be undertaken by all our parastatals. And we must work out for each enterprise the appropriate goals against which efficiency can be measured. These will vary from one kind of activity to another. They may be, for example, the ratio of buses on the road to the number being repaired, or the length of cloth, the number of ploughs, etc, produced and sold in relation to the capital investment and number of workers, and so on. This is a very serious matter. The fulfilment of our social goals, as well as an improvement in our people's personal consumption standards, depends upon the speed and efficiency with which we increase our total output.

Costs of Government

Since 1967, Government has been the fastest growing sector of the economy. In 1967 it accounted for 10.9 per cent of the National Income; in 1975 it was 16 per cent! Efficiency and economy of operation is therefore vital, for Government is not directly productive — which is not the same thing as saying it is unproductive! But in any case, Government is financed out of the wealth which the people produce on the farms, factories, and roads of this country, and it should be extracting the minimum necessary for effective operation and service to the people. Extravagance in Government hinders the peoples' development.

After 1967, some increase in the proportion of the national wealth which is used by Government was inevitable. For the Government of Tanzania is now actively engaged in promoting and organising economic and social development; it is not just an administrative and public security organisation. When the people decide to adopt a policy of universal primary education, they are at the same time deciding to increase the proportion of our wealth which is used in Government activities. When Government is told to initiate and control economic development, it must take the resources with which to do that work. And the amount of Government activity related to development must not be under-estimated. In 1974, for example, the Government, parastatals, and the East African Community together were responsible for over 70 per cent of the total capital formation of the year, and almost every aspect of that work involved Government servants as well as the parastatal and Community employees. It would therefore be absurd to talk as if the expansion of Government costs meant automatically an unjustified imposition on the directly-productive workers and peasants of this country.

Yet we must use the minimum amount of money on Government, and we must use it to best effect. Just now, for example, 80 per cent of the recurrent revenue allocated to the Regions is spent on wages and salaries of Government employees. This is absurd. It means that we pay people to work, and then cannot provide them with the facilities and equipment they need to do the jobs for which they are paid! Teachers do not get books and papers; there is a shortage of medicines in the dispensary; agricultural officers and development personnel do not tour their District or Region because there is no money for petrol.

This kind of thing must not continue. We are not able to increase the recurrent budget available to the Regions to any noticeable extent, so we have to tackle the problem from the other end. We have reduced some staff; we may have to leave other vacancies unfilled. And we must be more adaptive to our circumstances. There was a time, for example, when Agricultural Officers used to walk from village to village on duty, spending the nights in people's houses or in tents. Now we even scorn bicycles! And paper is wasted in our offices; the simplest letters are marked 'Secret' and put in two envelopes, circulars are duplicated on one side of the paper only, and so on. Such economies seem petty, and the amounts saved appear so small as to be unimportant in a single office; but they do mount up when

20 Regions and 72 Districts — to say nothing of the Ministries — are added together! Serious attention must be given to every detail of expenditure, and the question asked 'How can the job be done more cheaply?'

In Government generally we must also resist the temptation to establish a new institution every time we tackle a problem. By the end of 1967 we had 64 parastatal organisations; by 1974 we had 139 — and the number has been increased since. Some increase was necessary; we could not have carried out decisions without setting up the appropriate new institution. But still new parastatal corporations are proposed almost every month. And it is difficult to know the work that some of them do. There are two institutions dealing with sisal; one is called the Authority, and the other is called the Corporation! Why? It would be wrong to assume that the increased number of parastatals is just a sign of careless multiplication; we have learned from experience (e.g. with STC) that it is often better and easier to run a smaller specialised organisation than a large, multi-purpose one. Yet we must always remember that every parastatal involves extra administrative costs, and we should carefully consider whether a new one is necessary, or necessary now rather than in the future.

Further, some costs of government could be reduced if we helped the people in villages and towns to do more things for themselves. Training village members to do minor repairs and to service pumps, for example, would be better and cheaper than relying upon the District Engineer's staff for the work; other village members could be trained and then made responsible for the accounts, and the management. We must not rely solely on village managers, or village technicians provided by the State. Many of these people do a useful job, and this kind of technical and professional aid is now essential to the implementation of plans drawn up by Village Councils and Development Committees. But these people are not an integral part of the village, affected personally by its success or failure. Therefore, although it is necessary now to give the villages the help of trained government employees, eventually our aim should be to phase these out and gradually replace them by trained members of the village who are paid out of the village income. Then the Government should concentrate on providing 'consultants' and 'inspectors' whom the village technicians and members could call upon for advice, or who could be called in when a new project is being undertaken.

We have started training village people for work in their own villages. The National Service is doing a useful job training people in skills like carpentry, shoemaking, and basic mechanics. And the Ministry of Health takes people from the villages for a few months and trains them how to deal with the simplest illnesses and how to use the first aid boxes. When they return home, such people are able to join in the agricultural activities of the village at times of pressure, or do the other work on a part-time basis. We must give more emphasis to this approach to village development. We cannot yet support full time village specialists in every important field; what is important is that the skills should be available in the village to be applied as needed.

Leadership

Political and public service leadership has undoubtedly improved over the past ten years, in both commitment and in efficiency. But still leaders too often forget that the purpose of Government and Party and of ALL the laws and regulations in this country, is to serve people. And when we say 'serve the people' we do not just mean 'the masses' as an abstraction; we mean the people in large groups, and small groups, and as individuals.

It is inevitable that good and necessary social policies should sometimes bear hardly upon individuals. When that happens, it is the task of leadership to help people to adjust, and to arrange the implementation of the policy so that those who are willing to re-arrange their plans or their life have time to do it in dignity. And a good leader will always be able and willing to explain the purpose and the aims of the new policy, and why it has been adopted. That is part of the function of leadership; it is political education also.

Yet in practice leaders at all levels seem to delight in saying 'no' in response to even the most reasonable requests. Ask them why they have said something can be done in six days, or six months, but not now, and they have no answer; the truth is that by giving that decision they have demonstrated their authority. And in some cases they are also indicating that if a little *chai* (small bribe) is passed over, the matter can be speeded up!

All too often leaders in the Government and the Civil Service — and even in the Party — fail to show by their actions that they care for people. They do not act positively to help individuals who are in trouble even although this can be done without damage to our policies or to our security. There have been instances of gross ill-treatment of our people by Government and Party leaders who are supposed to serve the people. And when those instances of ill-treatment begin to surface, immense efforts are made to silence either the victims or those who have the courage to speak for them. This is a disgrace. This is an area where our Party must be extremely vigilant.

However, it is not only in respect of individual problems that some of our leaders fail to show a socialist commitment to people. Many of them also fail to fulfil the responsibilities with which they have been entrusted. Why is it, for example, that the numbers of buses on the road increases after the President has visited a depot and maintenance centre? How does sugar or something else appear in shops immediately after the President has called at a go-down? The President neither repaired a bus, nor manufactured sugar! These things mean that someone was not providing leadership, was failing to make necessary decisions, or was not ensuring that decisions were implemented.

Unfortunately, failures such as these are much more obvious than the more usual case of people carrying out their responsibilities and rising to the challenges made to them by the people. Consider, for example, the question of villagisation. In my Report to the 1973 TANU Conference I was able to say that 2,028,164 people were living in villages. Two years later, in June, 1975, I reported to the next TANU Conference that approximately 9,100,000 people were living in village communities. Now, there are about 13,065,000 people living together in 7,684 villages. This is a tremendous achievement. It is an achievement of TANU and Government leaders in cooperation with the people of Tanzania. It means that something like 70 per cent of our people moved their homes in the space of about three years! All these people now have a new opportunity to organise themselves for local democratic government, and to work with the Regional, District, and Central administrations to hasten the provision of basic educational, health, and other public services which are necessary for a life in dignity. Results are already becoming apparent. Universal Primary Education by the end of 1977, for example, would have been out of the question had the people not been living in village communities by now. As it is, we stand a good chance of achieving that objective.

We have become defensive about the villagisation exercise because there were widely publicised cases of maladministration, and even of mistreatment of people. Some few leaders did act without thinking, and without any consultation with the people who had to move. Therefore we did have cases of people being required to move from an area of permanent water to an area which is permanently dry. We had other cases where the new villages were made too large for the amount of land available. And there were cases where people were rounded up without notice, and dumped on the village site, without time to prepare shelter for themselves.

But it is absurd to pretend that these cases were typical of villagisation. They did occur; and they were bad examples of leadership failure. Of course they made people very angry — and rightly so. If one fish in a barrel goes bad, they all go bad. Yet it remains true that 11 million people could not have been moved by force in Tanzania; we do not have the physical capacity for such forced movement, any more than we have the desire for it. The vast bulk of our people moved on their own, with only persuasion and a little help from TANU and the administration. Many of them may have felt some initial reluctance to break the habits of a life-time in isolated homesteads, but they recognised that we had talked villagisation since 1962 and that it was time to act. And already, village life is proving itself to be beneficial and popular. Although rural life cannot be revolutionised in so short a time, the people now have a rational hope of improving their living conditions — at least of receiving clean water, simple medical care, and basic education for them-selves and their children within a few years.

It is time that tribute was paid to all those leaders, in TANU and in the Govern-ment, who worked with the people and for the people's benefit, over villagisation. This tremendous job was a real test of leadership, and the majority of our leaders came out of it well — some of them very well indeed.

And the leadership failures which were revealed at this time provide a lesson for all of us. In particular they demonstrate how much care people should give to the election of their representatives on District and Regional Development Councils, and how important it is that Regional and District Secretaries should be carefully selected.

There is still a tendency for all levels of Government to act as if the peasants were of no account, because our peasants are very patient people. Thus, for example. when houses are demolished in urban areas, compensation is always paid — even for shelters which are not more than temporary shacks. Compensation is paid even for trees. Yet very few of that minority of peasants who were required to leave houses made of cement blocks, or with a bati roof which could not be removed, have yet received even a token or 'first payment' in compensation. Such payments should be a priority charge on the Regional Development Funds. The purpose of villagisation is to lay the foundation for a permanent improvement in people's lives. When an individual had in good faith tried to carry out the injunctions of the Party, and spent his money on a house rather than on pombe, he should not be penalised for it because the village had to be sited elsewhere. We have neglected this matter too long.

Listening to the People

The truth is that despite our official policies, and despite all our democratic insti-tutions, some leaders still do not LISTEN to people. They find it much easier to TELL people what to do. Meetings are too often monologues, without much, if any, time being devoted to discussion; and even then the speech is usually an exhortation to work hard rather than an explanation of how to do things better.

Our leaders at all levels must make more effort to reach decisions by discussion. They must encourage the people to criticise mistakes which have been made, and they must be willing to work with the people in rectifying past mistakes and avoiding new ones. A willingness to discuss problems, to recognise mistakes made by themselves as well as those made by others, and to bring problems into the open, is a sign of real and confident leadership. The leaders of Tanzania must accept that democracy is at the heart of socialism.

Leadership by intimidation is not leadership. And it will work for a short time only. When people criticise stupid decisions they are exerting their rights as citizens. When they criticise decisions which are not stupid they can be brought to understand why the decision was taken, and what it implies. Leaders are acting for, and on behalf of the people; explaining things until the people understand is an important part of their work.

The real danger to ujamaa in this country does not come at all from the people's criticism of leaders. Our people support ujamaa; there are very very few individuals who oppose it, and these can be politically isolated and made ineffective when the masses of the people understand our policies. Detention of critics is not the answer; an Area or Regional Secretary who responds to a problem by detaining people — even within his legal powers — is almost always demonstrating his own incapacity for leadership. For it is very rare indeed that a peasant, a small trader or craftsman, or a junior official, is a danger to the security of the state or to our economic progress.

It is arrogance, incompetence, and slackness, among leaders which we have to guard against. And we must do so. Every leader should privately examine his own behaviour to see where he or she has fallen down. For everyone makes mistakes; if we hold important positions these mistakes are likely to have serious effects. But if we acknowledge a mistake, first to ourselves and then to those affected by it, it is usually possible for the error to be rectified or for its consequences to be minimised by cooperation between the leaders and the people. Leaders are not Gods; they are able to be effective, and to serve the people, only on a basis of mutual respect between themselves and those who have entrusted them with responsibility. A person who can admit a fault, and strive to do better, is both more worthy of trust, and more likely to be trusted, than one who pretends to be infallible and tries to shift the blame on to others.

The Need to be Serious

The basic aims of Tanzania are very clear. So is the need for dedication and discipline in working for them. We have undertaken a very difficult task, and it is necessary that we should be serious in pursuing it. But we do not always demonstrate that seriousness by our actions. For example, there have been very many occasions when new policy initiatives have been announced by local or national leaders, and all the other work is abandoned while these ideas are pursued in a great blaze of publicity or self-righteousness. After a week or two, the drive is called off, and the whole project dies a natural death.

Sometimes the reaction of any sensible person must be one of thankfulness that the announced policy has been abandoned. For new policies are too often made on the spur of the moment, either in the excitement of a public meeting or in anger at an emotional committee meeting, and have not been given any serious consideration at all. For example, it was once announced in a District that no peasant would be allowed to travel on a bus, or attend a market, unless he could prove that he, and each of his wives, was cultivating three hectares of land. Such a demand is itself obviously unconsidered; whether three hectares can be cultivated by a single person depends upon the tools used, the strength of the individual, and the type of crop. And in addition, such a regulation is quite unenforceable without an army of inspectors and a great deal of expensive red tape in the issuing of permits and so on.

Again; District or Regional Authorities lay down regulations to deal with temporary but urgent problems, and then they are enforced as a permanency, quite regardless of changed circumstances. An example of this is the prohibition on the movement of food out of a District at a time of local famine; if it is justified at all — which is doubtful — the ban should be strictly limited in time. Yet we find that for months and years after the danger of local famine is over, road blocks are still being erected, and peasants taking food to their relatives in the town — or even from their own shambas to their homes — are being harassed and abused. Indeed, in December 1976 this kind of thing was still happening, as if Tanzania were 72 different countries instead of one single nation with a single economy. No distinction is made between illegal movement of food from Tanzania to a neighbouring state and an ordinary and quite legitimate movement of food within Tanzania itself. The latter should be normal practice.

Actions such as these are a cause of much distress to law-abiding peasants and workers; they are an encouragement to petty corruption; and a drag on our development. They arise through lack of thought, and lack of vigilance by the people's representatives.

Yet on other occasions this lack of intelligent persistence in pursuing decisions means that good and necessary policies are made ineffective. It has been announced more times than it is easy to count that every able-bodied person in Tanzania must work, either on the land, in the factories and offices, or in some useful capacity in what is called the 'informal sector', (that is, as a carpenter, blacksmith, full-time trader, etc, etc.). I myself have been a leading advocate of the principle that every person must work. Then, on every occasion there is a great drive to 'round up' the unemployed in towns and repatriate them. For a week or so the criminals and idle parasites hide in their houses while respectable workers and peasants on legitimate business are harassed, and the people in paid employment otherwise carry on working hard or not as they did previously. Then the whole campaign dies away until it is realised that the problem of criminals in towns, and of people not doing a hard day's work, is still with us — and the process is repeated! The fault in such cases is not the decision itself; the Arusha Declaration says that in a socialist state 'everyone who is physically able to work does so; every worker obtains a just return for the labour he performs'. The fault was in trying to carry out the policy by a temporary 'drive' instead of a well-thought out and planned scheme which has the active support of the people. These hasty 'campaigns' are becoming a disease.

For we come back to the same problem. If our laws and regulations are to serve the people and to be effective, they cannot be adopted casually or in the heat of the moment. 'Platform policy-making' is not the answer to our problems. The people must be fully involved in drawing up policies. They must always be made to understand the need and the purpose of a particular public decision; and they must be involved in its implementation. Thus, for example, the Ten Cell leaders should know all the people who are living in their areas, and how they make their liveli-hood. Unless they are themselves criminals they could therefore be the spearhead of any campaign to re-settle on the land those who have no honest way of earning their living in towns. Similarly, the TANU branches in factories and offices should be acting to correct the faults of workers who slack or are negligent in the per-formance of their duties.

Further, Party and Government bodies, at all levels, must each fulfil their own functions. The Party lays down basic policy; through the machinery of Government, Parliament, the Civil Service, and Regional and District Development Committees, (all of which are made up of Pary members) these basic policies are turned into legislation and put into execution. Individual leaders do not make laws or policies. When they announce them, they are either speaking on behalf of the relevant Party or Government Committee — in which case they should say so and not try to take credit for themselves — or they are stating what they would like to see as a policy or a law. And sub-committees, whether of the Party or of Cabinet etc, can only make recommendations to the body which established them; their proceedings and announcements should be of interest as a contribution to public discussion, but they do not constitute law.

It is essential that we should approach this question of implementing Party policies with greater seriousness. We should give all legislation and rules more careful consideration through the machinery laid down. We may find that we are then making less laws and rules. But having made sure that they are practical and can win the support of the people, and having passed them, we must then enforce them properly — either permanently, or during the period for which they are to have effect before being renewed.

PROBLEMS CAN BE SOLVED

This brief survey of the past ten years shows two things. We have many problems to overcome, and many mistakes to correct; but we are moving in the right direction. Our problems are therefore soluble by serious effort and intelligent hard work, even if external events continue to hinder our rate of advance.

We have made good progress in very many respects, and especially in the move-ment towards greater equality, greater political understanding, and greater commit-ment to the principles of socialist cooperation. We have advanced a long way towards providing basic educational and health services for all our people; demo-cratic participation in decision-making and policy-implementation is greater than ever before. There has also been an increase in the personal consumption standards enjoyed by the mass of the people as evidenced by the per capita consumption of things like meat and other proteins, sugar, and cotton cloth. In other respects we have laid very useful foundations, on the basis of which we can improve our per-formances as regards production and distribution.

We have also seized control of our own economy. It is the people as a whole who determine the kind of society we shall create, and not foreign capitalists, or even local capitalists. And we have been able to use that control for our own benefit. Thus, for example, we were able to marshall all our foreign exchange resources to fight against the serious famines of 1973-1975, so that no one in this country died of hunger or was even seriously affected by it in the way which used to happen in the past. And we have been able to divert the impact of imported inflation, and the recession in the developed world, away from the poorest people, so that the heaviest part of the burden imposed on us was borne by those better able to carry it. Further, because we now control our own economic activities, we have been able to meet the economic difficulties of the last few years with a 'do battle' strategy.

In addition, we have now worked out a new Industrial Strategy, on the basis of which we shall be able to become more self-reliant as plans are implemented. The planned development of our coal and iron resources with the help of our Chinese friends is one aspect of this; another is our determination to expand our production in the basic and intermediate goods industries such as fertiliser, cement, spare parts, and simple agricultural and transport implements. We are able to make these new production plans because of our past infrastructural investments. More of these will be needed, for we began independent life grossly deficient in the public utilities which are essential to economic development. Indeed, when you consider the size of the country one might almost say that permanent roads and other means of communication, electricity, and water supplies hardly existed in 1961. But we may now be able to shift emphasis slightly on to investments which are directly productive; indeed, this has been the tendency in the last few years of the decade.

The Near Future

We used up all our foreign exchange reserves in fighting the drought and meeting the increased costs of essential fuel and development goods. Indeed, we have been forced to incur heavy overseas debts which will have to be repaid. Further, there is no sign that the world economy is likely to become more favourable for our development in the near future. On the contrary a further increase in oil prices has been announced, and inflation in the developed world continues to raise the prices of all our imports. And apart from coffee, which is enjoying a temporary boom, the prices of our exports are not keeping pace with the import prices.

We cannot give way to these difficulties. We must fight them. We have to increase our production of wealth, and our self-reliance, as a matter of great urgency. It is for this reason that Government is undertaking new investments in industry and in agriculture. We are concentrating on expanding the production of basic consumption goods, and on the processing of our own raw materials into manufactured commodities. But we must make a big export effort, so that we have more commodities to sell and can also break into the world market for simple manufactures. To do this we must produce more efficiently, and we must also learn and apply appropriate sales techniques for the different overseas markets.

But however hard we try it, it will take some time for our investments to bring results. That is why we have sought for, and welcome, a great increase in foreign assistance in recent years. It is now a high percentage of our development budget — in the current financial year it is likely to constitute something like 50 per cent of the total! This rate of dependence upon external aid is much·too high. It can be justified as an emergency operation in the existing circumstances, but only if it is used to increase our output and our ability to pay our way in the world. It must be used to increase production not to supplement our living standards. The intelligent farmer does not eat his seed-corn, and especially not borrowed seed! And this amount of foreign aid cannot be expected to last. Tanzania has many friends — the Scandinavian countries, China, and Canada are notable among them — but they are willing to help us only because they respect our determination to help ourselves, and to try to build a society based on human equality and dignity. If our effort slackens, they will — and they should — lose interest in cooperating with us for our benefit. And in any case, we have no right to rely upon these countries. We can accept their willingness to help us become self-reliant; we must not think of them as sources of charity which excuse us from work and sacrifice.

There is no doubt at all but that for the next three or four years Tanzania's economic circumstances will be very difficult indeed. Our effort has to be pro- portionate to these difficulties. We cannot expect early rewards from our work in the way of increased consumption — either of public or personal goods. We must be prepared to find our rewards for effort in increased national self-reliance and the maintenance of our independence of action. There is a time for planting and a time for harvesting. I am afraid for us it is still a time for planting.

CONCLUSION

We have cause for great satisfaction in our achievements of the past ten years. But we have no cause at all for complacency. We have done quite well; but with effort, and more intelligent effort, we could do better.

In the coming decade we must build on what we have achieved. We must increase our *discipline,* our *efficiency,* and our *self-reliance.* In particular we must put more effort into looking always to see what we can do for ourselves out of our own resources — and then doing it. As we celebrate the tenth anniversary of the Arusha Declaration, let us determine that the twentieth anniversary will find us more productive, and therefore more free, as a nation and as individuals.

Part II

RURAL DEVELOPMENT

CHAPTER 5

Kitumbi-Chanika and Kitumbi-Tibili: Two Ujamaa Villages that Refused to become one*

Michaela von Freyhold

Kitumbi-Chanika and Kitumbi-Tibili were less than three miles apart and about thirty miles south of Segara on the Tanga to Dar es Salaam tarmac road. The ecology was typical of Eastern Handeni: rolling hills, poor rainfall, and generally poor soils, although there were areas of moderately fertile grey-brown loamy sands in some of the valleys.

The Zigua people living in the area grew maize, kept cattle and went hunting. But the unreliable rainfall made growing annual crops — and particularly maize — very risky, and crop failure was common. More recently some of the farmers had started growing permanent crops — coconuts, cashewnuts, oranges and bananas. The villages were surrounded by thick bush so that farms which were not guarded were liable to lose their harvests to the monkeys and the wild pigs.

There were contradictory stories concerning the founding of the villages. It appears that in 1967 there was a meeting of the village development committee at which it was decided to start an ujamaa village. Later, on 3 June 1968, a meeting of district officials in Handeni decided that 12 ujamaa villages would be started in Mazingara Division, and Kitumbi was one of these. At this time only a few people had settled near to the new road, and there were five different clusters in the Kitumbi area.

According to the Tibili villagers it was the Tibili site that was intended to be the site of the ujamaa village all along. According to the Chanika villagers it was the Chanika site, and it was only when they went to cut poles to start house building that they realised that the village was to be at Tibili, for the government lorry dropped the poles at the Tibili site. When the villagers complained there was an argument during which the Divisional Executive Officer announced that Tibili was the approved site and that those who were not interested in building at Tibili could stay out.

At this point some people returned home and about 20 other families decided to build at another site altogether, Kwamkonga. They claimed that they were promised a letter to give them permission to join this village, but such a letter never arrived. Later in 1969 they were rounded up and locked up for 11 days on the grounds that they had opposed ujamaa by moving to Kwamkonga without permission. After their release they claimed that the chairman of the Kitumbi Village Development Committee had allowed them to start building at Chanika, and so they built their houses there. But the officials had not finished with them. They were told by the Divisional Executive Officer to demolish the houses they had built in Chanika, and when they did not do so the Divisional Executive Officer arrested them, and this time they were locked up for 14 days. Since he could think of no other charges the Divisional Executive Officer brought them before the primary court on charges of not growing cassava and millet and not paying the local rates (there were colonial

*From *The Communalisation of Peasant Agriculture in Tanzania* (Heinemann, London, 1979).

bye-laws still on the statute book which required each household to cultivate minimum acreages of certain crops). After investigation these charges were found to be false. A few who had not paid the taxes were imprisoned for six months and the rest were released. After their release the Divisional Executive Officer came and told them once again to pull down their buildings, but their leader (the present chairman of Chanika) replied by saying that according to TANU principles spelled out by the President on the radio villagers could decide where they wanted to have their villages and nobody could force them to go to a particular place. In fact he filed a court action against the Divisional Executive Officer in the Handeni District Court claiming that they were being wrongly forced to move.

The magistrate referred the case to the Area Commissioner's office, where it was decided (behind closed doors) that the Divisional Executive Officer had exceeded his authority. The villagers were told to handle the matter traditionally. So the DEO was made to slaughter a goat which was eaten by the villagers to signify his being forgiven. And eventually Chanika ujamaa village was officially recognised.

The official reason given by villagers who did not want to settle in Tibili was that to settle there would have meant crossing the clan boundary which separated Kitumbi in the West from Tibili in the East. According to Zigua tradition anyone who crossed the clan boundary might be punished by crop failures, illness or death. But since many people were no longer sure exactly where the clan boundaries lay, and since they had moved around a fair bit before the coming of ujamaa, it is hard to believe that this taboo was really so decisive. Moreover if a person wanted to start cultivating land where he feared the interference of his ancestors he could arrange for an oracle, but this had not been done when they had to decide about a site for the village.

The fears that existed were stirred up by some people who had property in Chanika and did not want to leave it. Some people claimed that the soils at Chanika were better than those at Tibili; others that Chanika was the one place with a reliable water supply. The situation was aggravated by the fact that the officials insisted that the new village should be built exactly on the site which a land surveyor had marked out, which meant that 20 households in Tibili in a cluster that already existed on the wrong side of the road were expected to build new houses across the road and only 100 metres from their old homes. When the pressure became too strong these people started building houses on the other side, but with no intention of completing them. However, their antagonism towards the new village which was to be created was still less than that of those people who were brought out of the bush with the help of the police and not even allowed to choose where along the road they would settle.

Whatever the strength of tradition and the interests of those who wanted the village in one place or another, people finally settled down in two different ujamaa villages under separate leaderships. One of these was Kitumbi-Tibili, officially founded in 1968. The other was Kitumbi-Chanika, registered in January 1971.

The conflict between the two as to which was the legitimate ujamaa village was important for two reasons. One was that the government had told the villagers that social facilities would only be built once, and in one village. The other was that there could be no proper land planning while both villages acted separately and claimed the same land. Although Tibili had been given a water supply in 1969, by 1971 the officials tended to favour Chanika. Tibili had initially had the better political connections, but by 1971 they had been eclipsed by the influence of the chairman of Chanika whose bar had become the favourite meeting place for all the officials who passed along the road.

KITUMBI-TIBILI

Some officials even started spreading rumours that Kitumbi-Tibili was about to disintegrate and that Chanika would soon be the only village left. But this was not the case. In 1971 membership was rising and those who had settled there intended to stay. In June 1971 there were 56 able-bodied men and 52 women there, and about 200 children, and about 200 more adults were expected to move into one of the two parts of the village before the end of the year.

It seems that after their initial difficulties the people became used to staying together: 'We were told that it was better to stay together, and we gradually started seeing that it actually was better to stay together. We realise this now — although it took us some time' (a villager). 'We are all one clan, we are all related, and even a new person who enters is accepted like a brother, the only difference is that we are not from the same parents' (an ex-chairman). .

In 1971 the village was not only settled and growing but had also cultivated a communal farm which was of reasonable size considering the environmental difficulties. They appeared determined to continue communal work in the coming seasons. The officials had noticed the farm, but they interpreted it their way: 'It seems that people in Tibili are doing something this year, but this is just because they feel they have to compete with Chanika'. The villagers themselves did not mention this motive of competition with Chanika when they discussed communal work.

All except a handful of people in the village were poor, and there was thus very little hiring of labour. One of the few relatively wealthy members was the shop-keeper, and he was very influential in the village. He had been a member of the village committee, but had recently resigned, claiming that he was too occupied with his private shop to attend the meetings of the committee. He was allowed to pay money to the village in place of communal work — and this same rule was applied to other members who had paid jobs outside the village, such as those working at the nearby building site of a micro-wave transmitter tower who were allowed to pay Sh. 4/- a month as a contribution, and in return were granted all the benefits given to active participants (such as famine relief food).

Although the villagers did not elect the shop owner to become their chairman they did not seem aware that there might be a class contradiction between them and the shop-keeper. When they were considering starting a communal shop they asked him for advice, and he told them that they ought not to start a shop because it would make losses and waste their time and money. He told them that he was not making any profit at all, and this discouraged the villagers.

Social differentiation also existed between the women and the men. The men were represented on every institution of the village government, but the women did not have any representatives. Most of the decisions were taken by the men and explained to the women, and the women accepted them. It was easy to see from the remarks of the men in meetings ('Keep quiet you women'; 'Listen you women') that they looked down on the women.

According to traditions which seemed to date from the colonial period, women were not allowed to speak in formal public gatherings. If they wanted to speak they had first to inform a man who would then address the meeting on their behalf. This did not stop the women expressing themselves when they felt they were wronged. When the village committee decided that the daily task on the communal field should be increased from two rows to three and that punishments for late-comers should be enforced, these changes were made without consulting the women (who were the ones mainly affected, since they were working in the fields while the men were building houses). A visitor at the meeting asked whether they thought the women might object, but the men considered this unlikely. However, the following day, when the women found out what had happened, they immediately went on strike and told the supervisor that they wanted the decision reversed. When they were told to work under the new arrangements until the committee could meet again they said they would go on working under the old arrangements until the committee met, and this they did. When the meeting was eventually held it was decided that the days of communal work should be reduced from five per week to two, but that the daily task should be three rows instead of two.

Traditionally women compensated themselves for their inferior status by paying more attention to each other than to the men, and the solidarity and hierarchy among them was strengthened by rituals and songs which were for women only. This did not make up for the fact that the women worked more than the men both in the fields and at home.

The years 1968 and 1969 were spent in house building. The villagers were given a plan of a suitable house, and one such house was built for them by a team from the District Headquarters to serve as a model for the rest. The houses were very large with a smaller kitchen area. The size was not varied according to family size, which meant that a bachelor had to built a much larger house than he needed. When the villagers protested they were told that trees were many and transport was free, and that they were to have big houses. Later the officials became more interested in getting new members into the village as quickly as possible, so emphasis was put on beginning with the kitchen building. Once this was ready a person could move into the village and live in the kitchen area while completing the rest of the house. Thus in 1971 there were many large unfinished houses in the village, but the new houses being built were small: the size intended to be just the kitchen had become the normal size of the dwelling houses.

During the 1970 long rains the villagers started a small block-farm of about 15 acres. This was planted with maize and bananas, but it failed due to drought and to selection of a bad piece of land. 1971 was thus the first year in which the village tried communal farming proper. The communal farm was about 32.5 acres in size, and nearly two thirds of this was taken up with maize (much of it interplanted with coconuts, cassave and bananas). There were also four acres of groundnuts, four acres of simsim, and some orange trees.

The area had been begun as a 'block-farm' with 30 members each preparing one acre. But the village was told that famine relief food would only be given if they worked communally, and so the block-farm was turned into a communal farm.

On the communal farm the villagers were willing to innovate. Fertilizer was used on five acres of the maize. The groundnuts were treated with insecticide. Somehow the *bwana shamba* (agricultural extension worker) managed to convince the villagers to thin the maize — in fact to such an extent that when a visitor failed to pull out superfluous maize plants during weeding women and small girls working in nearby rows came over and pulled the maize plants out!

The plot chosen was land that had already been cultivated but had been left fallow because of weeds. The *bwana shamba* encouraged them to try permanent cultivation on that plot. If it worked as he predicted — so that the weeds became more manageable after two years of cultivation — this would have been a major breakthrough in land-use in the area. Moreover, contrary to what happened on most private fields, the digging of the communal shamba was not delayed until the rains actually started in March, but was already done in January. When the people were reluctant to go to the fields without a sign of rain the *bwana shamba* started digging alone, and this example made the villagers follow him. As a result of the two new techniques — early digging and use of a previously cultivated field — a lot of labour had to be spent on weeding. Two weedings were needed before the rains really started, and three weedings after the seeds were planted. At the beginning of June the visitors were participating in the fifth weeding of the communal farm! Thus while 32 acres may not seem much, if one considers the intercropping and the labour spent in weeding, the labour performance was very reasonable.

The communal farm was a triumph for the *bwana shamba.* He was a local man, and an old-timer, whose quiet unassuming way and knowledge of the people were responsible for his success. Because he himself came from the area he did not rush to premature conclusions or start with prejudices. While staff from outside were quick to call the people subborn or lazy if they did not take advice, he looked for reasons, and if he did not find any he refrained from generalisation. His preference for ujamaa was technical: he said that it saved him the labour of looking for scattered farms in the bush and made it easier to demonstrate the benefits of new techniques and to persuade the people to use them. On non-agricultural matters he only spoke if consulted and he was careful not to pressure the people into accepting things they could not manage. Somehow he had succeeded in finding a role that was neither that of a villager, nor that of an outsider supervisor, but was that of an adviser whose word was listened to.

At the beginning communal labour was scheduled for three days in the week, and people were expected to work from 8.00 a.m. to 12.00. This continued until the planting was completed. The first weeding was done by setting a daily task, following official advice that three rows 100 steps long was the appropriate day's work for easy weeding, while two rows of the same length were appropriate for difficult weeding. In the middle of May the number of communal days per week was increased from three to five, and the third weeding was started by the women alone while the men began building houses. Where the maize had been interplanted with cassava weeding was much more difficult, so the task was reduced to two rows per day.

Although communal work took place on five days in the week, this did not mean that each person actually worked on all five days. Very often members of a household would take turns to attend, or choose particular days on which to work. As long as the leadership did not try to enforce attendance on every working day nobody minded having five working days in the week. As soon as there was an effort to get everyone to attend each day the members said that this was impossible since at least one member per household was needed to guard the private farms against wild animals, and in any case they felt that five days was too much. The issue was discussed on 19 June and it was decided that from then on the women should come on two days and the men on the other three days.

Thus during June 1971 there were two communal activities going on: the women were weeding and the men were building houses. Apart from the 112 adults in the village, 292 outsiders were also participating in communal work. They were doing so in order to get famine relief food, but were considered as potential members, and would receive a share of the communal harvest according to the work they had done, and a completed house in the village when they wanted to move.

Even though communal farming had only started in connection with famine relief there seemed to be a sense of responsibility towards the communal farm. For example a woman quietly volunteered to guard the farm from the monkeys when she found that the people who were supposed to guard it had not arrived on time. Another was seen weeding part of a row which had been forgotten by those to whom it had been allocated. When people worked they worked thoroughly and conscientiously on the communal field.

The way in which innovations were being introduced on the communal field has already been discussed. But apart from this there was no technical gain from farming all together with the same implements as before, except one: guarding the field against birds and wild animals was much easier and could be done by six people working in shifts.

The men were building houses. A rather elaborate division of labour had emerged in this work. For instance there was a group of people who cut grass for the roofs, another group bound it and transported it, while others thatched. The cutting, transporting and erection of poles to makes the structure of the houses was arranged in a similar manner. The villagers said that with this labour organisation it took a group of twelve men only six days to make the structure and roof, and another six days to build the walls of mud. The house was finished in two weeks. Whether this was in fact faster than private housebuilding could not be checked, but it would be reasonable to assume that, in the long run, division of labour of this kind would have clear advantages. In June 1971 there were about 60 houses in the village in various stages of completion, and most of them had been built within the previous two months.

There were supervisors who were responsible for ensuring that the work on the communal farm or on house building was well done. But up to May 1971 the village was governed by a council of twelve members and three small committees for building, farming and peace-making which functioned very informally if they functioned at all.

In May 1971 a three-day divisional training seminar for chairmen and secretaries of ujamaa villages was held. When the vice-chairman and secretary returned they told the villagers that the President had said that each village should have its own constitution, and small committees, one for each type of activitiy in the village. It was decided to set up four new committees.

But after the meeting many villagers were uncertain how many committees had actually been formed, how many members were on each committee, and whether the new 'committee for general affairs' would be under the old village council or in place of it. Regardless of the official composition, when a week later the agriculture committee met, about 15 people participated in the discussion, and later on this whole group discussed building (a building committee meeting was supposed to take place afterwards). It was evident that the way in which the villagers wanted to decide their issues did not fit easily into the formula received from above.

Nominally the village had a chairman, a vice-chairman, a secretary, and a person responsible for the distribution of famine relief. The chairman was the fifth holder of that office in three years. The villagers said that only the first had lost his job through bad leadership (he was too authoritarian) and that the others had given up their positions because they were not interested in holding official jobs. De facto leadership was exercised collectively by the present leaders together with the former leaders and a few other people of importance such as the shop-keeper. Discussion and decision-making was very democratic but not very effective. Discussions concentrated more on reconciling the people concerned and getting the problem out of the way than on finding the most rational solution to the problem itself.

Before ujamaa started, relationships between households required someone to settle conflicts, but the solution of problems of production was a matter for each individual household. It was probably significant that the solution of the dispute over the women's strike, and the new regulations for communal work which resulted, took the form of a *baraza,* or traditional court hearing. There was a prosecutor on behalf of the village, and a defence lawyer who spoke on behalf of the women. The changes that were made then emerged as a kind of judgement to settle the conflict. Such procedures could easily bring solutions to resolve disputes, but not necessarily solutions that were correct — it would be rather difficult to bring planning into this type of decision-making.

The role of the old *bwana shamba* in the village had already been mentioned. There was also a *bwana maendeleo* (rural development assistant) who did not seem to make much impact, and a villager had been sent to Handeni to be trained as a medical dresser (the nearest dispensary was 20 miles away).

The village was also served by a voluntary literacy teacher. He was a primary school leaver who worked without pay, who for years had been working in different villages starting TAPA schools while living on what he and his wife could grow on their farm (from the beginning of 1971 he was supposed to receive 30/- a month for his adult education work but often this did not seem to arrive). He was politically motivated although he did not make a lot of noise about it. He was accepted by the villagers but he kept himself in the background as far as the general affairs of the village were concerned. He was teaching about 40 children on a syllabus that did not differ much from that of other primary schools in Tanzania. Most of the children actually living in the village went to school, but there were only a handful of people in the village who could read and write.

The villagers were acutely conscious of their poverty. In no village was the gap between what villagers thought they needed and what they had greater. Most of them did not have more than a shilling a day to spend, and some even less than that. Yet in a group discussion on the minimum amount of cash a family would need there was an immediate consensus that a rather poor family would need five shillings a day for most of the year, and that fifteen shillings a day would not be too much. When asked whether they could provide themselves with five shillings a day they shrugged their shoulders. As things were they knew they could never earn that much.

The myth that the peasants of Eastern Handeni are satisfied with the life they have and do not want more was obviously untrue. They wanted a lot more, and realised that individually they could not get it. This was their main motivation towards ujamaa, and they had set out in a way which suggested that if they were helped to overcome their difficult environment, and were not given unrealistic targets or bad advice from outside, they would have the determination to succeed.

KITUMBI-CHANIKA

The early history of Chanika has already been described. In November 1970 the wife of the chairman of the village (by 1971 she had become the secretary) went to Handeni to request famine relief. She was told that it would be provided, but only after each villagers cultivated one acre of cassava according to the minimum acreage law. So the villagers started a block-farm, assisted by the *bwana shamba* from Tibili.

The secretary went back to Handeni to report that everyone had one acre of cassava, but this time she was told that if they were to be given famine relief they would have to do communal agricultural work. She explained this to the people but nobody paid any attention to her.

On 9 January 1971 a meeting was held at Chanika which was attended by the Rural Development Officer and Agricultural Officer from Handeni and the TANU Chairman of the Division. One of the Handeni MPs addressed the villagers to explain to them the meaning and requirements of ujamaa. He informed them that it had been decided to give them famine relief and to register Chanika as an ujamaa village, and this happened the same day.

In mid-1971 there were 358 people — 97 men, 141 women, and 120 children — living in Chanika, and another 600 or so were living in the area round about and were supposed to join the village later. However, only 57 villagers were listed as members of the ujamaa village — most of the women and many of the men were not yet officially members.

Seven of these 57 families were fairly rich compared to the extremely poor majority, having incomes of at least 1,000/- per year from their coconut and cashewnut trees. One member could have expected to earn as much as 10,000/- if his groundnut harvest was a success, while the chairman could have expected an income of about 7,000/- from his trees, but he was also misusing the license which his third wife (the village secretary) had negotiated to open a communal bar. Since the license was in his name he used it to run a private bar from which he earned about 20/- per day from the sale of tembo (a local gin). The chairman and one of the shop-keepers hired labour. A man coming from outside the village complained that the chairman had employed him to do a three week job for 40/- but had only paid him 25/-, and then used his position to threaten him when he complained. The chairman even exploited the villagers for his own purposes; for when they agreed to contribute money for a communal fund those who could not pay were offered work weeding his coconut farm at 1/- a day in order to earn the money to pay their contributions. Indeed the villagers often worked for the chairman for nothing in order to be allowed to accompany him on trips in his car.

Below the 7 households with incomes of over 1,000/- per year there were 14 households with at least 4 acres of maize and 40 coconut or cashewnut trees who could expect a cash income of over 300/- a year. At the bottom of the scale there were 36 households who earned less than 300/- a year. Perhaps five of them could make some money selling fruit from their trees. But ten households grew nothing or almost nothing and it was unclear how they would survive once famine relief was discontinued.

It was the property interests of the richest group that had made them resist the move to Tibili, for this would have meant a move away from their fine houses and permanent tree crops. This particularly applied to the chairman. After a life working in Mombasa, Tanga and on the docks in Zanzibar he had been one of the first people to settle at Kitumbi-Chanika, well before the coming of ujamaa. With the establishment of the ujamaa village in 1971 he automatically became the chairman. One of the villagers said that they had elected him because of his wealth — they were afraid that a poor chairman would sell or consume the famine relief.

The secretary, his third wife, was a member of TANU long before Independence, and had been on some important committee of UWT (the TANU women's organisation) in Dar-es-Salaam. She had completed Standard VIII — so that she was unusually well educated for a middle-aged woman in Handeni. For a time she had worked in a textile factory in Dar-es-Salaam, and then she had moved to this village with her former husband. When Chanika became an ujamaa village she was elected to be secretary, chairman of the woman's committee and *mama maendeleo* (community development adviser). In this area it was rare for a woman to hold a position that was more than symbolic. But this woman felt responsible for everything: she did the work of a midwife, replaced the medical dresser while he was on a training course, tried to persuade the villagers to use latrines, and introduced pottery as a communal activity. Her attempt to start a communal shop and a communal bar failed due to the opposition of the wealthy villagers including the two shop-keepers and her husband. She had tried in vain to establish a functioning women's committee. She had so little time that she had appointed a Standard VII leaver to assist her in her secretarial work, and another person to distribute the famine relief. She was highly esteemed by all the villagers, but she got little support in her work for ujamaa; even the note-books she needed for her secretarial work had to come from her own pocket. During meetings she stayed in the background.

Nominally the village government consisted of the chairman, the vice-chairman, the secretary, the assistant secretary, the agricultural leader and three ten-cell leaders, and there were supposed to be four sub-committees: the agricultural committee, the building committee, the peace-making committee and the village committee. This last was responsible for co-ordinating the other committees, deciding on working hours, distributing famine relief, and making plans such as the village's 'Five Year Plan 1970-1975' which was handed to the Economic Planning Committee of Handeni District and consisted of lists of crops and the acreages of each they would like to grow, the numbers of livestock they would like to have, and the infrastructure (a well, a school, a dispensary and a store) that they hoped the Government would give them.

All these committees met once a month. But decisions were often taken arbitrarily by the chairman. For instance one day the villagers returned from work to find that the chairman had cut some people's ration of famine relief by as much as one pound, while others had been specially favoured. Then his wife, the secretary, asked that there should be a fixed amount which would always be given out unless there was a shortage, and this was agreed. But on another occasion the secretary withdrew some women from watering the coconut trees to assist in some other task, and the chairman declared that those who were withdrawn would have to work without famine relief for three days to make up — which meant that they had almost nothing to eat for three days.

In 1971 Chanika had a communal plot of about 32 acres. This was about half an acre for each registered member, but only a quarter of an acre per member if the unregistered women were included. Of this, 28 acres were planted with maize, 1½ acres were planted with cassava, 1½ acres with groundnuts, 2½ acres with bananas, and there were 50 orange trees, 300 coconut trees and 500 cashewnut trees.

The plot was in good condition, but this was not really due to the work of the members. Few of those wanted ujamaa, and few participated actively (the secretary was a notable exception to this). Meanwhile work performance was guaranteed by what was effectively hired labour: non-ujamaa members from the area worked on the communal farm in order to get famine relief, while ujamaa members were given food without working because moving to the new site and registering was seen as more important than actual participation in communal work. The village leaders claimed that the village had exempted them from communal work. The chairman said that the villagers wished him to be clean and smart and ready to receive guests and respond to urgent messages without delay, and that for this reason they did not think he should be in the field.

Theoretically there were five days of communal work in the week, but as discussed above most of those who turned up were not ujamaa members, and many ujamaa members found excuses to stay away. On the plot the work was a set daily task — men and women did the same amount of work. A day's work was 2 steps by 70 steps of digging, or 3 steps by 70 steps of weeding (young people were given slightly less). Some men were employed in protecting the communal farm from attack by wild animals at night, while others were engaged in house building since most of the villagers were still living in very small temporary huts (only the few rich had big houses; the chairman and one of the shop-keepers had iron sheets on their roofs). Some women made pots, while others collected water for the young coconut trees. A simple shed had been built where meetings could be held and where the women made their pots.

From his bar on the main road, the chairman cultivated the government staff. The Agricultural Officer from Handeni came every two weeks, and the Rural Development Officer and Executive Officer from Handeni also visited frequently. The Rural Development Assistant of the Division visited the village very often.

Despite this, the village had not received all that much aid. Their biggest problem was the water supply, since the women had to go between three and four miles to collect buckets of incredibly bad water. Some steps had been taken to solve this problem, since the villagers had dug a well and this had been lined with rings from the Water Development Division. But in June this well was dry, and the villagers were hoping that well-digging would be more successful at another place. Two experts had been sent from Handeni to look for water, but the villagers were suspicious of them, especially as they required ten villagers each day to help them with their work.

Besides the rings for the (useless) well and the help of the water experts, the only assistance the village had received was famine relief food and seeds for the communal farm. They had asked the government for corrugated iron sheets, and tools such as axes, ploughs and oxen. They had also asked the government for help to provide a dispensary and a school. The dispensary was certainly needed, since the nearest dispensaries were at Manga and Kabuku, both about 20 miles from Chanika (and Tibili), and there were many cases of diarrhoea and eye infections in the village which were not treated.

There was also need for adult education, perhaps even more than for primary education since there was already a primary school about three miles away at Kwamkonga. Some villagers, including youths could barely speak Swahili, and illiteracy was very high. Practical education, for example in arithmetic, was also needed: on one occasion two people had 161/- to divide equally between them and they could not agree how much each one should get. There was also need for political education. The chairman and secretary had attended a leadership seminar held in the Division, and when they came back they read the *Mwongozo* (the 1971 TANU policy 'Guidelines') to the villagers. But the villagers complained that they could not understand it because of the difficult Swahili. In any case the chairman by his actions contradicted many of the conditions both of ujamaa and of the *Mwongozo*.

The villagers certainly did not see communal work as the solution to their problems. To them the foundation of the ujamaa village appeared to be the result of the struggle of their chairman against the government that wanted to move him to Kitumbi-Tibili. Ujamaa for them was an idea of the government. So they thought that the government was responsible for implementing it, and in exchange for this they were prepared to contribute the minimum required by the government. Despite their obvious exploitation at the hands of the chairman, very few of the villagers (with the exception of the secretary) saw the chairman and his small group of rich farmers as an exploiting class.

The village had started during famine, and ujamaa was a shelter for famine. Some of the villagers thought that famine relief would continue indefinitely. In June 1971 most of them had been settled in the village for at least nine months, but many had not started private farms, although there was no reason why they should not have started clearing and cultivating. On days without communal work they rested. It was surprising to find a group of healthy young men walking around the village for the whole day. To explain their laziness one of them asserted that Nyerere and the government were their parents and that for this reason they did not need to bother themselves with more than a bit of communal work, which was what these 'parents' wanted them to do.

CONCLUSION

Kitumbi-Tibili and Kitumbi-Chanika formed an interesting contrast. Tibili had been the original government choice, and Chanika had been a protest village led by a group of rich farmers who wished to preserve their fixed assets. Yet the government officials had allied themselves with Chanika, and overlooked all its weaknesses, just as they overlooked the strengths of Tibili. Tibili had settled down as a much smaller clan-village, and was just beginning to develop the commitment and resolution that could have made a success of communal work, while the life-style and actions of the chairman at Chanika prevented any possibility of responsible communal work.

The government of course wanted one village and not two at Kitumbi. The two villages were unable to agree on the boundary between them, and indeed the Chanika villagers had presented a map to the Handeni Economic Planning Committee which showed all the area of Tibili village as part of Chanika. In any case the government officials did not want to have two ujamaa villages so close together, since this would not have fitted in with their ideas about how to provide social services such as the school and dispensary which were obviously needed. The officials hoped that the two villages could solve the problem by negotiation, but there was no agreement in sight, and really no basis for an agreement. The possibility was always there that the government would intervene to solve their problem by force, and in doing so almost inevitably undermine the first steps towards learning about ujamaa.

CHAPTER 6

Rural Water Supply in Tanzania: Is Politics or Technique in Command?*

Gerhard Tschannerl**

In building up the country we — unlike the modern revisionists who one-sidedly stress the
material factor, mechanization and modernization — pay chief attention to the revolu-
tionalization of man's thinking and, through this command, quicken and promote the work
of mechanization and modernization.   (Mao Tse-tung)

INTRODUCTION

Water for domestic use is one of the basic necessities of life. Since man's existence
on earth the procurement of water to fulfil the various household needs has been
part of the struggle for existence. Water supplies for the majority of a town's
population began to be built only some 150 years ago. Before that only the wealthy
town residents were connected to supply networks, most of which were owned by
private water companies (Ridgeway, 1972, ch.2). At present about two thirds of
the world's population draws its water from sources which lie outside the compound
of the house. But in East Africa the proportion is about 90% (White, Bradley and
White 1972, p.1).

The availability of water from taps in several rooms of the house saves a good
deal of time and energy, particularly when compared to the drudgery of having to
carry water for the whole family in a container from a distance of one mile or
sometimes much further. But there are other problems with unimproved water
sources — such as dug holes, springs and rivers — which are not so readily apparent.
They concern the presence of certain diseases which could be strongly reduced or
even eliminated altogether with drastically improved supplies. They fall broadly
into two categories: infectious diseases which are passed on from one person to the
other through the water (i.e. related to water quality), and diseases which occur
because the quantity of water used is insufficient, be it for drinking or for washing.

Thus there is a wide range of per capita water consumption in East Africa. The
average in rural areas is 13 litres/day which means that many people use hardly
more than the minimum physiological requirement needed to replenish the bodily
water losses. At the other end of the scale lies the average per capita water consumption of 220 litres/day from houses with multiple taps in the wealthy parts of
East Africa's cities (White, Bradley and White, 1972, p.149). The Tanzanian government gives high priority to the provision of rural water supplies to the extent that
'within the next 20 years all Tanzanians living in rural areas should be provided
with adequate, readily accessible, clean and wholesome water throughout the year'
(Water Development 1971). The building of these supplies brings a considerable

---

* 'Politics in command' and 'technique in command' were two contending approaches to
Chinese development in the 1960s, the first held by Mao Tse-tung and the second by Liu
shao-ch'i. The struggle between these two lines was the main issue of the Cultural Revolution
(Hinton 1972, ch.3).

**Formerly Senior Research Fellow, Bureau of Resource Assessment & Land Use Planning,
University of Dar es Salaam.

improvement in the living conditions of the peasants. They save time and energy because of easier access to water, and the improved water quality has important implications for their health (see Tschannerl and Mujwahuzi 1975).

The fact that government-sponsored water supplies fulfil an urgent need of the peasants should, however, not prevent us from examining the role that the rural water supply programme plays in the context of the country's social formation. What objectively is the purpose of this programme? How does it relate to the ideology of the ruling class? How do the various aspects of the programme — the planning process, role of the staff, participation of the villages, etc. — reflect and at the same time reinforce the ruling class ideology?

The following discussion attempts to deal with some of these questions, and in particular to show that the nature of the process through which these supplies are created reflects the class formation in Tanzania. The government maintains close control over all phases of the schemes, from planning and construction up to maintenance. Local leaders are consulted at the planning stage, and when self-help is made a condition for including the scheme in the government's programme, the participation of the peasants is limited to the contribution of free labour under the supervision of the water development staff. The staff in turn tend to have a technocratic and bureaucratic attitude, putting primary emphasis on the establishment of technically sound structures rather than on close co-operation with the peasants. The large external component of the rural water programme in the form of funds, personnel, equipment, and consulting work, tends to reinforce the technocratic attitude of the local staff, while retarding the build-up of the country's capacity to undertake the needed construction work.

There is a larger question, however, that of the function of rural water supply in the total rural development programme, which is only touched upon in this paper. This subject requires a detailed analysis of Tanzania's social formation, including the production and appropriation of surplus and the nature and purpose of villagization. One important function of water supplies in this context is that they are offered by the government as an incentive for compliance with other programmes, such as moving into villages, cultivating cash crops, attending adult education classes, etc.

It should be clear from what is said above that the choice of the rural water supply programme for this analysis does not imply that it serves the ruling class exceptionally well in the pursuit of its objective class interest. Quite to the contrary, because it fulfils a pressing need of the peasantry and brings about an improvement in their living conditions, its other function — that of an instrument to pursue the ruling class ideology — is often overlooked. This dual nature, which the water supply programme has in common with the other services of health and education, reflects Tanzania's class formation and at the same time contributes to its regeneration.

COLONIAL RULE

Colonial conquest brought a drastic change to Tanzania's social formation with the introduction of capitalist production relations, which rapidly became the dominant mode of production. Arab traders brought rifles and manufactured goods in exchange for slaves and ivory, and were followed by missionaries, the colonial state, and white settlers, backed up by the colonial army. The colonial state served the metropolitan bourgeoisie in the exploitation of Africa. 'The first object of the government', wrote a British governor in 1926, 'is to induce the native to become a producer directly or indirectly, that is, to produce or to assist in producing something more than the crop of local foodstuffs that he requires for the sustenance of himself and his family'.[1]

This policy was carried out mainly in two ways. One was for Europeans to open plantations and farms which were run on capitalist principles and employed Africans as wage labourers. The other was the inducement of African cultivators to grow export crops, particularly coffee, cotton, and tobacco (Iliffe 1971, p.18). In addition, various kinds of taxes were introduced in an attempt to make the African peasants bear the administrative and military costs of colonial rule, while continuing to produce in small communities for the satisfaction of their own needs.

This two-fold colonial strategy, which was common throughout Africa, took on a different shape from one African country to another. In Kenya the white settlers drove many Africans off their land and established themselves as a dominant class. In Tanzania the settlers came into conflict with the German metropolitan bourgeoisie over the issue of encouraging Africans to grow cash crops (Hirji 1974, pp.27-31). The position of white settlers, and land ownership in general, was quite different in the two countries.

In Tanzania both plantation agriculture and smallholder cash crop farming coexisted. The approach taken in a particular area of the country depended on the ecological conditions:

a. Cash crops were introduced, sometimes by force (Rodney 1972, p.180, and Iliffe 1971, p.20) in relatively well-watered areas with good soils;
b. Cattle rearing was encouraged in dry areas where there were a lot of cattle, because cattle could be taxed and bought;
c. Areas which could neither commercialize part of their agriculture nor raise cattle were left to continue with subsistence production and became sources of labour for the plantations (Iliffe 1971, pp.12-18).

An important measure in the pursuit of this policy was to draw the African into the cash economy. The increasing penetration of capitalist production relations did, however, not lead to the elimination of other modes of production. On the contrary, the other modes remained and were made subservient to capitalism. As long as small communities consumed essentially all that they produced, it was not possible for an antagonistic class to appropriate whatever small surplus might be produced. Plantation farming and smallholder cash crop production could partly replace communal and feudal modes, but capitalism on the periphery of the international system was too weak to eliminate them. This process of *introducing capitalist production relations* to encircle and dominate the pre-capitalist modes has continued to play a central role in the underdeveloped counlries after independence (see Samir Amin 1974).

RURAL WATER SUPPLY IN THE COLONIAL PERIOD

Public expenditure on water supplies started in Tanzania around 1930, and the Water Development Division was established in 1946. The early concern of the colonial state was mainly with water rights for Europeans. The Germans drafted a water ordinance, which however was not enacted until 1923, during British rule. Water Boards were established to regulate the sharing of water between 'alienated' and 'customary' land. Attention was primarily given to four areas in the country: Kilimanjaro-Meru, Lushoto-Tanga, Kilosa-Morogoro, and Mbeya-Njombe-Iringa.

In 1934 a report by Teale and Gillman on the Kilimanjaro and Meru area expressed concern about the increasing alienation of land and water withdrawals. It described the predicament of the African farmers on the southern slopes of Mounts Kilimanjaro and Meru. Checked by the forest reserves uphill and faced with increasing alienation of land by Europeans downhill, they not only experienced an acute shortage of land for cultivation, but were also losing grazing land for their livestock at the foot of the mountain. The estates were cultivating only a small portion of the alienated land, yet they continually applied for additional water rights. The report therefore recommended a survey of the land and better utilization of alienated land holdings.

The hydrographic survey was completed in 1939 and made it quite clear who was to benefit from the water on the slopes of Kilimanjaro and Meru. A detailed survey of all the rivers, furrows, and water users were undertaken 'to make it possible to institute proper control of the use of water and to see that the available water is distributed in the most beneficial manner, to avoid unnecessary waste' (Water Executive 1939, p.2). It recommended prohibiting irrigation of the steeper slopes (i.e. largely in the zone of African cultivation), restricting the water use by Africans from large furrows, and allowing the European farmers to satisfy their demand and to pass on the excess, if there was any, to the African users. Thus the aim of water control in this area was clearly to *restrict the use of water by African cultivators,* so that enough water would reach the zone of European settlement to satisfy the water demand created by increased land alienation.

A review of the rural water supply projects surveyed or built in Tanganyika by the colonial administration from 1939 to the time of independence suggests that the following objectives guided the choice of projects:

a. to supply minor government settlements, such as bomas, prisons, labour camps, and schools;

b. to supply European farmers and other colonial outposts, such as missions;

c. to encourage the introduction of cash crops (including the commercialisation of cattle rearing) in certain selected areas for export or as food for the labourers and the Europeans on the plantations (Iliffe 1971, p.15);

d. as reward and pacification of the African population, and particularly those chiefs who co-operated with the colonial authorities.

The first two aims need no elaboration. The third falls within and reflects the aim of the metropolitan bourgeoisie of integrating the African farmer into the international capitalist system in order to exploit the country's resources. Water supply to Africans was one of the instruments to implement this policy, as is evident from the early emphasis on water supplies to Maasailand for cattle, Moshi and Bukoba for cash crops, and the related activities of agricultural experimental stations, ginneries, coffee pulping mills, etc. (Water Development 1946 and 1947). The first rural water supply project ever mentioned in a water report was built in Bukoba, and the report specifically states that coffee was grown in the area as a cash crop (Water Development 1946, pp.4-5). Documentary evidence for the fourth aim is more difficult to find, but the crucial role of incentives and rewards is obvious, particularly in a system of 'indirect' colonial rule through a caricature of traditional African Authorities. A specific reference to that aspect of water supplies was made in an Annual Report as late as 1958:

Water supplies, like all beneficial services, are their own best ambassadors, and the benefits

of a recently-installed supply are soon broadcast and lead to demands from other areas.
(Water Development 1958, p.8).

It should also be mentioned here that until 1955 irrigation was of no particular concern. From then on it gained rapidly in importance with the stated purpose of increasing agricultural output (Water Development 1955), but connected to the drive for cash crop production.

The heavy emphasis on Dodoma in the first years also suggests that it was meant to soften the impact of periodic famine in dry areas. There had been a bad drought in Dodoma in the three years preceding 1955, with the severity of the last year unprecedented for 30 years (Patton 1971 pp.4-5).

How did the colonial government make sure that only those water supplies were built which fulfilled these aims? Simply by *controlling the planning and construction of the schemes* and only approving those which served its interests. The materials and skills required for building a water supply are such that the project can in most cases not be carried out by the peasants without aid from the government. There was no need to apply force, as was done in the pursuit of other colonial aims; only minor improvements in the water supply could be carried out by the peasants themselves. Even delegating certain decisions to the 'Native Authorities'[2] did not change that pattern since local governments were made to serve as an arm of the colonial state. Self-help was at times encouraged, but only as a cost-saving device. While the 1947 Annual Report talks of the necessity 'to educate the native to build his own conservation works' (Water Development 1947, p.5), it regrets at the same time the shortage of European supervisers: 'The difficulty of securing competent supervision locally and the non-arrival of Inspectors of Works from the United Kingdom delayed work on a number of projects' (p.4). No wonder there was a poor turnout for this kind of self-help!

Another illustration of the colonial policy on water is provided by an early irrigation project planned for Turiani in Morogoro. The people of that place did not want an irrigation scheme and in fact threatened to leave the area altogether if the construction was started. The project was not built, but the government's reaction was that 'a considerable amount of prejudice has to be overcome in persuading the African villagers to accept the concepts of modern irrigation practice' (Water Development 1955, p.7).

POST-INDEPENDENCE

When the emerging national petty-bourgeoisie took over state power from the metropolitan bourgeoisie some important changes took place, but this did not alter the position of the country on the periphery of the international capitalist system. New contradictions emerged, which shaped subsequent developments. 'On the one hand there is the economic and political bureaucracy (objectively backed by the international bourgeoisie, the country being still in the neo-colonial framework), and on the other are the workers and peasants as represented in their most vocal and conscious elements — largely small groups of intelligensia, including a few enlightened leaders' (Shivji 1973a, p.22).

Many of the measures introduced after independence were initially progressive in the sense that they enhanced the well-being of the population as a whole, but soon began to retard the country's development. Some crucial developments were:

a. increased state control of the commercial sector, culminating in the defeat of the Asian commercial bourgeoisie (see Shivji 1976);

b. gradual expansion of certain activities[3] in the industrial sector through partnership arrangements between the Tanzanian government and monopoly companies;
   and
c. the moving or re-organising of peasants in part of the country into nuclear
   villages for the stated purpose of increased production and to facilitate the
   provision of social services (education, health and water supply) and economic
   infrastructure (roads, agricultural extension, marketing, etc.).

The villagisation programme started in the early sixties with a few selected
settlement schemes. It was greatly expanded after 1969 with the creation of hundreds of ujamaa villages which engaged in some collective activities (a collective plot,
a shop, a poultry farm, etc.).
  In most cases, however, the collective part formed only a small proportion of the
total activities in the village. The emphasis on ujamaa has recently been dropped in
favour of an accelerated movement of the rural population to so-called development
villages for increased farming on an individual basis. The villagisation programme,
however, has never significantly affected certain areas of the country, such as
Mt. Kilimanjaro, Mbeya, and Bukoba. They all have in common a relative high
population density, good soils and rainfall, and a relatively strong presence of
capitalist production relations. Villagisation has not taken place there because:

a. the cash crops produced there already provide the ruling class with a sizeable
   surplus;
b. a strong class of kulaks exists there who strongly resist any move towards land
   redistribution.

WATER SUPPLY AND SELF-HELP AFTER INDEPENDENCE
Rural water supply is given high priority in Tanzania. In 1971 a 20-year target for
supplying the entire rural population with an adequate supply of water was set.
It was estimated that in order to meet this target, the rate of construction would
have to be such that 810,000 people were newly supplied annually. This would
have to reach one million by 1976.[4] However the present rate of construction is
supplying only 300,000 people per year, which is only a small increase over the
annual average of 270,000 supplied from 1971 to 1973.
  One of the reasons for this failure to accelerate the programme faster is the
disruption caused to the operations of the Water Ministry in connection with the reorganisation of the government under decentralisation. For the Water Ministry this
has meant the loss of control over finances and project selection to the regional
administration. The co-ordination of the national budget, including water supply,
now lies primarily with the Prime Minister's Office and the Ministry of Finance.
  But even without the reorganisation of government the programme could not
have been accelerated much faster. The reason for this lies with the way in which
the programme is carried out. The government controls the projects from the
planning stage, through construction, and up to maintenance and operation. The
role of the villagers in the creation of a water supply is one of clients who will
later use the water that the government provides. They hardly ever participate in
decisions concerning the project, and even when they do, this is in the context of
the class relations between the petty bourgeoisie, which holds state power, and the
peasantry, which does not.
  That the contradictions between the classes hold back the progress of the rural

water supply programme can be seen from the poor performance of self-help in construction. People, of course, had always built their own water sources before the advent of government intervention. But schemes that constitute a considerable improvement over the old sources cannot be built by the villagers without outside assistance. There is, however, a fundamental difference in the class formation which assists the peasants with the work that they cannot do themselves, and one where every aspect of the scheme's creation is controlled by the state with the villagers participating only as unskilled labour when called upon to do so.

Soon after independence there was a climate of hope in Tanzania that the end of colonial rule would bring a drastic improvement in the position of the working class. There was an upsurge of self-help and nation-building activities. A considerable number of small rural water supply projects were built by local authorities, with the survey and exploratory work done by the Water Development and Irrigation Division (Water Development 1963, p.6).

Most of the projects were carried out at the request of the local authorities who were expected to pay for 25 per cent of the cost, with central government providing the remaining 75 per cent. One consequence of this division of the financial contribution was that wealthier district councils, such as that of Kilimanjaro District, were able to fund many more schemes than the poorer ones. The contribution of the local authorities was therefore abolished in 1965 to 'enable government to spread the development of supplies more evenly over the country' (Water Development 1965, p.9).

The reported shortage of government funds for construction in previous years was eased with the beginning of Swedish aid in 1966. Greater emphasis was placed in the following years on planning and financing (and on borehole construction), and no further reference to self-help was made in the WD & ID annual reports — the Arusha Declaration notwithstanding.

The question was again raised in 1970 by a firm of management consultants, Rimer and Associates, in connection with a recommended reduction in construction costs. They cited a WD & ID estimate that the labour component amounted on average to 27 percent of total construction costs, excluding overheads, and suggested that nearly all of this could be saved by utilising self-help labour[5] (Vol.II, Appendix 4). The Second Five-Year Plan also emphasised self-help: 'Top priority is to be given to low cost methods for providing rural water. All possible self-help will be mobilised' (Vol.IV, p.50). Instructions were accordingly issued to the regions, but only a few followed them.

The limited use of self-help labour in the past is also connected with the nature of the villagization programme. In the early years of the programme, services such as water supply were offered to the peasants *as an incentive* for moving into villages. In 1968-69 the people in Eastern Handeni were promised a water supply by the district and regional authorities if they formed ujamaa villages, but only very recently has the construction of a large nationally-sponsored scheme with self-help labour started in that area. Peasants in Rufiji District were promised a supply in 1968 by the national leadership if they moved their villages out of the floodplain to higher ground. Most of these schemes were accordingly built by the government between 1970 and 1972. The feeling of the villagers was that this formed part of the 'bargain' and the question of self-help therefore never arose.

Mainly to reduce the staggering expenditure needed for the big drive to build water supplies, a directive was issued by the Prime Minister's Office in July 1973, making it mandatory for all unskilled labour to be contributed by the villagers themselves. This directive has so far been strictly implemented. But according to estimates of some regional water engineers, the average cost saving obtained on piped schemes if all unskilled work is done by self-help amounts to only around 15 per cent for gravity supplies and 8 per cent for pumped supplies under the current mode of operations.

At present a project is built only if the future beneficiaries are willing to do all the unskilled labour without pay. The Regional Water Engineer's office carries out the survey and design work, and when the materials, transport, and the small team of skilled workers from the Water Ministry are ready, the construction work begins. The mobilisation of people to supply the daily number of unskilled labourers required is usually done by the Area Commissioner with the help of other political or administrative officials.

This form of self-help reflects the prevailing class relations. The high and middle-ranking government staff, and in their own way the kulaks, strive to maintain firm control over every aspect of the project. The peasants, on the other hand, want to obtain amenities, such as water supplies from the government without having to do anything in return. As long as this class conflict exists, there is no room for genuine self-help as described by President Nyerere in 1967:

> For an ujamaa village, as outlined in this paper, is both a socialist, and a self-reliant community. It will be using local resources and traditional knowledge, and working up from these to the simple improvements which are possible when people work together ... When the government and other national institutions come in they will do so to *supplement the activities of the members and assist them to help themselves* (**1968 p.176**, emphasis added).

A certain kind of self-help that is particularly popular in Kenya and known as *harambee* also needs to be mentioned as it can also be found in certain parts of Tanzania, such as Kilimanjaro and West Lake. It occurs almost exclusively in wealthier areas where the capitalist mode of production is relatively stronger. Many but not all people there have the money to contribute to the construction of services such as water supplies, schools, and dispensaries. They also see themselves as closer to the petty bourgeoisie than peasants in other parts of the country, a subjective condition which is in many cases reinforced by actual family ties to the national ruling class. The purpose of this form of self-help is to supplement the 'aid' programme of the government. By making a voluntary local contribution they are often able to attract more government funds than originally allocated. For example, after a school is built by self-help the government would be called upon to take it over, provide the teachers, and pay for its operation. In those areas people recognise that by joining *together* they are able to increase their *individual* chances of economic advancement in relation to the entire rural population of the country.

THE ROLES: EXPERTS, KULAKS AND PEASANTS

Three broad groups participate in the creation of rural water supplies: government staff, which includes the bureaucratic bourgeoisie as well as the upper, middle, and lower level salariat;[6] kulaks (well-to-do peasants); and peasants. One could further make a division of functions in the government staff between technical and non-technical (i.e. primarily political and economic) staff. The former category can be termed 'government technical staff', or more loosely 'experts'.

The different *roles* that these three groups play — experts, kulaks, and peasants — in the process of implementing the rural water-supply programme, and how they relate to the ideologies of the contending classes and further their class interests, are discussed below.[7]

a. **Experts.** The functional government staff — here called experts — engaged in the fields of agricultural extension, roads, water supply, sanitation, etc. consists primarily of members of the upper and middle salariat. In the water field this includes engineers, technicians, foremen, and regularly employed craftsmen *(fundis).* Although they have contradictions among themselves these groups possess a common objective interest in the class ideology of the petty bourgeoisie, of which they are a part. This interest is centred around a regular cash income, access to (urban) amenities, participation in decision-making, access to education, etc.[8] They occupy posts in a large hierarchial organisation — the state based on Weber's 'legal-rational' mode. Each member has to *legitimise* the occupancy of a place in the hierarchy primarily by how successful he is in performing the tasks allotted to him. The experts see their function primarily in terms of *physical accomplishments*: acreage under tea cultivation increased (Sender 1973), a road built without labour cost (Thoden van Velzen 1973, pp.157-158), and getting a certain number of ujamaa villages established (Cliffe 1973, pp.202-203). It is commonly believed that they achieve these tasks because of their specialised knowledge.

This is also the case for rural water supply. The progress reports on water supply talk about so many boreholes drilled, so many people supplied with water, so many kilometres of pipes laid, so many projects designed, etc. No mention is made of the process by which this was accomplished or of other results apart from the physical structure. One never reads, for example, that the engineers decided to spend more time with the peasants so that they could get better acquainted with their problems, or that so many plumbers in the village were trained in the course of construction, or that, as a result of suggestions from the villagers, a different, cheaper design for a particular item was adopted. Thus the role performance of experts fosters a dependancy relationship with the peasants and legitimises the existence of the government bureaucracy.

The dominant aspect of the expert's role performance is to provide technical knowledge. 'They don't know' and 'they don't understand' are frequently-used phrases in relation to the peasants.

> **There were no problems encountered with the villagers (during construction). They seemed to be well organised under their own group leadership. Our experts were there to ensure that they followed instructions,**

was the comment of one engineer. Indeed the 'need for close supervision' was often mentioned:

> **people have a tendency not to turn up for work when they are needed, and then they don't dig (the trench) deep enough. They think that covering the pipe with earth is sufficient. That makes it quite difficult for us.**

Another manifestation of this technocratic attitude is the tendency to look for a *technical* answer to any problem that arises, as illustrated by the following episode. During the study the researchers passed a place where people were taking water from a cattle trough to carry home for domestic use, although there was a tap only 30 metres away. When this was brought to the notice of an engineer in the regional office, his response was 'we have provided them with a tap, but they prefer to take water from the trough; it is easier for them'. The truth of the matter was that the pressure in the pipeline was so low during most of the day that even though water reached the trough, none ran out at the tap. It is as if the engineer's immediate reaction was to absolve himself of any responsibility, claiming that he had done all that could be expected of him — to provide the tap.

Reference is also sometimes made to high *professional* standards. Asked about the performance of some schemes which were built by self-help without the assistance of the Water Ministry (then WD & ID), one engineer lamented that the designs were 'not done in a professional way'. The pipe diameter was sometimes too small, he maintained, and the walls of the storage tank crooked. When challenged about the need for the storage tank to look nice as long as it served its purpose, he retorted 'but after all, there is something like professional pride!' Another engineer even referred to the supposed high standards of the trade in relationship to the non-technical staff in the regional administration: 'I have to convince many technically illiterate persons'.

The pre-occupation with technical matters at the expense of other, more people-centred problems might also be at the bottom of the unequal rate of progress made in the different phases of designing, building and maintaining a scheme. In many regions surveys and designs are one to two years ahead of implementation, and poor maintenance is also a problem. One technician's response to criticism about the disregard for people's wishes when preparing the design was 'How can we hope to meet the 20-year target if we take all the wishes of the villagers into account?'

Another case in point is a water scheme that was being built in a remote part of the country. The first plans for this piped gravity scheme to serve people and livestock were made in 1961 and the planned location of the pipe marked with pegs on the ground, but it was not built at that time. The original plans were recently revived and a team of surveyors sent there to place new pegs, marking the future location of the pipeline. The team asked the peasants to show them any of the old pegs that were left from 1961. The people told them at that time that the locations of water outlets shown by the old pegs were not good and suggested another lay-out. When the team left, the peasants found that the surveyors had put the new pegs close to the old ones, ignoring their suggestion without even informing them. When the foreman later arrived to supervise the construction (done by self-help labour), he referred to the drawings as his instructions and said: 'This is what I am authorised to do. I cannot make changes without the approval of the engineer. If you want to have something changed, you will have to see the people in charge at the office.'

At the regional water office the engineers and technicians were completely unaware of these discussions which had taken place at the project site. Neither of the field teams had reported anything. But when our research team pointed out the discrepancy between what the peasants wanted and what the field teams planned to do, the response was the same. Taking out the drawing, the engineer said 'This is how it is going to be. I don't care what is on the ground at the place now. We will see to it that the correct plans are being followed. Don't worry about it'. He was referring to the 1961 drawing! Not only were the wishes of the peasants ignored at every level, but it did not seem to occur to anybody that a plan that was a good one twelve years ago might not be the best now. When the reseachers looked into the matter at the site, they found that the peasants were right; the new locations were far better with little, if any, length of pipeline required in addition to what was provided in the plan.

Another aspect of the role of the experts evident from this example is an *insistence on procedure,* a *narrow definition of one's job,* and a *rigid chain of command.*

The surveyors and the foreman did not report the peoples' suggestions to the office, and the engineer did not try to find out if the old plan would serve the people best. A narrow view of the job reduces the risk of conflict with other members of the organisation, while at the same time enhancing the importance and status of each post in the hierarchy, and ultimately the organisation as a whole. *Plans* prepared and approved at a distance office, *authorisation* given to someone, being *in charge* of equipment. all serve as insignia of power to the experts in their dealings with the peasants.

The gap between them and the peasants created by the staff's narrow definition of its role is widened at times by misconceptions and misunderstandings. They range from simplistic social theories, such as 'People in places like Arusha and Moshi have a better appreciation of water because they are educationally more advanced', to a seemingly deliberate distortion of the people's behaviour, as shown by the following example.

A group of researchers arrived at a water point, accompanied by staff from the Water Department. The peasants who assembled started complaining immediately that there was not enough water coming through the pipe. The technician dismissed their complaints as routine requests for more water during peak demand time — usually early morning and later afternoon. He also mentioned that people there had a tendency to tamper with the pipe (one such incident had in fact recently occurred at that site), and so it was their own fault if there was not enough water. The party was about to leave when one villager urged us to go some distance uphill where a large quantity of water was spilling from a tank. It was then found that the pipe was partly blocked, presumably by some object which had fallen into the tank, resulting in a large overflow.

b. *Kulaks.* The introduction of market relations had progressed far enough in many areas of Tanzania during the colonial period to create a class of kulaks, explicitly encouraged by the colonial state in the years preceding independence (Iliffe 1971, pp.37-41, and Cliffe 1973a, p.37). The extent of rural class differentiation varies from area to area, but its existence has been documented in a number of case studies.[9] Kulaks have a *privileged position* mainly through a disproportionately large command over some or all of the following: (i) land holdings, (ii) hired labour, (iii) service facilities or trading (e.g. a shop, bar, flour mill, tractor, lorry), (iv) unequal access to education (Mbilinyi 1973, p.16), (v) salaried jobs, and (vi) access to funds. To exercise this control they tend to occupy local *leadership* positions, which give them greater power over land, employment, funds,[10] and access to the government staff. Holding leadership positions also enables them to make sure that the ujamaa village programme stops short of collectivisation and is not guided by a proletarian ideology. In many areas it is the traditional leaders who occupy the local TANU positions.[11]

It is in the interest of the government staff to have kulaks as local leaders for a variety of reasons. Kulaks are often the most 'progressive' and 'modernised' peasants, and most of them are in a better position than the poor peasants to show results in terms of the targets set by the government. And they provide the government staff at times with favours ranging from entertainment and presents to support in a dispute (Thoden van Velzen 1973, pp.167-168).

One might expect that the peasants are opposed to having the kulaks as their leaders, but this is only partly true. For the peasants, kulaks form a buffer to the government staff and act as agents to obtain the various services that the government staff can offer (von Freyhold 1973b, pp.14-15). Besides, a poor peasant can hardly survive as a leader since the kulaks often control some vital aspects of village life and generally enjoy the support of the government staff.

This seemingly ambivalent position of the kulaks, which leads many people to argue that they are just another group of peasants who *happen* to exercise a larger control over the means of production and distribution, can however be clarified by analysing their *objective* class interest.

In the Tanzanian context they are a part of the petty bourgeoisie, although in relation to the bureaucratic bourgeoisie they do not constitute a strong force (Shivji 1976, p.56). Shivji even suggests that 'there is evidence for important contradictions at the time of independence between the emerging "bureaucratic bourgeoisie" and the kulaks' (1976, p.56). In the pursuit of their *objective* class interest, the kulaks on certain issues form a temporary alliance with the bureaucratic bourgeoisie, as represented by the local government staff, and on other issues ally themselves with the peasants.

This phenomenon is important when examining the kulak's role in the field of domestic water supplies (but not necessarily in irrigation), where there is no major divergence of interests between kulaks and peasants. The nature of communal water supplies is such that no privileged group can enjoy a considerably larger share of the benefits. Minor opportunities for special privileges no doubt exist, but no significant inequality in the use of the water is possible, and most of them would only be deprived through the process of creating the scheme rather than through the apportionment of its benefits. Such privileges could include the location of a tap in closer proximity to a kulak's house, light or no manual work if the scheme is being built by self-help labour, control over the selection of who works on the scheme (particularly when the labour is paid), and a general boost to a kulak's position when he was the one who successfully negotiated with the government staff for the much-desired water supply. To what extent the kulaks can avail themselves of these possibilities varies from place to place, but with the possible exception of control over who gets employment, none would be in serious conflict with the peasants' short-term interests.

It appears therefore that for the purpose of obtaining a water supply scheme from the government, the kulaks' *subjective* interest is with the peasants, resulting in a *temporary alliance* with them on that issue. The kulaks then tend to act as spokesmen for the peasants in the negotiations with the government staff.

c. *Peasants.* There was a considerable variation in what the peasants said about the building of water supply projects, but they showed some agreement on the following points:

i. They had benefited greatly from the new supplies through improved water quality,[12] better ability of the schemes to deliver enough water every day, and reduced distances from their houses to the taps. There were frequent complaints, however, that the reliability, although much improved, was still inadequate.

ii. Some general meetings took place during the planning phases of the schemes which most peasants attended, but, it appears that their purpose was more to rouse the peasants to some action or to confirm their support of the leaders and the leaders' ideas, rather than to encourage a genuine discussion out of which a decision would emerge. More often than not the local leaders were consulted by the water department staff on a few technical matters, such as what source to use, but this advice was usually ignored.

iii. There were enthusiastic responses to the call for work, but the initially high attendance at the construction sites gradually diminished on most schemes, and the progress of some of them slowed down as a consequence. No clear explanation of this could be found except that there were pressing labour demands at certain times for other work, mostly on the fields.

iv. A certain deference to authority or expertise was sometimes in evidence. People would be 'grateful to the government' and would want to 'let the experts decide'. One response to a question about whether the communal outlet should have been built differently was, 'The government is the one to know, and it has experts who are the ones to make the plans, rather than asking people for suggestions'. On the other hand, demands on the government were sometimes stated in no unclear terms: 'We asked the government to give us water' — 'The government delayed this work'.

v. The local leaders figured prominently in the planning and construction process. 'The Diwani told us that the government had agreed (to finance the scheme). The leaders announced what days we should work on project'. The response of the peasants generally expressed support for their local leaders.

The following *conclusions* can be drawn about the peasants' role in regard to water supplies. They are aware of their needs, but have little confidence in their own abilities. They tend to look towards the government for solutions and seem to expect their leaders to negotiate for them. When they are given something that fulfils such a basic need as a water scheme they accept it without much question about the details of where the taps will be, whether there is a place to wash clothes, who will operate the scheme, etc. They are even willing to some extent to comply with conditions attached to the granting of a project, like their contribution of self-help labour. What they are willing to do in return, however, has its limits, as has been shown in the case of two villages which used the old water supply (for one village this was a polluted river) rather than shift to a new location, planned by the government, where water taps had been installed. The peasants seemed on the surface to accept the authority of the government without much question, but occasionally displayed a keen awareness of the conflict of interest between themselves and the government staff.

THE EXTERNAL COMPONENT

It remains to examine the international aspects of the Tanzanian water supply programme. This component should not be treated only as a by-product of the national scene, but as an integral part of it. The dominance of a neo-colony's economy by international capitalism requires the presence of a national ruling class which, in turn, can only pursue its direct class interest with the support of the international bourgeoisie.

When examining the external aspects of the rural water-supply programme, we immediately notice two things. One is the *large size* of this component and the other the *almost total absence of socialist countries.* Apart from a small contribution of personnel from Eastern Europe and a donation from the People's Republic of China all connections are with the advanced capitalist countries. The foreign component of rural water development mainly consists of funding, personnel, procurement of materials, and foreign consultants.

a. *Funding.* At present 75 per cent of the rural water supply development budget is covered by Swedish aid (it was 80 per cent previously). Some additional support was received from other governments, often to finance planning studies carried out by an agency of the donor country. Water master plans for each of the regions are now in various stages of completion, each plan being prepared by a team under the sponsorship of a different foreign government.

b. *Personnel.* A sizeable proportion of the senior officials in the Water Ministry, including those in the regions, are expatriates.[13] With the arrival of 40 Indian engineers, they numbered 220 in mid-1973. Swedish and Indian personnel constituted about one-third each, and the remainder were from Great Britain, Holland, Denmark, Bulgaria, Egypt, and some other countries (Hyden 1973, p.11). In spite of this large foreign contingent, the officials of the Ministry often pointed to the shortage of qualified manpower as the critical bottleneck in the acceleration of water supply development (Minister for Water Development 1971 and 1973). McKinsey Consultants (1973) estimated that in the regions only 70% of the required posts were filled, and not all of them with qualified personnel. As a partial remedy an additional 60 Indian engineers were expected to arrive.

The presence of such a large foreign contingent lends support to the technocratic attitude of the water staff. Foreigners are not part of the social and political fabric of the country (even though a few might try to be) and are thereby limited in their role to the 'offering of a skill'. Furthermore, the expatriates have grown up in a capitalist environment and possess a class interest which is opposed to a proletarian ideology. Some individuals, no doubt, have a progressive political outlook and are willing to learn, but they receive little or no encouragement. Technical and administrative competence, and an ability to get along with one's colleagues, seem to be all that is required (see Hyden 1973).

c. *Procurement of Materials.* Swedish loan agreements are modelled on those of the World Bank. Thus they do not restrict any portion of the loan to purchases from Sweden, but they stipulate that materials must be bought by *international tender* and the order given to the lowest bidder. For those few items which are being manufactured in Tanzania, the local manufacturer is usually the lowest bidder, but not always. A recent bulk order for plastic pipes went to a British firm, although there are two factories in Dar es Salaam making plastic pipes. (A small supplementary order to local firms is, however, stipulated in the aid agreement). This has dismayed many, including some Swedish aid officials, and efforts to bolster local production of plastic pipes — and later to start producing steel pipes — are underway.

The effect of these arrangements is likely to be a retardation in building up the local manufacture of these materials and a bias in the choice of technique in the design of water schemes. The requirement to shop in the international market deprives local industry of the protection and urgency that it needs to get started.

Another consequence of this ordering procedure has recently come to light with the sudden shortage of various raw materials on the international market. Tanzania has difficulty getting PVC (polyvinyl chloride), one of two alternative materials used to make plastic pipes. There is also a problem with steel. Access to vital raw materials such as these has become a new instrument of monopoly capitalism to dictate the terms of trade and control the establishment of industry in underdeveloped countries. A company which has a supply of a certain raw material, such as steel, guaranteed for a number of years, is in a strong position to obtain advantageous terms for a partnership agreement to establish a company in an under-developed country.

d. *Foreign Consultants.* The volume of planning work carried out by foreign consulting firms has increased considerably over the last few years. Many of these are Swedish, but their national origin is irrelevant because their role in Tanzania is not determined by nationality but by their basic function, which is to make a profit. Through that work they contribute in the following ways to increasing the contradictions in Tanzania:

i. The firm's employees bring to bear a capitalist framework in their analysis because of their personal background and the profit-making aim of the firm.

ii. They are likely to further the interests of international monopoly capitalism in an indirect way (e.g. capital-intensive equipment) or sometimes directly via business arrangements with other companies or financial conglomerates.

iii. They often do a poor job in an attempt to expend the minimum effort permissible under the contract, such as copying other researchers' data for their attractive-looking reports.

iv. The firms take a narrow view of their tasks, doing nothing to increase the potential of their clients which would enable them to independently solve similar problems in the future, unless this is specifically written into the contract.

v. The belief that consulting firms can offer superior knowledge and ability as compared to the Tanzanian staff leads to further dependency, because they are often called upon to perform tasks that only a local senior staff member can do, such as evaluate the report of a previously engaged consulting firm.

SWEDISH AID

Nearly all aid for rural water supply (especially in financing) comes from the Swedish government through the Swedish International Development Assistance (SIDA). The question has to be asked, therefore, what interest the Swedish government has in providing this aid. To answer this would require a detailed analysis of Swedish capitalism abroad and at home, which is outside the scope of this paper. The motivation for giving such large-scale aid with little direct returns is obviously a mixed one and partly reflects the presence of powerful progressive elements in Sweden. It would be a mistake, however, to neglect the role of *Swedish imperialism.*

From .1960 to 1965 Swedish capital export increased by 80 per cent. Between 1965 and 1970 it doubled. The number employed in Swedish companies abroad increased four times quicker than (in) Sweden during the 1960s. Of all Swedish investments abroad 15 concerns account for half the capital invested. Eight of these have more people employed than in Sweden. Most of the capital goes to EEC countries. But the proportion to the so-called under-developed countries is the one most rapidly increasing. In 1970 more than 21 per cent of all Swedish investment abroad went to these countries.

Of Swedish investments in underdeveloped countries the largest proportion goes to Africa. In 1965 the total market value of Swedish interests in Africa was estimated to be about six million dollars. Most of this was located in South Africa. Other countries subject to Swedish imperialism are Liberia, Ethiopia, Tunisia and Zambia. It is explicit Swedish government policy to promote and facilitate private Swedish investments abroad.

. . . In 1965, for instance, almost 10 per cent of all foreign investments in Portugal were Swedish. In 1971 there were around 60 companies in Portugal fully or partly owned by Swedes.
                                                                                            (Swedish Imperialism 1971)

The argument that Sweden gives aid to Tanzania because the latter is supposedly in transition to socialism is debatable. Swedish aid goes, for example, also to Botswana. The case of CADU, an experiment to 'develop' peasant farming in Ethiopia through a Swedish aid project (Nekby 1971) illustrates how Swedish aid adapts to the socio-economic conditions of the recipient country and supports the ruling class in power.

The considerable foreign involvement in the rural water supply programme supports to a certain extent the class interest of the government staff and retards the development of the country's capability to pursue the programme entirely on its own in the near future under the command of a proletarian ideology. The external component also lends support to the technocratic approach by placing primary emphasis on things like financing, organisational efficiency, job qualifications, design criteria, etc., rather than on political mobilisation, creativity of the masses, and ideological training of the cadres.

CHOICE OF TECHNIQUE

Technology is not neutral. A nation's material base is closely related to its production relations, and the choice of what level of technology to use for a particular activity depends to a large extent on the nature of that society. Indian capitalists manufacture cloth in urban centres on machines modelled after present-day British technology, while thousands of handloom weavers in the villages still engage in their household production. There are numerous examples of different techniques employed to do similar things in Tanzania: road and railway construction, textile manufacture (Shivji 1973b, p.18), and bread making in Dar es Salaam (see Chapter 13). There is a more fundamental difference between these alternatives than the proportion of labour and equipment employed: to present the choice exclusively in terms of capital-intensive versus labour-intensive techniques has meaning only under capitalist production (Wuyts 1973). In a socialist context the emphasis would be more on surplus generation, workers' control over production, learning skills, and confidence of the labouring population in their own abilities.[14]

Suppose rural water development was carried out by self-help (and not by self-help labour), the peasants were to take the initiative, the power of decision-making about the village was primarily in their own hands, the government's rule was one of assisting the peasants in their own efforts, and the country was disengaged from international capitalism. What would characterise the water supply technique in such a context?

The low level of productive forces would require that the small surplus generated in the country should not be spent primarily on services, but on expanding and rationalising production. As much of the resources as possible should therefore be generated on the spot, which means using *local materials* At this stage the technique should be labour-intensive.[15] The technique should also be *simple* to understand and build, so that the masses could do a good part on their own without the help of government experts. And it should give ample *scope for learning* through practice, and for improvement by the people themselves.

The technique presently chosen for rural water supplies in Tanzania meets hardly any of these characteristics. To a water engineer or technician, a good scheme is one that has been planned to the last detail by the experts and made of robust and well-tested materials. Technical excellence takes precedence over people's participation. The materials which are known to be most reliable to the foreign (and usually also to the national) experts are those used either in the past or the present in the advanced capitalist countries. Machines used for construction are also more controllable than people, and with the growing alienation and militancy of the low-level government staff, there has been some tendency towards acquiring more sophisticated construction equipment, such as powerful drilling rigs. Although some consideration is given to the labour component in the choice of technique so that government expenditure can be saved, the need for simplicity and learning opportunities for the villagers seems to be totally ignored.

It is risky to suggest concrete examples of alternative techniques which might be applicable in the East African environment, but are at present neglected. Some experts would immediately dismiss them as impractical or unworkable. But this is precisely what has prevented the introduction of any major innovation, with the exception of plastic pipes which came also from the capitalist world. Ideas for innovations which originate locally should be encouraged, whether they come from the masses or the experts, and then put to the test. Not only will some useful alternatives emerge this way, but the process of experimentation will itself be a learning experience.

Two designs which appear to the author to have some potential are a plastic rainwater catchment tank and a more systematic collection and storage of rainwater from rooftops. The first has been developed in the Sudan and later in Botswana by the Intermediate Technology Development Group of London (1969). It consists of a large hole dug in the ground, lined with an ingenious arrangement of plastic sheets, with the walls formed by hundreds of thin plastic bags filled with a weak cement-earth mixture and stacked like bricks. It has a cover, a silt trap, and is meant to collect surface runoff from rainstorms. It can be built by the peasants with minimal technical advice and with simple (but alas not really cheap) materials. People can easily learn how to build it by doing, and the knowledge can be passed from village to village.

In Africa water has been collected from rooftops for a long time, but it has only become viable as an adequate source for domestic use with the introduction of the tin roof. There are often several new buildings with tin roofs in a village which, when equipped with a proper water collection storage system, might provide a very good source of water. In areas with high rainfall it can cover all the domestic water needs throughout the year, in areas with less rainfall it might be able to provide only for cooking and drinking purposes, while people would bathe, wash clothes and vessels, and water cattle at an old source of poorer quality. Again these installations would be planned, built, and maintained by the villagers themselves with very little assistance from the government. Only systematic experimentation could show if and under what circumstances these designs are appropriate for Tanzania.

CONCLUSION

We can now return to the question posed in the title of the paper, is 'politics' or 'technique' in command? Hinton explains the difference:

> . . . "technique in command" is not some alternative way to build socialism but a way of building capitalism. And since in the modern world the capitalist road is truly barred to any underdeveloped nation by the overwhelming power of the already developed imperialist states who will not allow any new capitalist centres to develop but only satellite economies, this bourgeois road can only lead back to semi-colonial, semi-feudal status for China or any other developing nation.   (1972, p.45)

Building socialism means that a *proletarian ideology* guides all spheres of activity.

It means that advances in production must be based on the political consciousness of a revolutionary process to build socialism, with the masses firmly in power. To rely on advances in production to bring about socialism means in fact building capitalism. A one-sided emphasis on productive methods neglects class struggle and political consciousness, and fails to establish socialist production relations. Instead of engaging in class struggle and attacking the neo-colonial dependency relationship with the international bourgeoisie, one-sided emphasis on the development of the productive forces will sharpen class divisions and more firmly integrate the under-developed country into the international capitalist system.

In Tanzania there is a tendency for such services as water supply for rural areas to be used by the government as economic incentives to increase production. The underlying ideology of this process of rural development is that of the bureaucratic bourgeoisie, which holds the state power. In the limited context of the programme of providing water supplies, the dominant *ideology* is that of the *experts.* They emphasise the importance of physical structure, detailed engineering plans, rigid adherence to procedures and job responsibilities, and the efficiency of their organisation. They control the entire process of the creation of a scheme from planning to maintenance. The role of the peasants, if they are involved at all, is limited to some technical consultation (but the decision is made by the experts) and a contribution of unskilled labour under the experts' supervision.

For building socialism in Tanzania this mode of operation has to be changed, not only in the field of water, but in all spheres. The progressive elements who are willing to defend the proletarian ideology must lead the struggle for socialist transformation. This struggle must be based on a thorough understanding of existing reality. We conclude with Hinton again:

> Socialism is not simply a question of modern techniques and large-scale production; it involves the radical transformation of every kind of human relationship, of human motivation, of human consciousness; it involves the release of the enthusiasm, the energy, and the creativity of the masses and the development to the fullest of the capacity of each individual. Efficient modern mechanized production alone will not lead to socialism Only revolution can do that.   (1972, p.45)

NOTES

1. Sir Donald Cameron, 'Agriculture and Labour', 5 August 1926, TNA 215/121/48, quoted by Iliffe (1971), p.12.
2. During the colonial period and for a few years after independence the majority of projects of the Water Development Dept. were built at the request and with at least partial financing of the Native Authorities (later called Local Authorities).
3. This covers primarily the manufacture of light consumer goods which only a small segment of the population can afford to buy.
4. This calls for a large capital outlay. In 1960/61 the construction expenditure was 2.4 million shs. and had risen to 20 million shs. in 1970/71. To supply one million people annually will require an annual construction budget of 70 million shs. calculated on the basis of 1972 prices, a figure which will approximately double by 1979 at the present rate of inflation. In addition one has to consider the cost of maintenance, which will increase rapidly as the number of existing projects goes up (Water Development and Power 1972).
5. A distinction should be made between 'self-help' and 'self-help labour'. The latter constitutes 'free labour' in so far as the peasants work on construction like the labourers engaged by the water department, except that they receive no pay. It is therefore not different from 'alienated labour' in the sense that the people have no control over the product of their work and only perform unskilled tasks under the supervision of government technicians.

6. Adapted from Shivji's criteria for sub-dividing the petty bourgeoisie (1974, p.101).
7. Part of the empirical evidence presented here was collected in the course of a study on the impact of rural water supplies by Tschannerl and Mujwahuzi (1975). No distinction was made between the responses of expatriate and Tanzanian staff for the reasons that first, no clear difference between these two groups was evident from the study, and second, if a distinction between different groups had been made, the expatriates might have had to be further subdivided into Indians, Europeans, etc.
8. For details see Shivji (1974, p.100).
9. See especially Thoden van Velzen (1973), Awiti (1972), von Freyhold (1973b), and Sender (1973).
10. Misuse of village funds is not uncommon. See for example Sender (1973), pp.19-22.
11. Hill in Chapter 7 and Angwazi and Ndulu (1973) illustrate how more often than not leadership posts are still in traditional hands and further discussion of the general issue can be found in Cliffe (1973b) and Shivji (1976).
12. Almost all the people interviewed knew that there was a connection between health and water quality, although some had an incorrect notion of the precise nature of this relationship.
13. Here no distinction can be made between the Ministry's four main functions: rural water supply, urban water supply, irrigation and flood control, and power. But rural water supply is by far the largest of the four: nearly three-quarters of the development budget for 1972/73 and 1973/74 was for rural supplies (United Republic of Tanzania, 1972-73).
14. See Ngombale-Mwiru (1973, p.54) on encouraging the working people in Tanzania to regain self-confidence after colonial rule.
15. Baran (1957, pp.445-448) however, warns against an automatic option for labour-intensive techniques in underdeveloped countries. The choice must be made from case to case and not only be based on considerations of economic efficiency.

REFERENCES

Amin, Samir 1974, 'Modes of Production and Social Formations', *Ufahamu.*
Angwazi, J. and B. Ndulu 1973, 'An Evaluation of Ujamaa Villages in the Rufiji Area, 1968-1972', East African Universities' Annual Social Science Conference, Dar es Salaam, December 1973.
Awiti, Adhu 1975, 'Ismani and the Rise of Capitalism' in L. Cliffe *et al,* (eds), *Rural Cooperation in Tanzania,* (Dar es Salaam: Tanzania Publishing House).
Baran, Paul A. 1957, *The Political Economy of Growth,* (Harmondsworth: Penguin), 1973, (first published 1957).
Cliffe, L. 1973a, 'The Policy of Ujamaa Vijijini and the Class Struggle in Tanzania', in L. Cliffe and J. Saul (eds), *Socialism in Tanzania,* Vol.2, (Nairobi: East African Publishing House).
Cliffe, L. 1973b, 'Nationalism and the Reaction to Enforced Agricultural Change in Tanganyika during the Colonial Period', L. Cliffe and J. Saul (eds), *Socialism in Tanzania,* Vol.1, (Nairobi: East African Publishing House).
Hinton, William 1972, *Turning Point in China,* (New York: Monthly Review Press).
Hirji, Karim 1974, 'Colonial Ideological Apparatuses in Tanganyika under the Germans', mimeo, University of Dar es Salaam.
Hyden, G. *et al* 1973, 'Expatriate Effectiveness in Development Management in Tanzania', Report to the Ministry of Water Development and Power, Dar es Salaam.
Iliffe, J. 1971, *Agricultural Change in Modern Tanganyika,* Historical Association of Tanzania Paper No.10 (Nairobi: East African Publishing House).
Intermediate Technology Development Group 1969, 'The Introduction of Rainwater Catchment Tanks and Micro-Irrigation to Botswana', Report, London.
McKinsey Consultants 1973, 'Ministry of Water Development and Power, Reorganising to Increase Effectivness Under Decentralization', Report to the Government of Tanzania.
Mbilinyi, Marjorie H. 1973, 'The Problem of Unequal Access to Primary Education in Tanzania', African Universities' Annual Social Science Conference, Dar es Salaam, December 1973.
Nekby, Bengt 1971, *CADU, An Ethiopian Experiment in Developing Peasant Farming,* (Stockholm: Prisma Publishers).
Ngombale-Mwiru, K. 1973, 'The Arusha Declaration on Ujamaa na Kujitegemea and the Perspectives for Building Socialism in Tanzania', in L. Cliffe and J. Saul (eds), *Socialism in Tanzania,* Vol.2, (Nairobi: East African Publishing House), pp.52-61.
Nyerere, J.K. 1968, 'After the Arusha Declaration', in his *Ujamaa, Essays on Socialism,* (Dar es Salaam: Oxford University Press), pp.145-177.

Patton, M. 1971, 'Dodoma Region 1929-59: A History of Famine', Research Report No.44, University of Dar es Salaam, Bureau of Resource Assessment and Land Use Planning.
Ridgeway, James 1971, *The Politics of Ecology,* (New York: Dutton).
Rimer, Olle and Associates 1970, 'Tanzania Rural Water Supply Development', Vols.I and II, Report to the Government of Tanzania, Ministry of Agriculture.
Rodney, Walter 1972, *How Europe Underdeveloped Africa,* (Dar es Salaam: Tanzania Publishing House).
Sender, John 1973, 'Some Preliminary Notes on the Political Economy of Rural Development in Tanzania Based on a Case-Study in the West Usambaras', Economic Research Bureau Seminar Paper, University of Dar es Salaam.
Shivji, I.G. 1973a, 'Tanzania: The Silent Class Struggle', in his *The Silent Class Struggle,* (Dar es Salaam: Tanzania Publishing House).
Shivji, I.G. 1973b, 'Capitalism Unlimited: Public Corporations in partnership with Multinational Corporations', Conference on Public Corporations in Africa, Accra, May 1973.
Shivji, I.G. 1976, *Class Struggles in Tanzania,* (London: Heinemann).
'Swedish Imperialism in Africa and Portugal', *Maji Maji* No.6, Dar es Salaam, June 1972.
Tanzania, United Republic of, *Estimates of Public Development Expenditure,* July 1972-June 1973.
Teale, E.O. and C. Gillman 1934, *Report on the Investigation of the Proper Control of Water . . . ,* (Dar es Salaam: Government Printer).
Thoden van Velzen, H. 1973, 'Staff, Kulaks and Peasants: A study of a Political Field', in L. Cliffe and J. Saul (eds), *Socialism in Tanzania,* Vol.2, (Nairobi: East African Publishing House), pp.153-179.
Tschannerl, G. and M. Mujwahuzi 1975, 'Impact on Rural Water Supply: Eight Self-Help Schemes in Arumeru, Masai, and Lushoto Districts', Bureau of Resource Assessment and Land Use Planning, Research Paper No.37, University of Dar es Salaam.
von Freyhold, Michaela 1973, 'The Government Staff and Ujamaa Villages (The Tanga Experience)', East African Universities' Annual Social Science Conference, Dar es Salaam, December 1973.
Water Development, *Annual Report* 1946, 1947, 1955, 1958, 1963, 1968, Government of Tanzania (Formerly Tanganyika). Under various names: Water Development Department, Water Development and Irrigation Division (in Ministry of Agriculture or Ministry of Lands).
Water Development and Power, Minister for, 'Budget Speech', June 1971, and June 1973, Dar es Salaam.
Water Development and Power, Ministry of 1972, 'Review of the Rural Water Supply Development Programme', Internal memo, Dar es Salaam.
Water Executive, *Annual Report* 1939 and 1940, Tanganyika Territory, Dar es Salaam.
White C., J. Bradley and A. White 1972, *Drawers of Water,* (Chicago: Chicago University Press).
Wuyts, M.E. 1973, 'The Choice of Technique: Some Critical Questions', Conference of the East African Agriculture Economics Society, Dar es Salaam, June 1973.

CHAPTER 7
Operation Dodoma 1969-71*

Frances Hill

Until 1970 ujamaa villages were nationally approved local experiments. During 1970-71 ujamaa became a top priority effort by the central organisations of the party-state to mobilize the rural populations. These efforts centred on Dodoma Region as a potential showcase for the benefits of socialist transformation. Nyerere hoped to show that rural socialist transformation would increase local production and consolidate a peasant constituency for Tanzanian socialism. In March 1970 he ordered that the entire population of Dodoma Region should form socialist villages with 14 months.

Dodoma is truly marginal to the national economy. Its recurrent famines are considered a national embarrassment and resented as a drain on the national treasury. Table 1 shows how Dodoma ranked among the then 17 regions in the main production sectors.[1] National mobilizers clearly felt that they had nothing to lose by redoing Dodoma.

TABLE 1:
Dodoma Region Production Rankings

	Regional Rank	Percent of total
Manufacturing	11	0.9
Commerce	13	1.2
Export agriculture	17	0.0
Market agriculture	16	1.0
Subsistence agriculture	6	6.0
Food crops marketed	10	5.5
Stock sold	1	18.4
Gross domestic product	13	3.4

Source: Compiled by the author.

Rural socialist transformation can mean either *Ujamaa Vijijini* (socialism in the villages) or *Vijiji vya Ujamaa* (ujamaa villages). These two strategies do not necessarily differ in the ultimate degree of socialist transformation, the actual effect on production, or the consolidation of a constituency of peasant socialists. They do differ in the degree of initial perceived change, leaving open the question of the relation between change and socialist transformation. Ujamaa villages involve resettlement. *Ujamaa Vijijini* changes the social relations of production within existing settlements. In Dodoma Region the government began by encouraging

Ujamaa Vijijini, but soon committed its full resources to creating ujamaa villages. The change was a classic example of bureaucratic enthusiasm spurred on by the President. If Nyerere wanted ujamaa villages the bureaucracy would produce them. It is less clear whether administrators were as committed to socialism as they seemed to be to resettlement.

THE OPERATION IN KONDOA DISTRICT

The only area of Dodoma Region to make a serious effort to foster socialism in the villages was Irangi in Kondoa District.[2] The Rangi are reputed to be good farmers and astute politicians. Since colonial times their leaders have learned to interact successfully with whatever government was currently in power to extract benefits and to avoid reprisals. Both motives were involved in the attempts to foster ujamaa in the Rangi villages during 1969 and 1970.

Although the Rangi have a non-nucleated settlement pattern, there are identifiable villages. People live close enough to each other to cultivate a communal field, but this was not a living tradition by 1969. Instead, groups of kin and neighbours helped each other prepare their fields for planting. Each household head would provide meat or beer for these helpers. Under no circumstances did this aid give claim to part of the harvest. The use-right over land was absolute, as was control of the crop produced. Thus even the early experiments with ujamaa could not grow directly or spontaneously from the African communal heritage.

The early ujamaa experiments differed widely and generalizations are apt to be misleading. At this early stage it is more useful to explore the process of socialist transformation than to try to generalise about results. Since the process involved all party-state organizations and non-official local power systems, it would be impossible to discuss ujamaa in all of Irangi. Instead, I shall trace the change from *Ujamaa Vijijini* to *Vijiji vya Ujamaa* in one Rangi village that was at the centre of the controversy over rural socialist transformation.

Mnenia is a ward headquarters and thus the base for government services. Villagers had agreed to cultivate a communal field in 1969. Drought and then floods had meant famine in 1969. Mnenia had been more fortunate than some other areas of the district, but rumours that, in the future, government famine relief would go only to ujamaa village members provided an incentive for socialism. Rangi in this area were also positively disposed toward ujamaa because it was a TANU-Nyerere policy, and TANU had been strong and militant in the area during the independence struggle. Nevertheless, the people of Mnenia were not prepared for complete socialist transformation. Citizens and leaders alike were experimenting with a new way of life. At the very least the experiment could serve as a defensive compliance with government policy that would protect the existing way of life from government sanctions.

The first 55 workers, far less than one per cent of the population, cultivated about 30 acres. After troubles organizing work on the ujamaa field, 65 bags of maize were harvested and the entire crop sold to the cooperative for 22 shillings per bag, or a total of 1,430 shillings to be divided among the 55 workers. If it were divided equally, each person would get 26 shillings, a sum the Mnenia *wajamaa* dismissed as paltry, a certain indication that ujamaa did not lead to prospertiy. Dividing the cash caused severe strains among the members of Mnenia ujamaa village, some demanding equal shares, some demanding women's shares go to their husbands, some demanding pay according to work as recorded in the ujamaa village log.

Finally, there was an equal division, confirming the widespread fear that ujamaa was a social security scheme for the lazy.

Party-state leaders were also dissatisfied with the production levels reached in these early ujamaa experiments. Under pressure from a new Regional Commissioner and from the politician appointed to head the Economic Planning Team, sent by Presidential instruction into the District in 1970, the Kondoa Area Commissioner began to push for larger ujamaa villages that promised greater economic returns. This necessarily meant that local ujamaa experiments would come under increasing pressure to conform to national expectations. Since national ujamaa policy was by no means clearly or adequately specified, there was considerable confusion and mutual suspicion.

Tensions had been rising in the area since the President's Economic Planning Team began to work in Kondoa. In every district the team head was a politician, a member of the TANU National Executive Committee. The head of the Kondoa team was from Bukoba, in the far north-west of the country, and hoped to use his service in Kondoa as a stepping-stone to a high-level, well-paid government position. He thus demanded maximum results and sought to ascertain that full credit for these results devolve not on the Area Commissioner but on himself. As in other districts with similar teams, the team head and the Area Commissioner were soon locked in a political duel marked by reciprocal allegations and denunciations. Based on the President's March 1970 call for total socialist transformation of Dodoma region within 14 months, this man condemned the extent and nature of ujamaa in Kondoa, calling for ujamaa villages with at least 250 families, with each adult worker responsible for a minimum two acres of ujamaa field.[3] These demands necessarily meant amalgamation of numerous ujamaa villages. Technicians on the teams, under severe strain and unhappy about the Rangi's reluctance to aid their work, began denouncing villagers, telling them that soon recalcitrants would be jailed. At this point the Area Commissioner ordered the entire team to a remote corner of the district, where local complaints would have less direct impact on the district party-state. This was tantamount to banishment for technicians accustomed to larger cities. In their own words, many 'despaired'. They nevertheless produced plans for numerous ujamaa villages calling for greater production.

These plans caused apprehension among the local population. Those not living in ujamaa villages feared the government would take their land even though President Nyerere had repeatedly said ujamaa was voluntary. Even members of ujamaa villages regarded these plans as either threatening or ludicrous. The plans made erroneous estimates of both population and land area, set unrealistic targets of economic production, and expected fledgling ujamaa villages to assume a heavy burden of debt. The Area Commissioner, too, knew that these plans were worthless, but felt impelled to change from voluntary ujamaa that was a mere addition to the prevailing system of production to something more encompassing. He chose Mnenia as one of the high-priority targets for this new approach because he believed the local leadership was cooperative and effective. He did not expect the furore that soon erupted.

The Area Commissioner and the President's Economic Planning Team decided that Mnenia should enlarge its ujamaa field to 170 acres, a change requiring collectivization of adjoining private plots. In this effort, the Area Commissioner relied on the Ward Executive Officer and the TANU chairman to continue the operation of local government. He totally misjudged the people of Mnenia and its party-state leaders. In the ensuing crisis the Ward Executive Officer and TANU chairman opposed collectivization openly and actively, while the ujamaa village chairman manoeuvred for advantage in the ward power structure by allying himself with the Area Commissioner. This latter gamble failed, leaving ujamaa and the ujamaa village chairman weakened.

Public discontent surfaced in a special meeting called by the opponents of collectivization, led by the Mnenia Moslem sheikh. At this meeting no one except the ujamaa village chairman supported collectivization. All demanded instead that they clear new land, although no one had any idea where such could be found. They successfully insisted that ujamaa coexist with socio-economic patterns the Rangi now regard as normal, neither encroaching upon nor disrupting them. Those with little land were as insistent as those with more to lose. TANU leaders and ujamaa village members opposed collectivization as strongly as ordinary citizens not in ujamaa villages. Even a delegate to the ward development committee and member of the Mnenia Ujamaa Village Committee opposed collectivization because his private plot would have been among the first taken.

Opponents of collectivization all claimed to be good socialists intent upon building a 'proper' form of ujamaa. No one opposed ujamaa openly. Such debate was characteristic of the entire party-state. As long as a person limits his criticism to details of ujamaa implementation he can make plausible claim to being a good socialist. Anyone who suggests otherwise incurs general wrath. The young ward agricultural officer undertook to lecture the meeting on ujamaa, telling people of Mnenia that they did not understand ujamaa. He asserted that ujamaa was no longer a matter of discussion — ujamaa was mandatory and all-encompassing; citizens must follow the orders of 'leaders' like himself. This produced a furore and the agricultural officer was ignominiously expelled from the meeting. The people then agreed to draft a letter to the Area Commissioner stating categorical opposition to changing either their way of life or ujamaa as it currently existed. The letter was signed, 'People of Mnenia'.

This show of united opposition convinced the Area Commissioner that the situation was serious. He could do little to discipline the recalcitrant citizens since the entire local party-state apparatus was in disarray. In an effort to reassert his control, he transferred all Ward Executive Officers. The man assigned to Mnenia resigned rather than face an aroused populace. The Area Commissioner also sent the District TANU Chairman, both Members of Parliament from the district, and the District Council Executive Officer on tours to calm the situation and laud the virtues of ujamaa living. Irangi gradually became calm but not socialist. The district government had spent over \$200,000 to produce this impasse.[4] The Rangi continued a minimal level of defensive compliance, but their enthusiasn for ujamaa and their trust in the party-state were shaken.

THE OPERATION IN DODOMA DISTRICT

The Rangi had been able to turn aside a mobilization effort by district officials. The Gogo of Dodoma District had to capitulate to a mobilization effort by national officials led by the President himself. Operation Dodoma was conducted with the active opposition of numerous local officials, but TANU had never been strong in Dodoma District and the Gogo had never taken control of the local party-state the way the Rangi had. There were few leaders around whom they could rally in a confrontation with the government.

The Gogo live in scattered homesteads surrounded by their cattle. They are generally poor farmers in a harsh environment.[5] When there is adequate rain, the Gogo produce enough food for themselves. Droughts and famines are so regular that Gogo date their age grades accordingly.[6] Gogo society is characterized more by mutual suspicion than by cohesion and interaction. Everyone fears witchcraft; most leaders are thought to be wizards. Gogo from one ritual area do not readily interact with Gogo from another area.

Unlike the Rangi, who protect themselves from the government by interacting with it, the Gogo ignore the government. Until Operation Dodoma the government generally reciprocated by ignoring the Gogo. The only exception came during famines. Even the colonial government would have been embarrassed by mass starvation. The independence government also grudgingly kept the Gogo alive during such crises. The 1969 famine in Dodoma cost the government almost Sh.10 million.[7]

The costly and traumatic famine had numerous repercussions. The people had again faced starvation and some had died. Large numbers of stock had also died or been sold at very low prices to get money for food. While everyone recognized the Gogo's suffering, the Regional Commissioner and other officials also blamed the Gogo for their plight. The alcoholic Area Commissioner told the Gogo that the famine resulted from their tendency to prefer drinking local beer to cultivating their fields.[8] The 1969 famine created fear and uncertainty making people receptive or vulnerable to mobilization. The district party-state was too weak even to contemplate taking the primary responsibility for a serious mobilization effort. In both 1969 and 1970 area commissioners lost their postings for inadequate attention to ujamaa and for misleading President Nyerere about the true state of socialist transformation. Party leaders opposed ujamaa openly. The District TANU Chairman was warned about his opposition to ujamaa by President Nyerere during his November 1969 tour of Dodoma. A year later the chairman was removed from office and put under fairly lenient house arrest. The Member of Parliament for Dodoma South opposed ujamaa as openly as had the District TANU Chairman. He was not allowed to stand for re-election to Parliament and was also put under continual security surveillance. Other elected officials opposed socialism but were far less vocal or visible. At the Regional Development Committee they voted in 1969 that leaders should not join any particular ujamaa village but take general responsibility for all ujamaa villages,[9] an ingenious means of dissociating themselves from socialism. Others whose opposition was less subtle were jailed under preventive detention by the Area Commissioner in late 1970.

By early 1971 the new Regional Commissioner and new Area Commissioner were under intense pressure from Nyerere to make Dodoma both productive and socialist. The Area Commissioner was acutely aware that his two predecessors had been transferred and demoted. The Regional Commissioner, a former Cabinet Minister defeated in the 1970 general election, faced a bleak political future if Dodoma region continued its reputation as a centre of famine but not of ujamaa. Both undertook to mobilize their staffs to produce results consistent with the new idea of large, nucleated ujamaa settlements.

At this point the field staff began to circulate the rumour that during any future famine only those in ujamaa villages would receive government food. Ujamaa was not voluntary; it was required. All land would be allotted to ujamaa villages and there would be no place for those not joining ujamaa villages. These threats seemed especially menacing in 1971. The early rains had failed and another serious famine seemed imminent. The Gogo had no food reserves, for the 1970 harvest, coming after the 1969 famine, had been barely adequate. The Gogo were entirely dependent on the national government. In this atmosphere they decided to become socialists. Some began moving into ujamaa village sites on their own; others waited for government trucks to transport their goods.. Those who initially refused to move had government 'help' in demolishing their homes. At this point Dodoma District became the focus of the nation as President Nyerere chose to make Dodoma District, and especially Chamwino Ujamaa Village, a demonstration of his policy.

Presidential commitment meant mobilization of any resources Nyerere felt necessary. Thus, at Chamwino Ujamaa Village the National Service built a dispensary in two weeks even though there was a dispensary within two miles of the village centre. Everyone from secondary school students to local Members of Parliament came to Chamwino to make bricks for modern houses. Tractors cleared the ujamaa village plot. Three hundred trucks were called from other regions to move people into Chamwino. When the president was living at Chamwino, there would often be as many as 25 government Land Rovers there. Subsequently, the village was electrified, a convenience not enjoyed by Kondoa Town, a district headquarters. As Dodoma members of Parliament noted, things can always be financed if the president so orders. The total amount of aid given by Chamwino in this early phase is unknown. Neither are there reliable figures for the total cost of Operation Dodoma.[10] One Tanzanian economist estimated 50 million shillings for Chamwino alone.

CONCLUSIONS

The relationship between this enormous resettlement effort and either socialism or economic development remains uncertain. There was no attempt to introduce improved agricultural methods or even to adapt methods to the changed human-resource relationship caused by population concentration. Tractors merely meant that more land would be cultivated in the same way. There was also no attempt to limit stock numbers or to collectivize cattle. In response to prior rumours about cattle collectivization, some politically aware owners of large herds had discreetly sold stock on the assumption that no government could collectivize cash. However, most Gogo sought to replenish their herds after the drought. They thus demanded and received assurances from Vice-President Kawawa that stock would remain private property. Stock owners also bargained successfully for larger plots so they could have adequate room for cattle kraals attached to their new ujamaa village houses. Thus ujamaa villages would not impinge on the basis of economic stratification but would openly legitimate it from the outset.

The same was true for social stratification. At Mvumi Ujamaa Village, where about 600 families were living in temporary grass shelters, there was a neat line of brick houses being built up to deceased Chief Mazengo's home and headquarters. The *wajamaa* of Mvumi Ujamaa Village were building suitable accommodation for the deceased chief's close kinsmen.

There was a similar lack of change in the political sphere. If anything, Operation Dodoma intensified the party-state tendency toward elite initiative at the expense of participatory citizenship. During the initial phase of Operation Dodoma no official had time for questions of the future of these villages, for ensuring that they became self-reliant nuclei of democratic socialism rather than government relief operations. It was impossible to find officials who even thought that the composition of the ujamaa village committee, the modes of intra- and intervillage decision-making, channels of communication from ujamaa village to district and regional bodies, especially the District Development and Planning Committee and the Regional Development Committee, were important issues. When important meetings were held, one could find ujamaa village chairmen and TANU chairmen at their homes. Only government officials had been invited.

The experience with ujamaa in Dodoma and Kondoa Districts reveals certain problems of inducing fundamental change in rural Tanzania. The relatively uniform poverty of Dodoma Region eliminates expropriation as a tactic of inducing and financing at least the initial phases of the revolutionary dynamic. Unlike the early phases of the Chinese revolution where redistribution of economic assets within the villages provided the initial predisposition to revolution, the early phases of ujamaa mobilization could only be financed by government aid.[11]

Such a dependence on government aid brings its own problems and imposes its own limitations. The Tanzanian economy cannot finance many Chamwinos. The attempts to provide aid on that scale will only increase anti-ujamaa sentiment among the salariat entrusted with mobilizing and managing peasants. In the extreme, the managers could turn on the founder and stop any pretense that peasant pro-letarianization is a step toward Tanzanian socialism. In such a confrontation it is highly unlikely that the peasantry could save Nyerere. Ujamaa has become linked with proletarianization and productionism rather than with building the reliable socialist constituency that Nyerere still lacks.

Nyerere has not been able to convince Tanzanian peasants that their way of life will change even without socialist transformation and that non-socialist change would make conditions even worse than they are now in rural Tanzania. Population pressure on land has already exhausted the frontier that each of the local socio-economic systems relied on for economic survival and social flexibility. Slash-and-burn agriculture requires a continuously expanding resource base. Since no individual can play a full part in community affairs until he is an established household head, access to land is crucial to continued social flexibility. Until recently, there have been marked differences of wealth and status but no permanently landless and thus powerless class. Now, even within the poor but relatively equitable societies of Dodoma Region, one sees the beginnings of a class of landless labourers unable to find secure employment in any sector of the economy.

Ujamaa could solve the problems of impending rural change by establishing a new relationship between people and resources, thereby ensuring economic survival and continued social flexibility. The failure of Nyerere's African socialism would create the preconditions for a European-type socialism. It would be unduly romantic to see this as a positive opportunity to build socialism in Tanzania. European history has shown that the preconditions for class conflict do not produce socialism. African managerial elites, both civilian and military, have shown little tendency to let citizens threaten their privileged positions. If Tanzania is to become a socialist state, it will do so through ujamaa. The experience with Operation Dodoma suggests that the socialist content of rural change is being sacrificed to productionist ideo-logies that are economjcally unrealistic. A productionist ujamaa that sacrifices citizen participation to elite management will merely be a state capitalism that uses the rhetoric of 'modernization' and 'development' to legitimate elite consumption of the fruits of peasant labour.

NOTES

1. Based on data from United Republic of Tanzania, *District Data, 1967.*
2. All data on Kondoa and Dodoma Districts based on field research during 1970 and 1971. For a fuller treatment of these themes see Frances Hill, *Mobilization and Participation in Tanzania,* unpublished Ph.D. thesis, Harvard University, 1973.
3. This fitted the national policy guidelines of June 1970 proclaimed by the Dodoma Regional Commissioner when introducing the President's Economic Planning Teams.
4. Figure based on allocations by the District Development and Planning Committee, Kondoa District, 26 February, 1979, in Kondoa District Council File No.C.40/7.
5. Peter Rigby, *Cattle and Kinship among the Wagogo* (Syracuse, N.Y.: Syracuse University Press, 1969).
6. C. Brooke, 'The Heritage of Famine in Central Tanzania', *Tanzania Notes and Records,* No.67 (1967), 18-25. H.A. Fosbrooke, 'A Note on the Dating of Age Sets and Famines in "Historia, Mila na Desturia za Wagogo wa Tanzania"', by Mathias E. Mnyampala, in Tanzania National Archives File No.435/A2/24, 'Gogo History, Land Tenure and Cattle Tenure'.
7. Figure from a special report prepared by the Regional Development Officer, Dodoma Region, for the purpose of briefing President Nyerere during his tour of Dodoma. 19 February, 1970 *('Taarifa ya Maendeleo ya Mkoa wa Dodoma kwa Ajili ya Mazungumzo na Mheshimiwa Baba wa Taifa')* in Dodoma Region, Development Department File No.CD/RE/DO/1.
8. 'Speech of Area Commissioner for the People of Dodoma District for the Purpose of Increasing Agricultural Effort in 1969-1970', at the 30 October, 1969 meeting of the District Development Committee in Dodoma District Council File No.C.40/7, Vol.1, 'District Development and Planning Committee'.
9. Dodoma Regional Development Committee meeting of 16 May, 1969.
10. United Republic of Tanzania, *The Annual Plan for 1971/72* (Dar es Salaam, Government Printer 1971), p.57 and *The Economic Survey,* 1971/72 (Dar es Salaam, Government Printer, 1972), pp.62-64.
11. William Hinton, *Fanshen* (New York: Monthly Review Press, 1966).

CHAPTER 8

Operation Planned Villages in Rural Tanzania: A Revolutionary Strategy for Development *

Juma Volter Mwapachu**

With over ninety per cent of its 15 million people living in rural areas and involved in agricultural production, Tanzania could not choose a development path that was not based on its rural inhabitants and their main resource, land. Since independence in 1961, Tanzania has, therefore, been concerned with how it can evolve practically-oriented programmes to achieve speedy rural development. Its main problem has been what form of institutional arrangements to create for the purpose of activating this development process. For, as P.C. Mathur has correctly noted:

> With more and more developing countries launching programmes of planned development and acquiring first hand experience and processes, it is being increasingly recognised that these countries have to evolve new tools and techniques, if not new theories, to achieve and maintain a steady rate of economic growth. The centuries-old backlog of backwardness, the traditional ordering of social and political relationships, the primitive stage of agricultural economy, the widespread apathy and indifference to economic incentives, lack of well-knit administrative and institutional structures and a host of similar problems call for politico-economic innovations based on the conditions and circumstances prevailing in each developing country which seeks 'purposive utilisation of human and national resources'. This is all the more so because developing nations have to pursue the twin objectives of political evolution and economic development simultaneously . . .1

Writing on a similar theme, Professor Carl Rosberg has submitted that 'the problem [in Tanzania] is not to counter entrenched local patriotisms (as in Kenya) but rather to find the organizational means and resources for instilling in rural peasants the communal values of a new national socialist community'.2 Tanzania had, therefore, to evolve new tools and techniques in bringing about the development to which it aspired.

The first strategic move geared to the establishment of an institutional structure for promoting speedy rural development was taken by President Nyerere in 1962 when he urged rural peasants living in scattered homesteads to come together and live in villages so that they could be easily reached by social and agricultural services. Unfortunately this call was not backed up by policy, in the sense of committing Party and Government functionaries to its implementation. One can ascribe two main reasons for the subsequent failure. First, implementation was not planned; there was a call for voluntary acceptance of the programme and, having regard to peoples' traditional cultural values of community living, in 1962 (even perhaps in 1975), it was premature to expect an immediate positive response. Second, the fruits of communal living were not well known at that time. As Cliffe and Cunningham remarked, 'If the process [villagization] is to be voluntary, peasants must thus be

---

* The original version of this article appeared in *The African Review* (Dar es Salaam), Vol.6, No.1, 1976, reproduced with permission.
** When this paper was written, the author was District Development Director, Shinyanga.

convinced that real economic gains can be achieved through larger scale, collective production and that social advantages can be derived from living in communal settlements.[3] But a Presidential call had to be put into practice one way or another. It seems to me that the establishment of settlement schemes between 1963 and 1966 by Government Ministries and the TANU Youth League was in response to the President's plea. By 1966 all of these settlement schemes had failed miserably and the resultant financial loss to the Government was most pathetic. President Nyerere himself has explained the failure in very precise terms:

> When we tried to promote rural development in the past, we sometimes spent huge sums of money on establishing a settlement . . . All too often, therefore, we persuaded people to go to new settlements by promising them that they could grow rich there, or that the Government would give them services and equipment which they could not hope to receive either in the towns or in their traditional farming places. *In very few cases was any ideology involved.*[4] (emphasis added).

In other words, knowingly or unknowingly Tanzania, in spite of its TANU pledge to follow a socialist line of development, was creating what Professor Dumont has termed 'a semi-privileged rural class'.[5]

A pertinent question at this point is whether those who were involved in the creation of resettlement schemes were themselves ideologically aware of the purposes of these schemes. If in 1967 almost none of the Tanzanian leaders were leading socialist lives, how could they have appreciated the socialist intentions and organization of resettlement schemes? By 1966, therefore, the first experiment with a rural institutional arrangement for promoting rural development had failed.

In February 1967, Tanzania adopted a blueprint for socialist construction — the Arusha Declaration. This document firmly established the course of development that Tanzania must follow: the course of socialist development. Rural socialism was embodied in the ujamaa village institutional structure. Ujamaa villages have since been established almost throughout the country. Some of these have had reasonable success but others merely reflect a communal living pattern without much communal benefit accruing to the members. The problem with the less successful villages is really one of the villagers' concept of communal production and development. The concept of standard of living as an incentive for increased agricultural production has yet to permeate many minds. However, following the failures of the settlement schemes the ujamaa villages have at least survived without much government assistance. Their survival has depended on their voluntary character and on the acceptance of the socialist idea of communal living. But whilst ujamaa villages have survived, and in many cases succeeded, as of 1974 there were only 2,560,472 people living in them. Therefore, a great many people in the rural areas were not yet leading socialist lives.

As President Nyerere put it, it is one thing to argue the advantages of this type of rural development organization and yet another to force the rural peasant to live in ujamaa villages. For this reason he proposed the step by step transformation of rural living[6] and saw three stages to the process:

   i. persuasion of people to move their houses into a single village;
  ii. persuasion of a group of people, for example, the members of a ten-house cell, to start a small communal farm on which they work co-operatively, sharing the proceeds at harvest time;
 iii. confidence in the community farm under stage (ii) will lead to a full-fledged socialist village.

If rural transformation was to start, the first stage at least had to be on a national scale. The Operation Planned Villages that occurred in 1974, can therefore only be viewed and understood as a first stage of the process. The interesting point, however, is that the 1974 Operation Villages was not to be a matter of persuasion but of coercion. As Nyerere argued, the move had to be compulsory because Tanzania could not sit back and watch the majority of its people leading a 'life of death'. The State had, therefore, to take the role of the 'father' in ensuring that its peoples chose a better and more prosperous life for themselves. The purpose of this paper is to appraise this implementation strategy, with particular reference to Shinyanga District, looking at the problems and experiences which arose during the Operation and forecasting its potential for promoting rural development.

OPERATION PLANNED VILLAGES

Following the recommendation of the TANU National Executive, the 16th Biennial TANU Conference, meeting in Dar es Salaam between 24 September and 1 October 1973, agreed and resolved that the settlement of people in rural villages must henceforth be a compulsory matter. By 1976 the whole population of Tanzania was to be living in clustered villages.

Prior to this wholesale national operation, some areas of the country had already started moving people into planned villages (e.g. Dodoma and Kigoma Regions and Geita District). But their resettlement policy was more geared to the establishment of block farms to cultivate specific crops, or in the case of Dodoma, the movement was based on the need to reach the majority of the people in the area more easily, particularly after the famine experiences of 1971/72.

Why did TANU undertake this exercise in 1973 and not later? The answer is linked to the TANU and Government decision in June 1972 to overhaul the governmental administrative structure. In particular, the regional administration was to move away from its original law and order and revenue collection function into a more development-based management function with the people thoroughly involved in planning and implementation of development projects from grassroots level. Therefore, the people's participation had to be made more effective.[7] For, as Professor Rainer Scheckele has rightly asserted:

> **There are two fundamental goals which guide development policies in modern democratic nations: the goal of establishing civic rights, responsibilities, and opportunities for everyone's participation in public affairs: and the goal of increasing production for the main purpose of eliminating poverty. These twin goals are not in conflict but reinforce each other. They serve as beacons for steering national policies.[8]**

The 1972 Government decentralization programme aimed at the democratization of the development planning process in the hope that through the people being involved in planning their own development, they would be enthused to participate fully in the execution of development plans, including increasing their individual production. This policy was based on the assumption that measures for the mobilization of local resources for development can only be planned realistically in the context of the needs, aspirations and economic condition of the people. Therefore, one year after the decentralization programme was effected, TANU and Government saw the need to reinforce the participatory development notion by creating firmly established, participating institutions — planned villages. The scattered pattern of villages meant that participation in development was limited to a few elected individuals. If the majority of the people were to participate in their own development through established forums, these forums had to be within reach of a larger segment of the people. Also, the more the people participate, the greater the chances for changes in attitudes and values. For we must remember that the problems of the rural peasantry have been based fundamentally on their traditional outlook and unwillingness to accept change. As Professor Iqbal Narain has noted with regard to the Indian peasantry: 'The problem of development in India's rural context is one of inculcation of aspirations, building up attitudes and the development of a forward-looking, self-helping and action-oriented bent of mind which, cumulatively, constitutes what may be called the development conscience'.[9] The same applies to the Tanzanian situation. The 'development conscience' can only be developed through continuous participation by the people in socio-economic and political affairs.

Thus, whilst Operation Planned Villages must be seen in the context of a step by step rural transformation on the road towards rural socialism, its timing, in our view, seems to have been prompted by the need to reinforce the government decentralization programme and to make possible its participatory goal of evolving a development conscience amongst the rural inhabitants.

IMPLEMENTATION STRATEGY OF OPERATION PLANNED VILLAGES

Apart from declaring 1976 the target date for full rural villagization, neither TANU nor Government at the national level gave any guidelines for the implementation of the programme. The implementation strategy was virtually left to each region and to each district to formulate. Most districts throughout the country were, of course, perplexed as to how they could go about implementing the programme. Some districts sent teams of officials to see how Operation Kigoma (the World Bank supported project) was implemented; others sent their officials to Mara Region. Neither of the two districts I worked for, Bariadi and Shinyanga, sent out such teams. In retrospect, I am not sure that we took the right decision. However, considering the pace of the operation, visits to other Regions would probably not have helped make our particular operation any better. We decided not to send out teams to other areas on the advice of the then Regional Development Director of Shinyanga Region who was of the firm view that each district possessed its peculiar socio-cultural and ecological characteristics that necessitated special methods and strategies for resettlement.

The other implementation decision was whether the operation was to be implemented wholesale throughout the district at one go, or whether it should be on a selective basis with definite time schedules for each area, provided that by 1976 the whole district was covered. In both Bariadi and Shinyanga Districts the initial plan was to adopt a selective implementation strategy. Later, however, this was found to be unworkable, for two main reasons. First, there was a competitive attitude (particularly between regions) with all its political overtones. Here was a moment for self-aggrandizement by proving ability to mobilize a rural population wholesale. Reports were coming in from Mara Region that they were about to complete their operation when we had not started at all. Top party officials were heralding and positively reinforcing the achievements of resettlement in Geita District. Who, in such circumstances, would have wished to lag behind? Political leaders, therefore, called for quick measures to complete the resettlement exercise in a short time. Such a rushed exercise caused problems, of course, in the form of poorly planned villages, as we shall see later in the paper. Second, some districts, particularly

Shinyanga, began to experience the problem of 'refugees in one country'. Many people, not believing that Operation Villages was a national affair, began to move from their districts to neighbouring ones where resettlement was not yet in progress. Shinyanga District received quite a few 'refugees' from Geita and Kwimba Districts. Thus, the implementators realized that the selective strategy would in fact give rise to an intra-district refugee problem, with people moving from one division to another, depending on where the operation was being effected first. Thus, in both Bariadi and Shinyanga Districts, the decision was to undertake a frontal implementation strategy — an en masse resettlement of the rural population.

How was the operation actually conducted in Shinyanga District? Five steps were agreed upon and were embodied in a District Operation Villages Guideline of February 1974:

1. TANU and Government functionaries at the district, division and ward levels were to move throughout their areas of jurisdiction to politicize the masses on the economic, social and political gains of the Operation Villages. The politicization was to be conducted through public meetings, TANU branch and cell meetings, Ward Development Councils, etc. Bariadi District was very successful in this politicization aspect. Shinyanga District did not do so much. It should be noted that this kind of politicization or ideological orientation about the meaning, purposes and potential of these new villages was not conducted when creating resettlement centres in the early and mid-1960s. On the other hand, it must be admitted that even in 1974 some of the political leaders were not aware of the step by step rural socialist transformation and began to repeat the mistakes of the earlier resettlement schemes. Some of these leaders argued that the purpose of these planned villages was to get governmental facilities like schools, clean water, dispensaries, etc. And people did immediately ask for these facilities after being resettled. What ought to have been emphasized was the potential for increased agricultural production through communal living and, of course, that such living can bring about socialist co-operation in various ways. Government social services do not come like rain, as President Nyerere said recently. They are the products of a stable national economic situation whose firm basis is optimal agricultural production.

2. Ward Development Councils were to sit and discuss the best areas for locating planned villages. In choosing the most suitable areas for growth centres, the Guidelines required Ward Development Councils to look for the following criteria: (a) water, (b) land suitable for agriculture and livestock, (c) school, (d) dispensary, (e) co-operative society, (f) roads, (g) the capacity to accommodate between 250 and 500 families (approximately 1,500 and 3,000 people). By 'capacity' the Guidelines meant sufficient land for buildings (including a livestock boma), not less than one acre for a family without livestock and one and half acres for a family with livestock; and a minimum of two acres of agricultural land for each family.

3. District party and government officers were to visit all the selected village sites to see that the criteria for selection embodied in the Guidelines were followed.[10] And, indeed, in most cases they were. By the end of April 1974, all the proposed growth centres for planned villages had been visited and had been presented to the District Development and Planning Committee for approval.

4. The land accepted for building was to be properly planned in the sense of each plot being measured and allocated to a specific villager. This was done between May and July 1974. It took so much time because the period fell during the cotton

harvest season. From the beginning of July, peasants were asked to take plots and begin building.

5. A seminar for all party and government leaders in the district was to be held before the actual physical movement of people, to discuss the methodology of the exercise. In Shinyanga this seminar was held in August 1974. The seminar decided that for the movement exercise there should be a team for each division (Shinyanga District has seven divisions) led by a senior official either from the district party office or from the District Development Directorate. Each team was to include the Divisional Secretary (of the division where the team was going to undertake the movement) and the Ward Secretary (of the ward where the team was to work). The seminar also noted that the response of the people in taking plots for building was very poor; indeed some peasants had begun to spread rumours that the operation was not going to take place after all. In some instances it was the rural leadership itself that was spreading such rumours. We shall come back to this question of the effectiveness of the rural leadership later. The movement was to begin on 17 August. The seminar also discussed the utilization of funds available for the exercise. Shs. 200,000/- had been allocated by the Regional Government Office for the operation. It was decided that the money was to be used for hiring lorries to undertake the movement of people's goods and food. The seminar also resolved that the first people to be moved must be the leaders of villages, as an example to the others that leaders were not being favoured.

Between 17 August and 22 September 1974, Shinyanga District moved all its rural population of about 340,000 people into 149 villages. The actual physical movement did not cause much alarm although various problems arose as a result of the movement. In some instances houses were burnt down when it was realized that some people, after having been moved, returned to their former homes again after a few days. But this method was rarely used and in all cases officials concerned made sure that goods and food were removed from the houses prior to their being put on fire. Many more people moved on their own without waiting for Government assistance. There are two good reasons why this happened in Shinyanga District. First, there was news from neighbouring Geita and Maswa districts, that people's houses were being put on fire indiscriminately, sometimes with food and goods inside them. So the people decided not to wait for government help lest a similar catastrophe happened to them as well. Second, good leadership; for example, in the Tinde Ward, particularly the areas of Mwamkanga and Msalala, everybody had moved on his own and had started building by the time the 'moving squad' arrived. Moreover, the villagers there had adopted a self-motivated co-operative venture of clearing the ground, making bricks and building houses. It happened of course that the TANU chairman in this area, who hails from Mwamkanga village itself, is an excellent leader, notable in the district.

PROBLEMS IN RESETTLEMENT

The Operation Villages Programme was a huge exercise and some of the problems that arose were extremely serious, both on humanitarian grounds in terms of the direct impact on the peasants, and on the production side in that there was not always enough time after the completion of the operation for clearing farms and starting cultivation. There were also the problems associated with the sudden bringing together of large numbers of people.

One of the major problems when moving people into villages was how to deal with the old people without any family within reach, and the single women living by themselves. How were they to cope with a sudden move to a new place where they had to embark on putting up a new building? Unfortunately, because there had not been sufficient pre-planning, such questions arose at the actual time of the movement. In some places the help of local leaders was sought and houses were built through self-help by other villagers. But there must have been other places where the old and alone suffered a great deal without such assistance. This issue must be a lesson for the future.

There was also the problem of how people were to establish themselves in new homes and prepare their fields when they were moved near the start of the rainy season. It is interesting to note, however, the kind of vigour man adopts in a moment of crisis. Most people thought, in fact, that production would fall excessively as a result of the resettlement. They argued first, that people would be disillusioned, frustrated and annoyed because of the encroachment on their personal freedom and values, and second, that they would not have enough time to get production going. It is difficult to get a clear picture of what did happen for it has also been claimed that production was not as bad as had been anticipated because of the November 1974 Presidential national political mobilization to undertake agricultural production 'as a matter of life and death'. One point is certainly tenable: that peasants in Shinyanga District did not grow much cotton. This was a result of the belief that the President had emphasized food production rather than cash crop production because of the acute hunger problem that existed from three years' continuous adverse weather conditions.

The sudden influx of people into new villages had an immediate impact on water, medical, and education services. Sufficient services could not, of course, be provided overnight, but, as stated earlier, there had not been enough planning. In certain areas the water problem was acute and villagers had to walk again for miles to fetch water. As far as medical supplies were concerned, these were available in no time. The school problem, on the other hand, could not be solved immediately. This period, however, proved an exciting experience because it reflected an immediate awareness by peasants of the importance of social services, hitherto by and large neglected and distrusted.[11]

As a result of the peasants selecting the village sites they wanted, the TANU Ten Cell (the lowest grassroots political unit for affording exchange of political and development views) was immediately immobilized and Ten Cell leaders found themselves in new villages without their constituents. This immobilization of the Ten Cells happened at the time when the Ward Development Councils were considering what development projects should be included in the District's Five-Year Development Plan.

The most serious problem as we saw it at the time of the operation was that of dealing with agricultural land. The problem arose out of two situations:

a. Peasants being moved several miles from their former homes, making it difficult for them to return there for cultivation.
b. Former agricultural land being selected as the suitable site for setting up a new village. What was to happen to those who lost their agricultural land? Where and how were they likely to get other land?

In Shinyanga District in September a guideline for the allocation of agricultural land was drawn up and circulated to all Divisional and Ward Secretaries. It was explicitly stated that the document was but an aid:

The implementation of allocation of farms must adhere to the environmental situation obtaining in the local area and the Guideline should not be taken as a biblical implementation plan. It is therefore incumbent upon your Ward Development Councils to discuss the Guideline and allocate the farms fairly and equitably.

One of the important provisions of the Guideline was that in the case of shortage of land for allocation of those without, there should be redistribution of the land already under the control of other peasants. Fortunately, there was free land in most places and, therefore, the problem of shortage of land did not arise. Those whose land was taken over for village sites or who would have to move miles back to their former farms were offered virgin land close to the new villages. (Many peasants did in fact return to their former farms regardless of the distance. Of course, throughout Shinyanga District no peasant was moved more than five miles from his former home). But since these planned villages are one of the steps towards the creation of ujamaa villages, there is the question whether the time is not ripe to start thinking about equalization of land ownership.

A similar question arose during the rehabilitation period of the Chinese economy (1949-1952). Wheelright and McFarlane have asserted that 'a completely egalitarian land reform [in China 1949-1952] would have alienated the middle peasants and disrupted production'.[12] China did not, therefore, immediately socialize land distribution. But were the Chinese conditions in 1952 the same as ours? Do we have a similarly large middle peasant class as China had in 1952 to the extent of affecting production if we equalize land allocation? On the other hand, do we have a serious problem of shortage of arable land to go round? These are issues which the political hierarchy in Tanzania must seriously ponder as the step by step rural living transformation moves towards the achievement of rural socialism.

When President Nyerere visited Shinyanga District in February 1975 he criticized the siting of some of the villages and how they were planned — that they were just one long street of houses stretching for miles like the wagons of a locomotive. The problem here arose out of 'dumping' people at the village site areas, a result of a rushed job. Many villagers, therefore, took the plots on the main roadside and built their houses in the form they wanted. There was no supervision whatsoever in plot allocation and method of building. However, a village reorganization programme is now being undertaken in Shinyanga District to change the plans of the villages.

The other Presidential criticism was levelled at villages situated close to the granite rock hills (tors). But then the landscape of Shinyanga is by and large made up of granite rocky hills and *mbuga* (lowland plains which flood with water during the rainy season). We were faced with the dilemma of whether to site the villages on areas otherwise more suitable for agricultural purposes and therefore limit the acreage left for farming, or to site the villages on rocky hill areas or *mbuga* and leave a wide expanse of what would in fact be suitable land for building purposes, for agricultural use. We chose the latter alternative. But in response to Presidential criticism we are, of course, reviewing the sites again to see if a better solution can be found — this may mean, of course, moving people again and perhaps, this time, not merely five miles.

THE EFFECTIVENESS OF RURAL LEADERSHIP

Operation Villages provided an excellent test for the type and effectiveness of the leadership in the rural areas. Previously, evaluation of local leadership was limited to their participation in the various developmental discussions at district development forums. And at these forums it is difficult to discern the authenticity of purported development beliefs; in particular whether, given scope, a leader would really happily implement an idea he so emotionally advocates. The villages programme was not such an easy development idea to support against the deep cultural values of the people, particularly those of the Sukuma tribe of Shinyanga District. But here was a chance for the rural leadership to help the people to understand their development. For, as President Nyerere has so aptly put it, it is only through education and leadership:

> that people can be helped to understand both their own needs, and the things which TANU and Government officials should be giving the people . . . We should have taken the trouble to understand the development policies our Party is trying to pursue, and we should be explaining these policies to the people.[13]

This question of leadership commitment to party policies is so fundamental, particularly when it refers to rural leadership, because the greater part of the rural peasantry is unaware. And, though the party guidelines clearly stipulate that 'the duty of the party is to ensure that the leaders and experts implement the plans that have been agreed upon by the people themselves',[14] it will take time before the spirit of the guidelines, in terms of full and effective development control by the people, is achieved. Meanwhile, therefore, the people must continue to be led, though leading here specifically refers to talking and discussing with people, explaining and persuading — constructively. But what does the rural peasantry understand by 'being led'? Is it not true, as Professor Raanan Weitz has asserted, that in the rural environment of developing nations

> for better or for worse, the fate of a developing programme is often decreased by the judgement made upon it by the leaders . . . Whoever the leaders are, the position taken by them determines to a great extent the position that will be taken by the society at large regarding proposals for change and innovation.[15]

Our experience during Operation Villages indicated that where the leadership commitment to the purposes and intentions of the Operation was high, the implementation exercise went very smoothly, because the people were found sufficiently mobilized and politicized. It was quite obvious, for example, that where we had always felt that the leadership was strong and enlightened *vis-a-vis* party officials, the implementation process was quick and smooth. For example, in Tinde Ward where the ward party chairman is an excellent and committed leader, we found people had moved on their own and had embarked on a fantastic self-motivated co-operative venture of building new houses at the selected village site. On the other hand, it was quite obvious that in several places the leadership was against the operation. We would like to draw attention to two instances of bad leadership. First, quite a number of Ward Secretaries had informed the district that all preparations for moving people had been effected. But when the district officials arrived to start the movement, it was found that the selected sites had not in fact been planned in terms of allocating specific plots to individuals, and some of the peasants were complaining that they had not been told about the operation, where they would be moved to and when. 'We would have moved on our own a long time ago', they claimed. Clyde Ingle may, therefore, be justified in concluding that:

> It is open to question . . . how effectively the cell leader delivered the views of the people to higher posts in the hierarchy. [And presumably vice versa]. In fact, my findings suggest that if the message was critical of government policy or revealed poor response to official directives, it was likely that the information simply would not be communicated beyond the ward level.[16]

In this particular instance the weakness of the leadership was founded either on its own attitude — not agreeing with the policy — or on its fear of annoying the peasantry under its jurisdiction. In fact the second example is more related to this 'fear' attitude and was more common amongst TANU Ward Chairmen and Councillors who had previously been chiefs or sub-chiefs in the areas they supervize. It also applied to Members of Parliament elected from local constituences. These three cadres of people are elected functionaries and their fear was of losing the next election. As one Member of Parliament who continuously managed not to participate in the moving exercise confided to me, 'how to do you expect me to do something that threatens the continuance of my monthly Parliamentary salary?' I suppose he was right but is he the kind of leader Tanzania wants? As regards the former chiefs, though chiefdoms were abolished in Tanzania in 1962, the Sukumas still have a special place and respect for these people and it is because of this respect that some of these rural leaders find themselves in a difficult position when trying to reconcile their roles. They still 'psychologically' believe they exercise royal roles. There was one particular TANU Chairman who went to the extent of introducing the district team as 'these are the people who have come from Shinyanga to move you', completely excluding himself from the operation.

We have raised this question of the effectiveness of rural leadership because we believe that TANU has been able to reach down to the masses at grassroots level in their own development. Institutionally this is well and good, and, in fact, following the amendment of the Interim Constitution of Tanzania giving TANU supremacy over all political and governmental activities,[17] the party grassroots institutions have been further strengthened in their powers and functional confidence. But the pertinent question is how effectively managed will these grassroots institutions be? Do we really have the right type of rural leadership or, are Cliffe and Saul correct in concluding that in the party leadership discipline has in fact been hijacked by 'intra-party diplomacy', for how otherwise can one judge the behaviour of certain political leaders during Operation Planned Villages in Shinyanga District? TANU must seriously address itself to the question of rural party leadership if mass mobilization and politicization of the peasantry for development is to succeed.

PLANNED VILLAGES AND DEVELOPMENT

We now turn to the important subject of the potential of planned villages in the promotion of rural development. Perhaps we should begin with a quotation from Professor René Dumont:

> **It is true that the scattered population characteristic of the Tanzanian countryside is an obstacle to the spread of technical progress, to the commercialisation of crop production and to easy access to schools, dispensaries, mosques and churches. The creation of villages throughout Tanzania would also bring down the cost of community services . . .[18]**

We agree with Dumont's summary of the development problems associated with dispersed homestead patterns in rural areas. Unfortunately he does not go into detail as to how planned villages will promote the political and socio-economic development of Tanzania.

As to the political dimension, undoubtedly planned villages will contribute to the birth of a development conscience so crucial in the development planning system and production process. Development consciousness is a function of continuous political mobilization and education. On the other hand, such consciousness is almost impossible to develop or inculcate if people are scattered. The creation of planned villages, therefore, makes possible the bringing of the seat of power and nucleus of participation nearer to the people. As a result, inculcation of the modernization consciousness will be made easier and people's participation in development at planning and implementation levels will become more efficient. As Iqbal Narain has correctly put it, it is critical to build up an 'adequate institutional model for decentralisation which may make it an equally efficacious instrument both of development and democracy'.[19] There will, of course, be the usual problem of the type of leadership available. Our view is, however, that leadership selection will be better conducted and made more effective, in time, through people living together and daily coming into contact with each other and learning each other's strengths and weaknesses.

Each planned village must, therefore, be turned into an institutional structure for development planning and even take up more powers to become a village government agency in every respect. The Ward Development Councils have not been effective tools for mobilization of the people for two main reasons. First, mobilization was rendered difficult because of the scattered nature of homesteads. This was not the fault of the Councils as such. Secondly, the leadership became too bureaucratic and non-representative in the sense that it lost touch with the people because of the power it wielded, and its failure to continuously consult the people. It is in recognition of these problems that TANU and government have decided to establish Village Development Councils in every village that has the minimum 250 families. These changes are embodied in the Village (Registration Designation and Administration) Act, 1975. As a result of their being legally registered, the villages, through their Councils, will be bodies corporate capable of holding and alienating property and entering into contracts with any other body corporate. Since June 1975 TANU has decentralized political powers from the ward level to the village level. Each village with the minimum 250 families must have a full TANU branch. In fact, as far as TANU powers are concerned, the ward no longer exists. The Ward Development Council will, in our view, similarly not be essential under the proposed changed participatory system, as planned villages can forward all their development programmes direct to the District Development Directorate. Each Village Development Council will then elect their representatives to sit on the District Development Council.

In the socio-economic dimension, enormous advantages arise out of the planned village system. Perhaps we can review these advantages by first looking at what conditions, facilities and services a rural peasant needs for increased production and motivation. For we are really trying to see how planned villages will facilitate the provision of those facilities, services and conditions so important for promoting rural development that would otherwise not have been possible under the previous scattered pattern. Professor Rainer Scheckele sees five such conditions or facilities:[20]

i. Provision of effective transportation of peasants' goods into and out of his village, for getting modern inputs in time, for storage, etc.

ii. He needs research and extension services to demonstration modern techniques and adapt them to local conditions.

iii. He needs credit and marketing services at favourable terms.

iv. He needs economic incentives like subsidized fertilizers.

v. He needs a rural social environment that encourages the development of his managerial capacities and civic responsibilities, his opportunities for self-improvement and his participation in public affairs. (This particular condition we have commented upon already).

It should be noted that none of the above-mentioned conditions or facilities can be provided to individual scattered homesteads. In fact the provisions of these facilities, including the provision of a rural social environment endowed with piped water, dispensaries, schools, etc., goes to the crux of area development planning strategy. How can one effectively plan the development of an area where people do not live in communities? Where would the focal points be for placing the rural social infrastructure? In fact, there already exists in most parts of Tanzania signs of development confusion where the scattered village pattern prevailed, of irregular location of various infrastructural social services where people have to walk many miles to use them. All the motivational conditions listed by Scheckele would, therefore, be difficult to provide unless peasants live in village communities which have recognizable growth centres. Note, for example, the question of provision of credit facilities for purposes of intensifying and modernizing agricultural production. There is no doubt that if proven agricultural techniques are to be implemented on a planned basis, peasants will need capital. This necessitates the availability of credit. But which bank will trust an isolated peasant living all alone somewhere deep in the bush? Most of the loans of this type would, therefore, normally be in the form of group loans, issued

in cash or in kind, or both, to formally or informally established groups of farmers. Credit will generally be granted for productive purposes, and the responsibility for obtaining a loan, field disbursement, and repayment, will be vested in either an individual as group leader of a small informal group, or a committee where larger more formal groups are concerned.[21]

Likewise, when it comes to extension services, these cannot be effective unless you have a village community situation. As time goes by, Tanzania will in fact need to establish rural extension training centres[22] for training peasants in modern methods of agriculture and animal husbandry, and these centres will have to be established in focal village nuclei so that actual farming demonstration can benefit the maximum number of people.

In 1971, Tanzania committed itself to the eradication of illiteracy by the end of 1975. This is as it ought to be because literacy is a crucial factor in the evolution of a development conscience. J.A. Ziolkowski has described literacy education as an important ingredient of the 'psycho-social infrastructure'. As if writing on the Tanzanian situation, Ziolkowski has stated: 'It would not be fanciful to imagine that one of the reasons why this institution of "participatory democracy" implying a high degree of social awareness and knowledge has not gained ground is the fact of illiteracy among peasants'.[23] We raise this point specifically because the creation of planned villages has had a fantastic impact on literacy education in rural areas. For four years up to October 1974, Shinyanga District had recruited 60,095 illiterates into literacy classes. Between the completion of Operation Planned Villages in November 1974 and April 1975, the number of those recruited rose to 81,439, a rise of 21,344 over a period of six months. What we are trying to prove is that we have been able, through planned villages, to effectively mobilize the rural peasantry to achieve a very crucial tool for development, an exercise which would have been extremely difficult to achieve in such a short time with a scattered village pattern.

We stated at the beginning of this paper that agriculture is the mainstay of

Tanzania's development. A forward thrust in agriculture is, therefore, the basic essential for promoting development. We believe that with the creation of planned villages in rural Tanzania, we have achieved the institution of an organizational structure necessary for the implementation of schemes and programmes of socio-economic and political change. Coupled with the decentralization of development planning and implementation powers to the grass-roots levels, there is no doubt that speedier development, particularly in rural areas, will henceforth become a positive reality.

NOTES

1. P.C. Mathur, 'Economic Planning and Panchayati Raj', in *Panchayati Raj, Planning and Democracy*, M.V. Mathur and Iqbal Narain (eds.) (Asia Publishing House, 1959), p.109.

2. Carl G. Rosberg, 'National Identity in African States', *The African Review*, Vol.I, No.1 (March 1971), p.89.

3. Lionel Cliffe and G. Cunningham, 'Ideology, Organisation and the Settlement Experience In Tanzania', *Socialism in Tanzania*, Vol.2. *Policies* by L. Cliffe and J. Saul (eds.) (Nairobi: East African Publishing House, 1973), p.131.

4. Julius K. Nyerere, 'Freedom and Development', in *Freedom and Development: A Selection from Writings and Speeches 1968-1973* (Oxford University Press, 1973), p.66. Jack Potter has elucidated on this ideology issue: 'ideology is important in rural development . . . because the social force needed to overcome social resistance and to mobilise a conservative peasantry to participate in development programmes can apparently come in no other way'. 'Modernisation Processes and Rural Development in Developing Countries: An Anthropolitical View', in *Rural Development in a Changing World* by Raanan Weitz, ed. (Cambridge: M.I.T. Press, 1971), p.358.

5. René Dumont, *Socialisms and Development* (London: Andre Deutsch, 1973), p.146.

6. 'Socialism and Rural Development', in *Ujamaa — Essays on Socialism* (Oxford University Press, 1968), pp.132-135.

7. For a good review of the law and order and tax collection administrative system on the eve of the Government Decentralization Programme, see James R. Finucane, 'Hierarchy and Participation in Development: A Case Study of Tanzania', *The African Review*, Vol.2, No.4 (1972), pp.573-595.

8. Rainer Scheckele, 'National Policies for Rural Development', in *Rural Development in a Changing World*, *op.cit.*, p.57.

9. Iqbal Narain, 'Introduction', *Panchayati Raj, Planning and Democracy*, *op.cit.*, p.xi.

10. Compared with the Department of Community Development in India, the district officials did not go into elaborate and sophisticated details in analysing the selected growth centres. For details of the Indian exercise see S.M. Shah, 'Growth Centres as a Strategy for Rural Development: Indian Experience', *Economic Development and Cultural Change* (University of Chicago), Vol.22, No.2 (January 1974), pp.215-228.

11. This experience is in line with the views of Professor Raanan Weitz who has noted that 'in the rural areas of the poor nations of the world, a change is taking place in the peasant's evaluation of his worth to himself and his society and in how he wishes to express that evaluation. This is manifested by his increasingly expressed demands for improved material conditions, for more and better services, and for a change to ensure his children a better future than could have been promised to them in the past. These desires and aspirations can and must be used to further the acceptance of change and hasten the pace of development', *From Peasant to Farmer: A Revolutionary Strategy for Development*, A Twentiety Century Fund Study (1971), p.69.

12. E.L. Wheelwright and B. McFarlane, *The Chinese Road to Socialism* (Harmondsworth: Pelican, 1973), p.331.

13. Julius K. Nyerere, 'Freedom and Development', *op.cit.*, pp.61-62.

14. *TANU Guidelines on Guarding, Consolidating and Advancing The Revolution of Tanzania, and of Africa* (Dar es Salaam: Government Printer, 1971), paragraph 28.

15. *From Peasant to Farmer, op.cit.*, p.71.

16. Clyde P. Ingle, *From Village to State in Tanzania: The Politics of Rural Development* (Ithaca: Cornell University Press, 1972), p.172.

17. See *Daily News* (Dar es Salaam), 4 June 1975.

18. Dumont, *Socialisms and Development, op.cit.*, p.145.
19. Narain, 'Introduction', *Panchayati Raj, Planning and Democracy, op.cit.*, p.xxxi. The creation of these planned villages also facilitates an 'institutional framework in which the people will not only be able to absorb innovations in the production process, but will be interested in doing so'.
20. See 'Regional Planning for Rural Development', in Weitz, *Rural Development in a Changing World, op.cit.*, p.64.
21. R.M. Sturgeon, 'Group Loans to Small Farmers', FAO/Finland Regional Seminar on Agricultural Credit for Africa, pp.1-2.
22. For an excellent exposition on educational needs for rural development and approaches to rural extension and training, see P.H. Coombs and Manzoor Ahmed, *Attacking Rural Poverty: Now Informal Education can Help* (Baltimore: The Johns Hopkins University Press, 1974), pp.15, 24-26.
23. J.A. Ziolkowsky, 'Illteracy and Rural Economy', *The Economic Times* (India and Asia), *Annual Supplement*, 1973, p.159.

CHAPTER 9

Large-Scale-Villagization: Operation Sogeza in Iringa Region*

James De Vries and Louise P. Fortmann

After the Arusha declaration, ujamaa villages were established, both through the people's own initiative but also at the instigation of the party and government. By 1973 about 15 per cent of the population was living in such communities, but the general feeling was that progress was too slow and the party therefore resolved that all regions should be concerned about moving people into villages. The President declared the end of 1976 as the deadline for the completion of this move. As a result *Operation Vijiji* (Villages) or *Operation Sogeza* (Moving) was started in various parts of the country. By August, 1974 the *Daily News* was enthusing that:

> . . . it is quite possible to move a whole district into planned villages all at once and at minimum expense. There are regions like Mara which have already completed moving the peasants into planned villages. But we have 19 others on the mainland. It would be a good idea if they seriously considered adopting the system adopted in Geita which is quicker, cheaper, and puts the entire population into gear instead of doing so on a piecemeal basis.

This system was soon adopted by other regions including Iringa. There, the move was made in the last half of 1974. Iringa Region is located in the Southern Highlands of Tanzania. It is a large region of approximately 56,000 square kilometres containing some 800,000 people. Its altitude varies between 500-2,400 metres and rainfall varies from 400 millimetres per year in the lower areas to 1,800 millimetres in the high zone.

The major cash crops of the region are tobacco, tea and pyrethrum. There are two major maize producing areas. In the highlands around Njombe, a temperate area with reliable rainfall, hybrid maize is grown, often with fertilizer and with very high yields. The Ismani plains area near Iringa town is also a noted maize producing area, but rainfall is less reliable than at Njombe and fertilizer often does not pay. Much of the region is semi-arid and has not yet been agriculturally exploited.

Ujamaa development in Iringa up to the time of *Operation Sogeza* varied a great deal between different areas. In the sparsely populated Ismani area, large-scale Tanzanian-owned farms had been established and most of the people had been turned into labourers on these and Greek settler farms. As can be expected, here there was strong opposition to the establishment of ujamaa communities by the larger farmers. Dr Kleruu, the Regional Commissioner who had organised *Operation Vijiji* in Mtwara Region and was now transferred to Iringa, was assassinated by one of the Ismani farmers whose land was being nationalised. Elsewhere in the Region there was much less resistance and especially in Njombe a large number of villages were established 'voluntarily'. By the middle of 1974 the region had 645 ujamaa villages. Of these 79 were registered producer co-operatives and 21 were in the process of being registered. Most of the remainder were ujamaa villages in little more than name and intent, with women often forming the majority of the members as the men were away seeking wage employment.

*This paper was written when the authors were lecturers in the University of Dar es Salaam's Faculty of Agriculture at Morogoro.

THE STUDY

During October-November 1974, following the peak of *Operation Sogeza,* people were interviewed in 15 development villages in Iringa Region. Twelve had been existing ujamaa villages to which new people had been moved. Three villages (one in each district) were newly-formed autonomous *vijiji vya maendeleo* (development villages). Data collection was hampered by an atmosphere rife with rumour, fear and hostility. Villagers feared the interviewers might be government agents to whom it would be unwise to talk. A prevalent rumour at the time was that the next act of the government would be to nationalise all the cattle. Some were therefore eating or selling their cattle to avoid nationalisation (a more exotic version of the rumour held that all wives were going to be nationalised as well). People were therefore reluctant to discuss their possessions or feelings with strangers. However a reasonable amount of information was collected and a picture emerged of a well-intentioned policy hurriedly implemented by a rigid, non-accountable bureaucracy.

SITING OF VILLAGES

The first problem of *Operation Sogeza* was siting the new villages. While guidelines were issued at the regional and district levels, this task was left primarily to ward level political and administrative personnel. They were expected to consult the villagers and technical experts, but due to the rapid and large scale nature of the move, very little consultation took place and sites were often chosen rather arbitrarily. Errors in siting resulted in some villagers having to move two or three times and became a major source of complaints.

Guidelines issued in late 1973 specified among other things that: villages should be located near roads, the railway, schools, dispensaries, sources of water and enough fertile land; villages must have a minimum of 300 resident families; people should, where possible, be moved to already existing ujamaa villages; each family should have a minimum of one acre for their homestead garden. The move was scheduled to commence in May 1974 and to be completed by the end of the year.

Misinterpretation of the guidelines, their too rigid application, and the fact that in many areas sites meeting all the above qualifications just were not available, had a number of unfortunate results. Many people knowing that they would have to move by the end of 1974 moved 'voluntarily' to those places they thought would become villages in order to get first choice of a home site. The result was that in many cases new houses were built for miles along either side of major roads. Once the official site was chosen most of these people were forced to start all over again. Often the gathering of over 300 families into one village resulted in a lack of fertile land within easy walking distance. In Njombe District farmers traditionally lived in scattered settlements along fertile valley bottoms. There the move took the form of moving them to the barren hill tops, contrary to agricultural commonsense. As shown in Table 1, in Njombe 24% of those interviewed complained about the inadequacy of land at the new site. In other villages, due to a lack of land at the village site, homesteads were only allowed as little as one-eighth of an acre each. One had so many inhabitants that if each person had received 4 acres as required to meet the targets laid down for agriculture, some would have had to travel 8 miles to their fields!

While the intention of *Operation Sogeza* was to give people better access to clean water and various social services, in the short run the opposite seemed to happen.

Due to poor planning, some setttlements were located as much as six miles from the nearest water source. This bore hardest on the women who were faced with having to walk increased distances both to fetch water and to work in their fields. Many new villages had no services to offer and pre-existing services became quickly overloaded by the large population influx. As can be seen from Table 2 only four villages had dispensaries, and two of these were overloaded by the additional population.

TABLE 1: Number of Villagers reporting problems as a result of Operation Sogeza

PROBLEM	Iringa District N = 35		Mufindi District N = 15		Njombe District N = 25		Total N = 75	
	No.	%*	No.	%*	No.	%*	No.	%*
A. Problems related to siting:								
Individual farms not adequate	4	11.4	1	6.7	6	24.0	11	14.7
Cannot care for permanent crops since former farms are too far away	3	8.6	2	13.3	5	20.0	10	13.3
Further from water/ lack of water	6	17.1	1	6.7	3	12.0	10	13.3
Further from school	4	11.4	1	6.7	—	—	5	6.7
Not enough grazing area	3	8.6	1	6.7	—	—	4	5.3
Further from dispensary	1	2.9	—	—	—	—	1	1.3
B. Problems related to moving:								
Building a house/ sleeping outside	23	60.0	9	53.3	16	60.0	48	58.7
Lost, stolen, or damaged property	5	14.3	11	73.3	7	28.0	23	30.7
Problems in moving property	6	17.1	7	46.7	7	28.0	20	26.7
Increased incidence of disease	—	—	—	—	3	12.0	3	4.0
Income in the Ujamaa village is very low	1	2.9	—	—	—	—	1	1.3

*Sums to more than 100 percent due to multiple responses.

THE MOVE

Many people objected not so much to the move as to the way it was done. 'We were treated like animals', some said. Government representatives (militia, Tanu Youth League members, government and party employees) simply told people they must move to a particular place by a given date. While available transport was mobilised to help move people and possessions, this was often inadequate and people were therefore forced to move themselves. Over one fourth of those sampled had difficulties moving their property (Table 1). To assure that people remained in the new villages, former homes were usually made uninhabitable by ripping our doors and windows and knocking holes in the mud walls or by setting fire to the thatch roofs. In some cases grain stored in or near the house also caught fire and the family's food supply was destroyed. The forced haste and large-scale nature of the move caused numerous problems. Lacking transport many people could not move all their possessions in one trip. No longer being able to secure their goods in window-less and doorless houses, they often returned to find some or all of their remaining possessions gone. As shown in Table 1, over 30% reported having property stolen or damaged during the move. People reported cases where the lorries which came to move the grain stored in their *vihenge* (traditional grain stores) either never delivered it, or part of it was missing by the time they reached the new site.

TABLE 2: Distance in Miles to Facilities Available in Sample Development Villages

Village	Market	Dispensary	Primary School	Cattle Dip	Maize Mill
A	3	4 (overloaded)	4 (overloaded)	4	(overloaded)
B	—	1½	1½	1	x
C	6	(overloaded)	(overloaded)	x	x
D	8	8	7	3	2
E	6	6	5	5	x
F	x	1½	1½	5	x
G	x	4	x	x	x
H	2	2	2	6	x
I	30	(overloaded)	(overloaded)	x	x
J	4	4	4	5	3
K	—	x	x	x	x
L	25	6	6	x	x
M	30	5	x	5	x
N	30	x	—	3	x
O	6	10	8	12	6
Percent with facility, excluding overloaded facilities N = 15	13.3%	13.3%	20.0%	26.6%	66.6%
Percent including overloaded facilities N = 15	13.3%	26.6%	33.3%	26.6%	73.3%

KEY:
x — present in the village
Overloaded — present but overloaded
Numbers — miles to nearest facility

THE IMMEDIATE AFTERMATH

In the short run the problems created by *Operation Sogeza* outweighed any benefits it might have bestowed. If the major goal was to bring people to services, the movement was premature and the siting often poorly done. As was recognised by members of the TANU Central Committee sent out to evaluate progress in November 1974, planning was often done haphazardly due to a serious lack of qualified personnel. Existing facilities were also completely inadequate to meet the large increase in demand, and very little could be done to improve this situation in the short term. The only bright spot was the increased availability of maize mills which lightened the staggering work load of the women who formerly had to prepare their grain by pounding it with a mortar and pestal.

The problems experienced by the respondents as a result of *Operation Sogeza* are presented in Table 1. Nearly 90% reported at least one problem. The move in most areas took place during the dry season, a time when lack of water made it impossible to produce enough mud for building, but when nights, especially in the higher altitude areas, were cold and damp. Lack of housing necessitated sleeping outdoors or in temporary grass huts, which often resulted in illness due to exposure. (There were several unconfirmed reports of deaths from pneumonia). Grass huts and open fires for cooking and warmth also posed a serious fire hazard. When the rains started, people were then faced with the dilemma of choosing between building a house and planting their crops late (which might result in a serious food shortage), and planting their crops and suffering the cold and rain in completely inadequate shelters. Most resolved this in favour of the most pressing need — housing.

The people who moved were not the only victims of theft. People already living in the villages at the time *Sogeza* was initiated complained that in the confusion and disruption caused by the move, village theft had increased. Members of one village were particularly bitter. They had for some time followed a policy of systematically expelling from the village known and habitual thieves. When in one fell swoop *Operation Sogeza* moved all these people back into the village and theft increased, the villagers felt not a little upset.

The move also created a whole host of problems centred around agriculture. As shown in Table 1, many farmers had been moved too far from their old fields to cultivate them and at the time of the survey had not been given an adequate amount of new land. In at least 60% of the villages very little or nothing had been done to prepare the land for the coming rains. Farmers said they had not begun to cultivate because they were waiting for the government to tell them where to farm or, they were waiting to see what the government would do next. Previous residents of the villages also suffered. In many cases the houses of new settlers were jammed together on the farms of the old residents, thus doubling the problem of finding new farms. In the end, officials recognising the impossible situation they had created, allowed some people to return to live at their old farms for a short time.

Owners of livestock also encountered difficulties due to the concentration of traditionally scattered herds. Many feared that diseases would spread more readily. Getting water for the animals was a problem for 21%. 32% reported difficulties in confining their animals at night. Overgrazing near the villages seemed inevitable while it was felt that more distant areas might be undergrazed and thus revert to bush. Damage to crops either from trampling or eating became a source of tension between old and new residents. Increases in theft of livestock, especially of chickens, were reported. The sole bright spot appeared to be that veterinary services became more readily available.

To get an idea of the likely short term changes in acreages cultivated, farmers were asked about their plans for the current season compared to the previous years. As can be seen in Table 3, most farmers claimed that they would either cultivate the same number of acres or increase the acreage. This is not surprising as at the time of the survey *Operation Kilimo* (the agricultural programme), which required each adult to grow a minimum of 3 acres of food crops and one acre of cash crops, had just been launched. This Operation was launched largely because regional leaders feared that farmers would fail to cultivate adequate food crops due to the problems of *Operation Sogeza* and that this would result in a serious food shortage.

TABLE 3: Planned Changes in Crop acreage due to Operation Sogeza

CHANGE IN ACREAGE

CROP	Increase			Decrease			No change		Don't know		Total	
	N	%	Acres	N	%	Acres	N	%	N	%	N*	%
Maize	35	47	1.9	13	17	2.3	22	29	5	7	75	100
Beans	7	20	2.3	2	6	1.4	20	59	5	15	34	100
Sunflower	9	43	2.1	4	19	2.4	3	14	5	24	21	100
Cowpeas	7	35	1.4	1	5	1.0	9	45	3	15	20	100

*N for different crops varies as not all farms grew all crops.

As regards village organisation, the situation was somewhat brighter. 60% of the new villages had elected a chairperson; 53.3% had a village committee; and 66.7% had elected ten-cell (the smallest political units) leaders at the time of the survey. Only four villages had no formal organisation at all.

Respondents were asked what help they thought the government would provide them. The answers are presented in Table 4. There was some evidence of wishful thinking that the government would lower the price of corrugated iron for roofing or provide poles for housing. However, most respondents who thought that government aid would be forthcoming thought it would be what the government had in fact promised, i.e. water, dispensaries, schools and so on. The credibility of the government did not appear to be terribly high, however. Only 34.7% thought the government would provide piped water and 22.7% thought it would establish a dispensary in their village. No more than 20% thought the government would provide any other single promised item.

TABLE 4: Aid Villages Expected the Government to Provide

AID	Iringa N = 35*		Mufindi N = 15*		Njombe N = 25*		Total N = 75*	
	Number	Percent	Number	Percent	Number	Percent	Number	Percent
Water	10	28.6	10	66.7	6	24.0	26	34.7
Fertiliser	5	14.3	4	26.7	3	12.0	12	16.0
Food	8	22.9	0	0	0	0	8	10.7
Dispensary	8	22.9	4	26.7	5	20.0	17	22.7
School	5	14.3	7	46.7	2	8.2	14	18.7
Building houses	5	14.3	2	13.3	3	12.0	10	13.3
Agricultural developments	4	11.4	1	6.7	1	4.0	6	8.0
Seed	1	2.9	0	0	0	0	1	1.3
Dipping	1	2.9	0	0	0	0	1	2.7
Transport	3	8.6	4	26.7	0	0	7	9.3
Provide farms near village	4	11.4	1	6.7	0	0	5	6.7
Provide poles	2	5.7	0	0	0	0	2	2.7
Lower price of iron sheets	2	5.7	0	0	1	4.0	3	4.0

*Sums to more than 100 percent due to multiple responses.

IMPACT ON UJAMAA DEVELOPMENT

A great deal of confusion was generated over whether *Operation Sogeza* was a step towards ujamaa, part of ujamaa, or a step away from ujamaa. Comments such as 'we like ujamaa but don't like the way it is being implemented', and *'Operation Sogeza* has changed the meaning of ujamaa' showed this confusion. In addition, members of small ujamaa villages which had been consolidated with larger villages expressed bitterness about having to move when they were already following government ujamaa policy. At the time the move was started, most ujamaa villages lacked the necessary 300 families and many of the larger villages consisted of several settlements of 50-100 families which allowed easy access to land and facilitated work organisation. The net effect on ujamaa development was that the negative feelings generated by the move, especially towards the way it was implemented, were directed towards the ujamaa policy and ujamaa villages which were the visible sign of this policy. Many people, in fact, blamed the move on ujamaa villages because, as they saw it, they would not have been moved to these villages (as was the case in many parts of Iringa Region) had they not existed. Interviewers noted a lot of hostility towards the ujamaa villagers by the newcomers. In a meeting in one village they went so far as to threaten the life of the chairperson.

Although a small percent of the newcomers had applied for ujamaa membership, most people at the time of the survey were taking a wait-and-see attitude, expecting that the government might require them to engaged in communal farming. The motivation for joining appeared to be mixed. Some were likely to be attracted by the prospect of receiving government help and benefiting from communal enterprises. It also seemed likely that others would seek membership simply as a sort of insurance policy against further government interference in their lives.

The existing ujamaa groups appeared to welcome the prospect of new members. Only one village was reported to be opposed to any newcomers joining. A critical problem for ujamaa groups was a shortage of communal labour and a number of the chairpersons interviewed felt that increased membership would help to solve this problem. The influx of new settlers also created land problems for the ujamaa villagers. In some cases in Njombe they complained that the communal farms on which they had spent a lot of time and money to clear, cultivate and build up fertility, were now taken over by newcomers who had contributed nothing. In one village people were told that individuals would have priority in assignment of suitable land, near the village, in accordance with *Operation Kilimo.* This meant that land for communal activities would be both scarce and at some distance from the village.

A more serious problem for the long term development of existing ujamaa groups was that many, government staff and farmers alike, saw *Operation Sogeza* as a change in policy from communal production to communal living. As a result emphasis shifted back to encouraging private production. *Operation Kilimo* was interpreted to mean private production of at least 4 acres of crops. If this was implemented there would be little if any surplus labour for communal production.

CONCLUSION

It was clear that in the short term, *Operation Sogeza* in Iringa generated both a lot of problems and an increased demand for government services. The longer term impact remained to be seen, but government and party officials were convinced that a step towards the rapid development of the rural sector had been taken. While any move of this magnitude is bound to create problems and generate hostility as people are uprooted from their traditional settlements, several things might have made the process less painful and the results better.

First, more time could have been taken in moving people. The national deadline for completion of the move had been stated as the end of 1976, not 1975. This extra year would have allowed more careful planning of sites and more assistance during the actual move. The need for the use of brute force would also have been considerably lessened. Designation of home sites six months to one year before the actual move was to take place would have allowed farmers to begin building homes on the new sites and to prepare the land. This would have considerably lessened the burden of the move and the danger of famine, and would have been much closer to traditional methods of moving home sites which require much less outside help.

Secondly, a more flexible approach should have been taken in the design of villages. A lot of complaints resulted from rigid enforcement of village boundaries and bureaucrats' desire to have houses in straight lines. Some people were forced to move their house as little as 50 feet! More importantly, it should have been realised that as topography, soil fertility, water availability, farming systems, etc. varied a great deal within the region, not all villages could follow the same pattern. For example, the system in use in some of the larger ujamaa villages in Njombe of having several small settlements within a radius of say 3 miles from a central one associated in a single ujamaa group was well adapted to the local environment. It allowed easy access to scattered fertile land as well as to social services and essential infrastructure. Close consultation with the peasants might have revealed similar opportunities in other areas. Such local adaptations within broad national guidelines would not only have lessened resistance to the move, but also provided a better basis for the future development of viable ujamaa communities.

CHAPTER 10

Some Crucial Aspects of the Maasai Predicament*

M. L. ole Parkipuny

The Maasai are the largest and most widely known of the pastoral ethnic groups in East Africa. However this knowledge is superficial. It is hardly more than an awareness of the existence of a people whose image has been subjected to distortion and romanticism. In discussions of development, the livestock herds have tended to attract more attention than the people who raise them.

There are three related groups which constitute the Maasai population in East Africa. These are the Maasai proper, the Sambur and the Baraguyu. In talking about development and change a great deal of confusion has resulted from the tendency among government officials and outsiders in general to confuse these with semi-pastoralists such as the Wa-arusha who, although they speak a dialect of the Maasai language, have a completely different culture reflecting an economic base predominantly of crops. Thus in Tanzania Wa-arusha practices have been wrongly quoted time and again as illustrations of Maasai 'taking to agriculture', 'proper dressing', or 'voluntarily sending their children to school'.

THE GEOGRAPHY OF MAASAILAND

Maasailand proper is a large land area of over 100,000 square kilometres, dissected by a stretch of the Tanzania/Kenya border some 400 kilometres in length. As a result of close proximity to the equator, temperatures are generally uniform and high throughout the year, implying high evaporation. Overall average rainfall is in the range 500-750 millimetres. Below 750mm it is generally accepted that crop cultivation becomes marginal, so by and large extensive agricultural production is not suitable for Maasailand. But knowledge of the true rainfall is extremely scanty, and this will remain a real problem in the immediate future since there are few gauging stations in the area and those few in existence are very poorly utilised. As a consequence reliance on impressions is inevitable. Still certain things are clear: that the total rainfall is low on average while potential evaporation is high; that, as in most of the rest of East Africa, the actual rainfall is very variable not only in respect of the total amount falling in a year but also seasonally, and from place to place as well as in timing; and finally, that the influence of elevation on the annual amount of rainfall and its reliability, and thus on temperatures and vegetation cover, is very substantial indeed.

The altitude factor makes the crucial difference between the wet and cool highlands, where rainfall is reliable, and the scorching heat of the lowlands where rainfall is very patchy and hardly ever spreads over all the country at any one time. Elevation varies between 645 metres above sea level around the Rift Valley lakes, to well over 3,300 metres in the Ngorongoro and Mao highland blocks. There is a large

*A shortened version of a paper presented United Nations Environmental Programme seminar in Mauritius, April 1976.

highland plateau covering Narok District in Kenya and the adjacent area in the sub-district of Loliondo in Tanzania. There are also several isolated mountains, covered at the top by thick forest caps, which are more important as water catchment areas than as sources of pasture, though they also constitute essential dry season grazing areas. All in all, roughly 40% of Maasailand is high altitude land of over 1,200 metres above sea level.

In short the range of diversity in topography, ecological zones, soils, and in the climate of Maasailand is remarkable. Lowlands, elevated steppes and parklands, extensive highlands of varying magnitudes, numerous isolated mountains, and the volcanic complex comprising the Great Rift Valley with its saline lakes, craters, one active volcano and several extinct cones, have given the countryside a landscape of unexcelled beauty and very diverse land-use potentialities. The immediate economic potentialities of the cooler, higher and water surplus areas present a glaring contrast to those of the warmer, lower and water deficient areas. Thus Maasailand is far from being the type of monotonous semi-arid country that many assume the homeland of a pastoral people to be.

Of even greater magnitude than the range of land-use possibilities is the intensity and complexity of the problems facing the Maasai people, for whom this land of contrast is the only home they know. The problems hinge on the agency of forces external to the society itself.

The high potential cool uplands, fertile plains and valleys, are suitable for the production of a wide range of cash crops such as wheat and other cereals, beans and other legumes, and tree crops. These areas have been the focus of land alien-ation ever since the time when the first foreign administration set foot in Maasai-land. As early as 1911 the British colonial administration removed the Maasai from huge tracts of their best pasture in the Kenya highlands and drove them south to the semi-arid waterless plains of Kajiado where the rigours of incessant drought have become their lot. The process has continued in both Kenya and Tanzania up till this day.

Secondly, Maasailand has retained one of the world's largest concentrations of wild animal population. Free, unmolested game grazing side by side with cattle herds and donkeys in the forest margins and in the open plains can be seen in many parts of Maasailand. Virtually the whole of Maasailand is designated as either game controlled areas or game reserves, and almost all the famous National Parks and Game Reserves in Kenya and Tanzania are within or on the borders of Maasai country.

The third cause of pressure on the land resources available to stock has been disease vectors, the most outstanding being the tsetse fly. The fly has its own uncontested reserves in Maasai country. It has successfully kept livestock away from large tracts of high potential pasture which are only, and very rarely, used by the stock of highly daring stockmen in periods of acute drought when the choice available has narrowed down to one between definite mass starvation of the animals and accepting the unknown tolls of trypanosomiasis and sleeping sickness.

THE MAASAI ECONOMY

Before going on to explore how external forces directed at the improvement of the Maasai production system are in actual fact worsening the state of affairs, we must examine some of the internal shortcomings of the indigenous Maasai socio-economic order.

The Maasai variant of pastoralism is still for the most part not embroiled in a state of social class exploitation *internally.* This does now, however, mean that exploitation is not an important element of the internal structure of the society. It is primarily exploitation of child and women's labour that is dominant. It is boys, and to a lesser extent girls, of school-going age or even younger, who normally tend the family herds. And it is the women folk, in the service of men, as is the case generally with pre-capitalist societies, who look after the animals at home in addition to their numerous chores.

The Maasai people are grouped into distinct sections each confined to a specific portion of the tribal land. The outer boundaries of these sub-tribal sections constitute the limits of livestock movements in pursuit of grass and water.

The most prevalent pattern of pasture utilisation is transhumance, and this is ideally suited to the areas where open plains are backed by mountains. It involves regular cyclical movements of livestock over substantial distances, up to 20 kilometres at times, between two or three places in response to seasonal climatic changes. The driving force is the need to secure adequate supplies of good quality pasture and water simultaneously and continuously. At the onset of the rains the main cattle herd is moved to open, short-grass plains. In such short-grass rangelands the new green shoots sprout and grow very quickly, almost overnight soon after the first rains have fallen, but they dry up equally rapidly and get depleted fast at the end of the rains. Usually the only water available in such places is rain water in numerous water-holes which fill up after one night's downpour and dry up almost immediately at the end of the rains. It is this depletion of water in the water-holes which triggers off the next stage in the cycle. The youths who take the cattle to the plains begin to trek the herds back home to where there is permanent water. The herds may stay there throughout the dry season. But more frequently after a couple of months they are driven to another outpost in the mountains where they remain until the rains begin to fall again. Then the cycle is repeated.

A second pattern differs rather significantly in that movement from one area to another involves the movement of whole families instead of just a few herders with the livestock. At the beginning of the rainy season *all* the families are expected to move from the vicinity of the permanent water and the surrounding pasture land. At the end of the rains all return to their permanent water area homes. This pattern is prevalent where there is only one permanent watering point which necessarily means heavy concentrations of livestock in the immediate neighbourhood of the watering point.

This modified transhumance pattern imposes a lot more strain not only on the land but on the cattle as well during the dry season. Since thousands of cattle rely on only one watering point during the dry spells the surrounding grass gets depleted very fast. As time goes on the distances that cattle have to travel to reach pasture increase. Ever widening circles of land around the watering points turn into bare soil dissected by the tracks made by herds trekking to and from the watering points. In due course these furrows get enlarged by surface run-off, and turn into gullies. Just before the rains the radius of the area being grazed can be as much as 15 kilometres. With the increasing distance between water and grass, cattle drink less frequently. The pattern becomes as follows. On the first day the cattle are driven to water, and they hardly graze at all on that day as the area they pass through is bare soil virtually all the way, and at the water there are endless queues of herds waiting their turn to drink. A herd might queue up for six or even eight hours. The following day they again pass long stretches of bare ground before they reach the nearest pasture. Two 'dry' days, i.e. two consecutive days in which the cattle go without water, are not unknown, but the high temperatures and low humidity make it almost unbearable particularly since the cattle are feeding on very dry forage.

There are also what are termed 'drought year disorders'. During such hard times the pasture is exhausted in most parts of the district, and the regular cycles and systems of grazing are thrown into chaos as cattle from the lowlands flock into the few cool mountains with pasture reserves. In the worst of such years many families in fact evacuate to distant lands far from their traditional localities. These chaotic movements of desperation hasten the depletion of pasture reserves in the better off areas. The result is almost invariably a calamity, as the combination of water and pasture disappears over a widening area. Confusion and discouragement, hunger and accelerating loss of cattle, become the order of the day, and the nightmare of famine haunts the whole region. With more frequent rain failures since the 1961 drought, this has now become a common experience in various parts of Maasailand.

Irrespective of the dominant pattern of pasture utilisation the setting aside of a certain part of pastureland in each grazing unit for yearlings during the dry season is a practice common throughout Maasailand. This portion of land is invariably near the village and water. The idea is to avoid subjecting yearlings to the strains of long distance trekking, but goats and sheep and weak cows or bulls are also let into this pasture.

The problem of soil erosion is accentuated by the heavy downpours of the tropics. The result is rapid and severe washing away of a fragile soil, trampled to fine dust and raped of grass cover by the herds moving in thousands. We mentioned earlier the numerous animal paths to and from watering points and grazing areas that turn into ever deepening gullies. Another problem is silt which is likely to cover any depression holding surface run-off, so useful to the animals during the wet season. Soil erosion and depletion of the palatable grass species have been major agents facilitating the advance of bush. This process is accelerating from year to year. The advance of bush in turn has speeded up territorial conquest by the tsetse fly. In this advance the fly wins important watering points as well, and these are lost to the growing animal population and to the people.

Shortage of water appears on the surface to be the most crucial problem of the Maasai. Four basic factors define the nature of this problem and the difficulties involved. First, good permanent water is very scarce. There are few rivers and lakes, and a number of those which exist are not as useful as they have the potential to be. The few big permanent rivers, such as the Uasin Nyiro, Mara and Pangani, provide breeding areas for the tsetse fly. There are a good number of sizeable lakes, mostly on the rift valley floor or at the bottom of craters, but most of these are either too saline to be of any use for consumption or their accessibility is restricted by sharp rocky escarpments separating them from major pastures in the vicinity. Thus seasonal rain-filled pools, man-made wells, boreholes and dams, together with springs and short streams have become the pivots of Maasai socio-political life and the means for exploiting the surrounding pastures. Underground water, surface run-off collection using dams, and piping the few streams for more efficient utilisation, are alternatives for the future. But underground water resources are apparently scarce and large-scale collection of rainwater is impaired in many parts of Maasailand by the porous quality of the volcanic soils.

Secondly, no really detailed inventory of the water resource potential has been undertaken. Thirdly, high construction costs have become a major problem — mainly because of the failure to mobilise local resources and to deploy these for the benefit of the people. The overall implication of all these physical considerations is important, but it cannot be over-emphasised that however generous government might be in investment in the provision of water, the contradictions of the Maasai situation will continue to frustrate even the biggest inputs until these people and the resources they control have been mobilised to meet the challenge of their own situation in its totality.

It is low productivity and extreme uncertainities rather than prestige that necessitates keeping livestock in large numbers to meet family subsistence needs. As it is now, food consumption and the quality of life for that matter is determined by the weather conditions. Thus the rainy season is the time of bounty — there is almost too much and all live and feed very happily. As the dry season sets in, the supply of milk (the principal and favourite food) dwindles and consumption falls very low. In drought periods all subsist at almost starvation level: hardly a drop of milk, and the animals are so weak and boney that those which still cling to life can neither be slaughtered, nor sold to earn cash with which to buy maize flour, the principal food of the dry season. Yet during the rainy and normal dry seasons there remains considerable surplus that could be channelled to the market, had hard cash or money savings been more important to these people as a medium of exchange and for security than livestock and lineage are, even in the monetarised societies of today.

Yet it is only the security of the individual that is ensured in this social order, and that itself is true only so long as the extended family has security. There is no insurance against calamities which hit the whole group. The system has very shaky safeguards against weather abnormalities even when bitter experience has demonstrated how notoriously erratic the weather is. In time of calamities — severe drought or epidemic in particular — the system of security, pegged to livestock on the hoof and embedded in the fabric of the society, collapses. Hence the cry for famine relief, year after year. Rescue operations from outside thus constitute the ultimate security.

A system which cannot guarantee itself adequate supplies of daily bread throughout the seasons (whatever its other merits) is indeed an ailing system. It is here, and not in who controls the means of production, that the principal contradiction of the pre-capitalist Maasai situation is rooted. That is, while production is orientated to internal consumption and internal security with the surplus primarily retained within, the ultimate security is sought from without. The surplus remains within because involvement in the wider market is simply marginal in extent, even in the hardest of times.

Beyond doubt pastoral societies, the Maasai included, have over the years adapted themselves well to the hard conditions of production characteristing their physical environment. But they have gone no farther than that. Their achievements have merely enabled them to intelligently exploit the physical resources around them rather than to develop the productive forces at the same time. Technology describes the mode by which man in society deals with nature in the process of production by which he sustains his life, and thereby also lays bare the mode of formation of his social relations as well as of the mental occupations that flow from them. As in virtually all other pre-capitalist communal social formations, labour is the principal source of available power, and it is geared almost entirely to livestock production and domestic chores, none of which involve extended reproduction of capital goods. Precisely, the Maasai relationship to nature is exploitative. Gatherers and hunters reap what they have not planted. The Maasai mode is a step up as they plant before they harvest, but they are far from effectively treating the wounds that their animals inflict on the range land, their sole means of production. Even the spears and knives which constitute the main tools and weaponry of these people are not made by artisans from within. This technological bankruptcy has deprived the social order of the basis for internally generated development, and hence its continued direct dependence on nature, manifest in the inevitable susceptibility to the vagaries of nature and subsequent recourse to metaphysics for relief.

The incapacity of the Maasai type of socio-economic formation to overcome the basic contradiction between man and nature, in a world in which the totality of humanity has attained unprecedented scientific know-how, makes this subsistence economy and its superstructure definitely out-moded.

THE MAASAI PROJECT

The idea of bringing development to the Maasai dates back to the arrival of Europeans in the area in the second half of the 19th century. The most ambitious attempt since is the current Maasai Range Management and Development Project in Tanzania in which the key unit to solve the problems of Maasailand is the ranching association. Ranching associations are conceptualised as corporate bodies to provide the framework for the development, management, conservation and rehabilitation of the resources and the welfare of the people. The official procedure for the registration of an association involves eliciting the consent of at least 60% of the prospective members, the posting of a full-time resident range officer to work in the area, a census of potential members and their stock, and the election by the members of a ten-man steering committee to see to the smooth running of the association. Following the achievement of these stipulations the ranching association can be granted the rights of occupancy to all land and water within the area demarcated and declared to be for range use by the association, in accordance with the Range Development and Management Act of 1964.

The first pilot ranching association, namely Kolomonik, was formed in 1966 by Ministry of Agriculture staff in the area immediately around the headquarters of what was then known as Maasai District. The Ministry made an initial investment of some one million shillings in the construction of two dips and a pipeline system to supply water to Mfereji, the driest section of the association area. However, the government could not afford to pump more money into the pilot association, and as a result the necessary facilities were not provided in the rest of the area, which, incidentally, was of higher potential. Besides, in less than a year it had become starkly clear that a new problem had already been created. Not only was the rest of the area without adequate dry season water and dips, but even the other dry areas bordering on the part which now had water, had hardly any reliable sources of water for the dry season. The island of abundant water created in Mfereji became the focus of livestock convergence in the dry season as herds from all directions streamed in to drink water. The result was acute over-grazing. The area was in danger of turning into a dust bowl. Furthermore, without grass the water is of hardly any use to Mfereji. The damage continues to date, a testimony to negative development.

After the disappointments of the Komolonik fiasco, a beam of hope shone for a short time as the US Agency for International Development moved in, in 1970, to take over the financing and direct running of ranching in the area, following the signing of an agreement for a ten year programme called the Maasai Range Development and Management Project. USAID went ahead and set up an office for the project, recruited five US range development experts, committed funds under a loan of $1.7 million to the Tanzanian government to supply heavy equipment for the construction of dams, boreholes, roads, and for bush clearing, and undertook to train in the United States (up to BSc and MSc level) 30 Tanzanian counterpart personnel. The major task for the Maasai Project was to initiate ranching associations and to organise the development of water and the construction of dips within the associations, and to establish efficient marketing of livestock from the associations.

When USAID replaced the original programme, Komolonik, and particularly Mfereji, had come to be viewed as a bad pilot association. Talamai in southern Maasailand was chosen as the new pilot ranching association. The people responded well, and for two years Talamai was the pet association, constantly quoted as the shining example guiding the way towards the ultimate destination for Maasailand. But the bottlenecks which had brought Komolonik to a halt were present and towards the end of those years it became increasingly embarrassing for the 'well-intentioned' experts to go on lavishing praise on it. Even so, important visitors who wanted to see the accomplishments of the Maasai Project were taken to Talamai to see the Maasai dipping their cattle and the imposing boran bulls which had been dished out to certain members of the association.

Today it is no longer possible to close one's eyes and pretend that things are under control. The land has gone on deteriorating at an incredible rate. Pasture and water are no longer adequate. The bush and unpalatable weeds have kept steadily advancing at the expense of edible grasses in many parts of Talamai, but most intensively in the neighbourhood of watering points and dips. Poor planning of the location of the initial infrastructural investments by a project with 'Highly Qualified Experts' has created bottlenecks to the implementation of further development projects at a higher stage. In spite of the existence of 6 dips and 6 fairly reliable watering points for an area of 120,000 hectares, Talamai is proving yet another failure.

In view of the importance of the current Project for Maasailand, a look at what has actually been going on is timely. But first some points must be clarified. Firstly, that for the Maasai the hour to embark on a new life on a mass scale is long overdue. Secondly, that for such a new life to materialise adequate water supply in the area constitutes a pre-requisite of the first order. Thirdly, the current livestock and range development project, particularly the $1.7 million loan agreement with USAID, is by far the most ambitious government investment input in the history of Maasailand. And finally, that considering the amount and sophistication of the equipment at the disposal of the Project there is no reason whatsoever why it should not be possible to develop all the exploitable water resources in Maasailand over the next few years. Indeed its sheer magnitude is indicative of a major determination on the part of the government, a commitment to a far reaching objective of no less than national significance. At least it seems to answer the description of the mammoth programme proposed by Denis Branagan some twenty years back, and to correspond with the fact that the provision of an adequate supply of stock water in the area is beyond doubt very demanding. It would certainly be difficult to imagine the validity of any arguments denying the appropriateness of the extensive use of heavy equipment to solve the water problems of Maasailand.

The terms of the loan are very generous at face value. The annual interest rate is as low as 2% for the first 10 years and rises thereafter to 3% on the outstanding balance of both interest and principal. The repayment period is 40 years commencing from the date of the first disbursement. But to stop there would be totally missing the point. The soft terms should not screen from us the fundamental issues emanating from such a transaction. To start with, the credit is not free from strings. The borrower is bound to purchase equipment and operational components as well as services 'required' for the Project exclusively from the US. It is the USAID Project technicians who specify and define what is required. Secondly the loan agreement stipulates that all repayments must be effected in US dollars. Even more important in the long run is the package of disadvantages to the recipient and gains to the donor from such a deal. Among the gains to the donor must be included market conquest and monopoly in the long run through technological lock-in and skilled labour training. The basic problem must be perceived as the internationalisation of the structural base for the establishment of roots of exploitation by the international capitalist system. In this connection the alienation effects of gigantic machinery to the exclusion of the mobilisation of the internal resources of the society, human and material, cannot be over-emphasised.

THE 'EXPERTS'

Since 1970 the Maasai Project has sustained stresses and criticisms levelled at its failure to realise its goals. The principal bones of contention have been the structure and methodology of work organisation, as well as the issue of control and the relationship of ranching organisations to ujamaa villages. Thus an American Project Manager had this to say:

> **The Project was almost continuously under reconsideration, either by Tanzanian leaders or by USAID. To both sides . . . the project represented a controversial experiment. Among Tanzanians there were fears that the American technicians might oppose ujamaa in the field; and when the 015 loan equipment was greatly delayed in arriving, it was said that this was a deliberate US action to impede Tanzanian development. Among USAID officials in Washington too there were some who were disturbed at the size of the Project's investment in a country where most land was not privately owned and where technical programmes were clearly subject to close political control by the nation's socialist leaders.**

The issue of accountability and control became the focus of controversy because the Project started off as a 'national' project but predominantly foreign financed. By definition a 'national' project is accountable to Dar es Salaam ministerial headquarters, the Ministry of Agriculture in this case. Therefore the Project was not part and parcel of the administration and planning system of the district it was situated in. Worse still USAID control of the purse strings and the power of the 'experts' completed the detachment of the project from the people. As if that was not bad enough the American experts were all along resident in Arusha town and had an office there rather than at the headquarters of the district they were supposed to work in. The experts only went to the district headquarters occasionally and for the rest of the time it was not known where they were or what they were doing.

The second problem arose as a result of USAID and its team going on strike in reaction to a problem which had already led to the termination of a similar UNDP project in Dodoma Region and Sukumaland. This was the conflict between agricultural ujamaa villages and ranching associations. Though both were to prove inadequate to the challenge of raising productivity and unable to revolutionise the mode of life of the people in the area, nevertheless the controversy precipitated was immense. The problem centred on the right of occupancy that the ranching associations were securing to land and water under the Range Management Act

1964, versus the TANU policy of giving supreme priority to ujamaa villages over the use of land and water. Thus in protest against the attempt of regional and district officials to follow the latter imperative, USAID froze the ordering of the heavy equipment early in 1971.

The first effect of the crisis was the accentuation of the feeling in the district that the expatriates were not part and parcel of the district team. The strike strengthened the feeling that the expatriates were just holidaying in Arusha or in the scenic Maasai countryside or hunting or collecting precious stones or all of these. These rumours became widespread. The second effect was a delay in the water programme and hence a frustration of the hopes of stockmen all over the district, as everywhere they had been told of the big water procuring machinery and so their dreams were all pegged to the arrival of the machines. Clearly effective control of the USAID personnel and of the Project at large had not been achieved by the district, and certainly not by the people. This remained true despite amendments to the Project Agreement in 1972 which included creation of the post of Project Co-Manager, as well as the incorporation of the Range and Veterinary Departments into a new Department of Livestock.

The third problem was related to the above conflict but more particularly to the bourgeois pretence of separating politics from technical work. The result was the development of a mutual distrust between politicians and technicians which in turn created numerous contradictions, bottlenecks, and a lack of co-ordination. The problem was that the Project separated the animal aspect from the totality of the livestock-based human order. The Agreement between the Tanzanian Government and USAID defined the Project in the context of the livestock industry only, and was therefore confined to plans to develop the livestock industry in Maasailand rather than to bring development to the people as a whole. The Government did not provide a corresponding social development project. Consequently there was merely an investment project in Maasailand and not a development project, for as the Arusha Declaration aptly points out, development means more than the development of material things.

As a result there came into existence two extreme lines of thinking. It was the viewpoint of the range technicians that the role of the Project was solely limited to livestock and rangeland resources. This implied that any kind of work on the human aspects was to be handled by the Project sociologist and was merely in order to clear the ground for the principal objective, the development of the live-stock industry. This has not necessarily meant that none of the USAID personnel have had a genuine interest in the human aspects of development in Maasailand. What it has meant is that such people are contravening the ethics of their ideological grounding and taking an interest in issues outside their assignment, and are there-fore undesirable in the team. Such individuals have risked the danger of antagonising their bosses and being thrown out. The local government and party bureaucracy has tended to take the opposite position, holding the technicians responsible for the totality of misdevelopment in the area. In the shadow of it all the stockmen became mere objects rather than an active control force.

THE RANCHING ASSOCIATIONS

Initially the ranching association was meant to function as the smallest unit of organisation for the Project. The possibility that the associations were just too large to function as the primary village unit was not considered. The truth was that the associations cover even larger areas than the indigenous rotational grazing units within which overgrazing had become widespread.

The principal bait used initially to induce the stockmen all over Maasailand to form ranching associations was the promise that once they had done so the Project would send one of its experts to ascertain what they needed in terms of livestock services. Then the Project would proceed to undertake the capital works and provide the livestock services.

Generally speaking anything new needs a convincing advantage and also time for the experience to be evaluated before it can be accepted comfortably. This is even more true in a situation in which risks are costly, as in the case of the production conditions and cultural integrity of pastoral societies. The Maasai response to the official appeal for the formation of associations was initially slow. But once account was taken of the initial experience with dipping and word had travelled across the land, and news travels fast and far in Maasailand, in no time the problem changed to being one of how to meet the numerous requests for the registration of new associations and how to provide the promised dips and water. 'Range' became the magic word, overshadowing everything else including the government and party in the minds of the stockmen. That is how in some parts of Maasailand the newest age group was given the name Range.

But almost as soon as the extent of the response from the people began to be revealed, and the stockmen in different corners of Maasailand clamoured to be recognised and given the association title, the true colour of things began to unravel. The promised facilities could not be provided to the new associations immediately. Word to that effect began to travel and the clamour subsided slowly. It was only the lie used by the USAID experts that the heavy water equipment was in transit from the US that saved the Project from complete disgrace and collapse. The burning issue became the arrival of the equipment.

Providing adequate water and dipping facilities for the livestock, so as to eliminate tick-borne infections and cut down the heavy annual losses of animals through other diseases and drought by spreading out cattle with new watering points, these have been accepted by both sides as top priority undertakings. As a US expert put it:

> While technicians in some areas may be labouring to get herdsmen to dip stock, in Maasailand we are often trying to explain to *Wafugaji* (herdsmen) why they do not yet have a dip to use. In some associations the members have paid or are willing to pay for large portions of water and dip construction. In spite of apparent conservatism the Maasai express opennesss to extension work in disease control and other issues in livestock management. This does not mean that they follow all advice given, but that at least their's and the technician's interest in better livestock coincide.

Beyond that point the objectives diverged. On the one hand the stockmen wanted to see an end to the animal losses because in their view of the world the mark of prosperity was the large size of the herd. The other side conversely saw in the Maasai herds ideal wealth which only needed to be delivered to the market to materialise into cash and protein. The Project's men had come to Maasailand with goals dictated by their view of what livestock should be raised for. Hence the declared official goal was the development of a prosperous livestock industry to pay back all the investment and generate more surplus for growth and 'development', whatever the meaning of the latter term.

The stockmen's primary purpose for their family herds was family/tribal community utility in non-cash terms, while that of the investor was 'national utility' through the cash medium. Yet to this day official policy has not found a means of resolving the problems of habitat destruction which arise from the two opposite views.

Plainly the problem of overgrazing in the neighbourhood of watering points and dips has become the drawback to the success of the undertaking. Mention any of the flat land in Maasailand with permanent water, or a dip, or both — Engikaret, Engaruka, Mfereji, Tiga Tinga, Malambo, Talamai — and these once productive pastures, the 'granaries' of animal production in the whole Maasai country, are inevitably now either bare of natural grass cover or bush and weeds have taken over. My own recollection of the rich grass varieties and good health of the livestock in Malambo in the 1950s is vivid, and affords a glaring contrast to the continuous bush with hardly any grass cover today. The continuous depletion of grass and degeneration of highly productive pasturelands into desolate bush thickets, following the installation of dips for the livestock, has spread tens of kilometres around the existing watering places all over Maasailand.

The problem began to take shape as far back as the 1930s when the first major investment in stock water was undertaken by the British colonial administration. But until the 1950s such watering points were still relatively few and far apart. Since then the situation has changed drastically. There are many more watering points. And dips have been introduced to make water use even more effective by saving an increasing number of animals from loss through diseases. The process of installation of means of destruction under the label of 'development' continues to gain momentum. And the rate of destruction is also accelerating. The magnitude of the cumulative damage to the national forage and soil that can result from the free movement of livestock over areas as big as the average ranching association must not be underestimated. In the past the alarming destruction of the habitat came about as a consequence of unregulated livestock movements and use of grass and water within locations often even smaller than those occupied by the average associations today.

So far it has been mainly the lowlands which have been adversely affected. The uplands which were historically the cattle refuge in the dry season and drought years are now being lined up for an assault on their habitat. The prevalence of disease there previously put an effective brake on the numbers of animals in the mountains. But now dipping is making the most devastating diseases a problem of the past and livestock numbers have begun to multiply rapidly there too. It is a well-known fact that the highlands with their steep gradients are a great deal more susceptible to soil erosion. And once the process has begun, who knows the cost of stopping it, not to mention the cost of rehabilitation? It is beyond dispute that the time is now overdue for the establishment of rational grazing patterns as part of an integrated socio-economic transformation of the Maasai social order — a liberation struggle from the realm of necessity to one of freedom — and to save the land from irreparable damage.

The ranching associations in Maasailand are a dead letter. The Project itself has become a monster in our land. Some of the associations have existed on paper for almost ten years but what are the accomplishments? Hardly one has taken a stride beyond the original aim that induced the people to accept the title — the securing of government financial inputs. Who is to blame? Certainly not the stockmen! The ranching associations were conceived as the basic functional units for investment in the area: corporate bodies for the operationalisation of livestock production and range land management, conservation and rehabilitation for greater productivity to benefit the 'national' economy and the producers. But first, the associations lack the basic structure, organisation and planning capacity to initiate and sustain the rapid self-sustained socio-economic transformation that is desired. Secondly, they lack the strategy and appropriate ideological approach to the problem. Thirdly they need the support of a socially dynamic base, a crucial missing link (though the recent idea of 'livestock-based villages' might provide this — see the discussion of these later in this paper).

The result is stalemate and non-functional ranching associations. The activities undertaken have been limited and narrow in scope. The initial enthusiasm has died out and apathy has taken hold. One of the crippling ailments in the life of the associations has been the question of revenue disbursement. Hardly a single association follows a systematic accounting system. There is neither internal nor external auditing, unlike other forms of co-operatives. Consequently embezzlement of people's funds is a debilitating problem of the first order in virtually all the ranching associations. In one of them nearly Shs. 50,000/- originally raised by members as a support fund for a loan the association had requested from the Rural Development Bank was shared out among a few members some three years ago. Among the main benefactors were the secretary of the association who pocketed Shs. 10,000/-, the treasurer Shs. 5,000/-, and two big cattle dealers, both members of the association, one of whom took Shs. 17,000/- and the other Shs. 23,000/-. The scandal is known to district officials, and to the Project. Yet none of these men have been arrested, and the former secretary of the association has even been appointed as a District Secretary of TAPA (the Tanganyika Parents Association, an affiliated body of TANU). This is the worst example, but the practice of misappropriation is common to virtually all the associations. In fact annual fees are no longer paid regularly in any of the assocations primarily because it has become impossible to persuade members to part with their money when they know very well that it will find its way into the pockets of a few greedy individuals. Besides there is no plan for the productive use of the funds. The main recorded expenditure of the assocations is petty expenses.

The associations have not been able to regulate livestock numbers to the quotas that the rangeland can support. This is because no Maasai will really lend a hand in keeping out the livestock of his kinsmen or neighbours from using water or dips simply because he happens to possess a title. There are two reasons for this. One is the strength of the social ties which supersede any legal regulations originating outside the ethnic group. A Maasai who deprives his neighbours' animals of water is believed to be bound for misfortune, particularly when the issue boils down to a matter of one group of people and their animals living in hardship and deprivation while another is enjoying happiness and abundance that could be shared. The second is the problem of the distribution of animals. It is not easy to achieve a cut in the size of the animal population by 10% when ownership is unevenly distributed, so that some families have hundreds or even thousands while others have a hundred and even far less.

It is difficult to establish the actual distribution in terms of who owns what number. As would be expected the surveys carried out by the experts working for the Project have not attempted to expose the details of animal distribution among families. Besides there is the problem of identifying who actually owns all the animals in a herd; often two or more families combine their animals into one herd; and even within a single family the herd distribution among individual members can be very uneven. Thus when it comes to the reduction of the number of livestock in the ranch, the inevitable question is *who* reduces *what number?* That is a touchy question. The big owners are of course against the idea. Once in 1972 I asked the Chairman of Talamai Ranching Association, who at the time had a herd of 800 cattle, why association members paid annual and membership fees on a flat rate basis since this did not reflect the wealth distribution among the families. He answered, 'it would have been unfair and alien to our custom to do otherwise'. He meant what he was saying. The point is, obviously, that it is not possible to regulate the animal population without hitting the big owners, and to hit the rich stockmen involves shaking the whole social fabric.

In the current stalemate in the development of associations at least one thing is clear, that the range officers and government officials misled the people in their campaigns to sell them the idea of ranching associations, as they went about promising free capital works and services. Consequently, the Maasai have remained ignorant of the actual costs incurred in the provision and running of dips, water projects, etc. Secondly to them the government has not only unlimited political power but also unlimited financial resources. Therefore why should they bother with thoughts of the need to make the investment pay back? In a nutshell they have felt no responsibility to this nation. But is this failure unique to the Maasai? Is it not the general character of a people brought together into a nation by colonialism? Is it not true that there has to be a re-creation of a nation other than by the colonial inheritance? Full answers to these questions would be a long and major digression from the narrow confines of this paper.

To come back to our point, the people have not been educated about their responsibilities and mutualities with the rest of the nation. The prevailing government development approach is actually an investment approach, not at all educative of the people. In actual fact it is opposed to any popular initiative and self-reliance. Knowledge can be gained through practice, the actual grappling with real problems, and not mere chat or speech-making. If responsibility and repayment of government investment in this case meant producing and selling more livestock so as to improve the protein intake of fellow countrymen in areas of low animal protein consumption, do the stockmen in this country know this? Or do they even know that there exists a problem of inadequate protein consumption in large parts of this country? The answers to both questions are categorically no. Secondly, it is indulging in self-deception to talk in terms of the 'national economy' in the case of a country like Tanzania where production is either geared to local subsistence goals or to the external, metropolitan markets of the imperialist world giants.

THE IMPROVED BULLS

Another prestigious preoccupation of the learned, Yankee livestock experts of the Range Project in Maasailand has been the haphazard distribution of improved bulls. Most of these bulls are Mpwapwa type borans. The adventure is considered 'a modest up-grading programme aimed at boosting milk yields and beef production capacity in one and the same animal — the dual purpose beast'. It commenced early in 1971 with free dishing out of an assortment of animals obtained from the Malya and Tanga livestock research stations. As might have been expected, most of the bulls died, having been shipped from research station conditions and dumped in their new habitat at Komolonik or Talamai. Both were, and still are, infested with east coast fever, as disease control facilities are neither adequate nor regularly functioning. Yet in the following five years the experts made hardly any attempt to evaluate the impact of the adventure. Besides, the learned experts embraced the fallacy of the dual purpose animal as the type of beast ideally suited to Maasailand conditions.

Maasai herds are predominantly of the indigenous Tanzanian, short-horn zebu breed. As indicated already the main merits of this animal are sturdiness and adaptability to the prevailing unfavourable livestock production conditions. Its qualities are measured in terms of the ability to trek long distances, survive on meagre feed and little water, and resistance to high temperatures and tropical diseases. These merits must be weighed not only against the demerits of the breed — the small maximum weight and the slow rate of growth — but also against the purpose of production. The breed is ideal only in a subsistence economy — i.e. where low productivity is an accepted norm. One of the binding constraints to raising the breed for a purpose other than subsistence is the low genetic potential for high rates of weight gain and early maturity that are such important elements in high productivity livestock production. This low genetic capacity has decisive implications for any serious livestock development programme capable of sustaining rapid socio-economic transformation in any situation, be it an underdeveloped economy of the Tanzanian type or an already industrialised one.

Contrary to widespread thinking, pastoral people, the Maasai included, are not interested in large cattle herds. Indeed their focus of interest is in the best quality animals attainable. The desire for large numbers is motivated by security reasons, and the poverty of the production conditions limits the realisation of good quality animals. The Maasai try to raise herds which combine high quality in beef and milk production with big size. Thus their preference is for heavily-built, well-muscled and fat castrates. In the case of cows, families with outstanding reputations for milk yield are considered the best.

It is on the basis of features indicative of these dual characteristics, high milk yield and high beef potential, that calves to be raised as breeding bulls are selected at an early age, before castration of the rest begins. But, ignorant of this, the learned livestock experts assumed the stupidity and ineptness of the stockmen. As one of the experts admitted: 'We anticipated that the major considerations in animal desirability would be in morphologically peripheral features which might conform to certain traditional or idiosyncratic concepts of attractiveness: colour, horns, hump, etc'. Thus is was with surprise that they came to realise that these aesthetic features had little meaning, and that the Maasai criteria were correct: 'The Maasai appear to consider the potential of the animal far more important than traditional or personal aesthetic features'.

When the bulls were distributed preference was given to so-called 'progressive' stockmen, most of whom were members of their associations' steering committees, had large herds, and were involved in political and business activities at the extra-association level.

The introduction of exotic bulls can never bring about mass genetic transformation of the Maasai herds. The size of the livestock population in Maasailand alone is large enough to absorb more than the bull output of all the breeding stations in the country producing at their full capacity. The situation becomes even more hopeless when the requirement for bulls to transform herds is viewed on a national scale. For sure, the output of exotic bulls could easily be stepped up. But, obviously, exorbitant financial and skilled manpower resources would be demanded by such an undertaking.

So the only context in which distribution of improved bulls could be viable is for a few selected or pilot projects. Alternatively they could assist in the goal of transforming the whole national herd if they were used for the production of semen for a national artificial insemination programme. But in the ears of the learned livestock development experts, true to their bourgeois confusion in training and commitment, artificial insemination brings technical complexity beyond the comprehension of the peasant livestock owners. As they put it: '(A.I.) . . . is so replete with technical requirements . . . ascertaining when the cow was in heat requires a well trained and experienced technician'. This is absurd. Lack of respect for the knowledge and mental abilities of the broad mass of the people is part and parcel of decadent bourgeois thinking. Where the proletarian ideology is supreme the approach to problems of any specific social situation takes into consideration the whole as well as the parts, and the point of departure is faith in the people. The first task of technicians with regard to this particular issue would be to forge simple easily understood teaching materials, and to use them in mass education programmes. After all, even those experts who came here with preconceived, negative ideas about the Maasai have seen that the knowledge of these people about livestock and their habitat is significant.

It required only a short time for the Maasai to learn from experience the pros and cons of the bulls initially received with enthusiasm. News spread like a prairie fire to the effect that the bulls were not what they had been claimed to be: the pathway to the era of better herds for Maasailand.

Three broad categories of shortcomings were noted by the stockmen. Foremost, the bulls were not strong enough to withstand the rigours of rangeland in which the indigenous zebu stock show such a high capability. Thus the bulls succumbed to long trekking for grass and water; they required more food and water than the local hardy beasts; and the improved stock were particularly susceptible to east coast fever and other diseases.

Secondly, misgivings were expressed over the low servicing capability of the exotic bulls relative to the locals. One man was quoted as saying that while his local bulls mounted about five cows a day in the season, the imbecile exotics barely managed one. Cases were reported of the large alien bulls harming the smaller local heifers while mounting, an occurrence not at all uncommon with the larger Maasai zebu bulls too.

Thirdly, the stockmen expressed their fears that, given dips which were constantly malfunctioning, erratic water supplies, and verterinary assistance far from being available when needed, the probability of survival for the bulls was very low. As it turned out, the loss in the distributions between early 1971 and the end of 1973, involving some 110 bulls, was on average 50%.

These shortcomings were accepted by the livestock experts as all generally valid points. But the experts were still mesmerised by the passivity of the stockmen and their lack of enthusiasm. Yet all except a few of the experts failed to see that this negative state of affairs was a consequence of the working principles they have been brought up with, tutored to follow, and the bourgeois system they work within and belong to. Precisely, the crucial problem was not only that the stockmen had been spoon-fed, but worse still that this had been done to the exclusion of any form of local initiative or self-reliance. So they continued to treat the stockmen as an ignorant and unresponsive lot, simpletons, objects to be acted on.

THE COUNTERPARTS

The functional life and death of the Maasai Range and Livestock Development

Project is founded on the loose sands of the heavy water construction equipment and on a battalion of USAID-financed, US-trained, so-called experts. Though the training programme is not even half-way through, today Maasailand has the largest concentration of skilled livestock and range manpower found in any one region in the country. The revised Project Agreement of 1973 provides for, as well as locally trained certificate and diploma level field officers, 9 US livestock and range management specialists and 30 Tanzanian counterpart officers to be trained in the US. The American task force comprises the Project Manager and a specialist in each of the following: animal production, range management, marketing, veterinary, water engineering, hydrology, heavy equipment and sociology. When the original agreement was signed in 1970 the provision was for 6 Americans and 13 Tanzanians. That committed Tanzania to a salary bill for the Yankees estimated at Shs. 340,000/- annually. The bill is currently about Shs. 500,000/- per annum and rising as a result of salary increments. But this could well turn out a relatively minor loss.

The greatest loss (second only to the destruction of the habitat) is the idleness of the battalion. Prodigious of learning as it is, the range team has become notorious for being idle for most of the time. The morale and work output of most of the Tanzanians working in the Project is poor. It is no exaggeration to say that for the majority of the field officers the focus of interest in working with, or aspiring to join the project, is the scholarships to the US. The Project has become the doorway to the Cowboy Universities of the US.

The idleness of the range officers is conspicuous enough for anybody to see. In Maasailand and Arusha people talk about it openly and widely. Besides, the officers themselves admit it with apparent bitterness and apathy. The inevitable question is how such a state of affairs is possible when there is concentration of such high level know-how face to face with the most challenging problems of their profession.

The men responsible for the state of affairs put the blame on the shortage of vehicles, and on financial bottlenecks arising (they say) from too much politics getting in the way of orderly progress of technical work. The politicians attribute the problem to sabotage by the Americans and laziness together with lack of courage among the Tanzanian learned young men in the project.

To be sure, the primary cause of the problem is the imposition of a development strategy and work organisation which are at variance with the needs of the concrete situation. The development strategy and philosophy of the Project is typically bourgeois. The Project operates on the basis of eight specialist lines. Each specialist American, with his counterparts, is then supposed to spread out his activities and cover the whole length of Maasailand, and produce results. No wonder the problem is made to appear so complex and prodigious. Development will not come without mass mobilisation. No specialist can cover Maasailand in a few years and generate results. Only the Maasai can transform Maasailand in a fraction of ten years. The narrow specialisation on which the Project operates is not only inappropriate to the present stage in the development of Maasailand, it actually acts as a stumbling block to the success of ranching among the people. Presumably the approach is very suitable to US ranching conditions but not to those prevailing in Maasailand.

At our present stage of development the type of personnel needed are broad-minded certificate and diploma level cadres recruited from within Maasailand and equipped with the basic range, livestock and ideological precepts relevant to the transformation of pastoralism. That is, cadres to spur and to mobilise the people to liberate productive forces rather than to seek themselves to administer development on paternalistic lines. These would be participant educators spearheading mass campaigns instead of castigating locals for 'political interference' like the big brothers from the land of cowboys.

The problem of idleness is a product of the work organisation. The nature of the Project operation necessitates the deployment of large numbers of land-rovers or other light vehicles for each officer to be mobile. Without transport the officer is not functional. The Americans have each a Jeep purchased with USAID special funds. Only the Americans are good enough to drive the Jeeps. No Tanzanians, not even the respective counterparts, are allowed to drive the Jeeps. So if the American is for one reason or another not ready to drive, the Jeep will wait for him and to hell with the counterpart who might be desperately in need of means to get to some distant part of Maasailand.

With this structure, each counterpart needs a vehicle to be able to do his work properly. Whether the American or Tanzanian does his work once he is mobile is another question. Arriving by a land-rover gives the range officers a dominance over the elected leaders of the ranching associations, even if the range officers are mere distributors of acaricides and drugs, and convenors of meetings. When they have no dynamic role to play, when their major role is merely administration of the status quo, it is wanton wastage to dish out land-rovers to the associations or to range officers.

While the Americans are given grade A houses and Jeeps irrespective of need, their Tanzanian counterparts, again irrespective of need, are without means of transport and hardly with shelter for their families. That is, having imposed a system of officers with 'officer' expectations, the American system leaves the Tanzanians to grapple with the mess. It does not even solve the problems it creates. The result is bitter disenchantment, apathy and frustration for the counterparts.

Even more revealing is the fact that since 1970 while officers are flying across the continents to New Mexico every year to scoop up B.Sc's, the training of the Maasai herdsmen was not even part of the Project Agreement. Apart from a two-day seminar held at Talamai in April 1972 there has not been any mass education campaign for the stock-owners. The Project, true to its bourgeois grounding, has been relying on a feeble extension system which, as we have seen, is not functional. Consequently even very simple operations, such as minor repairs to dips and water systems, are still done by people from outside the ranching associations who are paid by the Project. Shame upon these experts! What knowledge are they passing on to the Maasai?

The expert/counterpart relationship has no time limit. The usual pattern for a project like this would be for qualified Tanzanians to be heads, overall and depart-mentally. But here the order is reversed. The Project Manager is American, while his counterpart is an experienced and academically qualified field officer who has the extra advantage of knowing the area and the Maasai, himself being a product of *that* society. Why should he be counterpart to the Project Manager, and not the Project Manager? Among the other counterparts too the majority are no less competent than the Americans though they have lower academic qualifications. The primary reason for their being kept subordinate is simply because the Americans are ex-patriates with the mystical 'Dr' label.

Development will remain elusive for us until we throw off the blanket of that inferiority complex that smothers the productive forces and dissipates the spirit of self-reliance, confidence and initiative among us. Just as it does not provide for mass education, the Project Agreement is mute on the question of the phasing out of the American personnel. They are here until the end of the Project and probably intend to remain after. Consequently Tanzanians are expected to remain counterparts to successive teams of confused US bourgeois 'experts'. It is time we learnt the basic dictum concerning knowledge: that knowledge comes from practice, and that more practice generates more knowledge. If our own personnel remain idle and subordinate indefinitely, when will they come to grips with real problems, when will they have the chance to learn through practice?

The ideal kind of assignment for the expatriates would be in marshalling research in their respective fields. It is often claimed that one of our problems is lack of basic information. It is much more a problem of failure to utilise past research findings — just as it is with the glaring failure to learn from past experience in general. Hence repetition of the same mistakes time and again. Research must certainly mean more than sociological and livestock censuses, since these could be left to ranching associations and their cadres once everything no longer depended on the experts — i.e. if the strategy was one of a mass line. Of course it would be wild fantasy to expect the Americans and US trained personnel to follow a mass line. That defines a crucial problem of our situation. Drastic change is necessary, not only in Maasailand but in the country as a whole, away from the confusions inolved in hiring capitalist bodies for the building of socialism.

Our viewpoint is thus that the Tanzanian Project Co-Manager should become the Project Manager, and that all USAID experts should be relieved of administrative work and confined to specialist and advisory functions. Whatever relevant skills they might have could be utilised if they were given specific technical assignments requiring specialised knowledge and advice to assist counterparts in preparing mass educational materials.

Finally there is an urgent need to examine the relevance of the different posts in the Project. In the districts the District Livestock Officer should at the same time be in charge of range management and animal production: thus six posts could be covered by two, one in each district. Secondly, a US trained sociologist is the least desirable adviser, let alone organiser of a development programme directed at socialist transformation. It is only because we are still deeply entangled in cultural confusion that such expatriates can be employed. The post of sociologist is in fact totally unnecessary. What is needed in its place is more co-operation between the livestock development personnel and the Ujamaa and Co-operative Division. This should be re-constituted. To have in such districts a department devoted to co-operatives (which do not include ranching associations) is a glaring illustration of administration rigidity and failure to meet the needs of concrete situations. It would be better to recognise ranching associations as livestock co-operatives.

All the specialists should operate from the Monduli Rural Training Centre. Their functions should centre on three areas. One is feeding the officers stationed in the associations with mass education materials and raising their technical knowledge to cope with problems as the frontiers of production widen. This of course means that they must spend a considerable time in the field face to face with practical problems. Second, it is to undertake research. Third, it is to teach the producers at the Rural Training Centre, transmitting superior livestock production techniques to both the broad masses and to grass-roots cadres. The motto should be that of the FRELIMO militant, Jorge Rebelo, to 'forge simple words which will enter every house like the wind, and fall like red hot embers, on our people's souls'.

UJAMAA VILLAGIZATION AND THE MAASAI

The preceding critique of the Maasai Project leads us to an analysis of the latest attempt by the supreme national agencies of change, the ruling party TANU, and the Government of Tanzania, to bring development to the Maasai by forming them into proper ranching villages in line with the national struggle to villagize the whole rural population.

Ujamaa villagization was adopted as a national policy in 1967. Between then and 1974 the translation of this policy to the pastoral way of life was dominated by the tendency among policy makers and implementors to make these people abandon 'primitive nomadism' and switch to crop agriculture which was to them a system of production superior to livestock raising. 1971 and 1972 in particular witnessed some debate on the issue in the national press. The most significant result of that debate was the acceptance by the supreme national agencies that the development of pastoral societies is possible without turning the people into agriculturalists.

Thus when villagization took a frontal turn the idea of ranching villages was taken up as official policy for predominantly pastoral people. A ranching village was defined as a village whose main commodity was livestock, the implication being that other economic activities are only subsidiary and meant for subsistence. Under this policy, the grazing area available for the livestock of all the individuals in a village would range from 32,000-40,000 hectares, depending on the carrying capacity of the rangeland. The estimated average initial livestock population for a village was 10,000 animal units. Each kraal would consist of three families, and 25-35 kraals, or 75-100 families, would constitute an average village. Initially each family would be allowed to keep no more than 130 animal units — so there would be about 400 animal units per kraal. Ideally the distance between kraals in a village would be half a kilometre, and the kraals would be arranged in a circular or semi-circular layout with village service units such as the school, dispensary, shop, workshop, etc., located at the centre of the circle. The scheme also stipulated that the rangeland should be divided into three parts for the proper utilisation of the pasture. Two of these were the wet and dry season grazing areas, and the third was to be situated near the village centre and set aside for a small herd of milk cows and calves.

Operation Imparnati (permanent settlements) was launched in September 1974 in and around Monduli, and was scheduled to be completed within two years, by which time all the residents of Maasailand would be in villages. By mid-1975 more than 2,000 Maasai were reported to have been moved into ranching villages.

Beyond the drawing board stage, the implementation of the operation was not a mass transformation campaign. It was precisely an 'Operation' — a programme implemented by the government and ruling party officials — and not a systematic programme to enable the people, be they in Maasailand or elsewhere in the country, to undertake their own all-round development. People were collected into villages, without this move being at the same time part of a bigger continuous process of mass mobilisation, education and transformation. There was no overall long-term programme. Thus even those villages like Upper Monduli established nearly three years ago have not embarked on any programme to take them beyond the mere lumping of kraals together. Apparently they have to await the time when everybody else in the district has moved into a village before the next undefined step is taken *by the officials* at the district headquarters. It would not therefore be surprising to find the people moving again as soon as the dry season conditions intensified long before the next step had been taken. The other danger is that one or two years of heavy concentration of livestock could easily damage the rangeland beyond repair. The level of persuasion used has been very crude.

There was little politicization as such, and what was called politicization was in fact sterile argument to the effect that since the government had decided that people should move into villages it was better for them to do this voluntarily rather than risk the use of force. Besides, not all the government employees with essential immediate roles to play were listed in the implementation of the operation. It was, for instance, surprising that range officers were not always utilised when it came to establishing livestock villages in their respective associations. Teams of officials sent from the district headquarters organised and ran the movement of people. In one case, at least, such a team led by an administrative officer went out burning houses and kraals and ordering people to squeeze kraals into a narrow valley in the Loliondo area. The same gang burnt down villages of cultivators in a neighbouring ward. Yet such a gang, whose actions caused ordinary peasants to flee across the border to Kenya, to flee away from ujamaa, is still working for the ujamaa-aspiring Tanzania government. When I suggested to the TANU District Secretary that the party should investigate the circumstances of the harassment and take disciplinary measures against the members of the team, who should be made to apologise to the people who had been so badly mishandled, his reply was that such proceedings would unnecessarily delay the implementation of the operation.

Finally there is gross failure to comprehend the essential need to separate two basic requirements — the need to concentrate human population so as to facilitate the procurement of social services and provide viable units of production and co-operation on the one hand, and on the other the need to spread out the livestock population to safeguard the range-land from the destructive power of large herds, while meantime ensuring full use of the pasture for high quality output. This failure is demonstrated by the tendency to widen the radii of the circle of kraals of the ranching villages. In a number of cases, e.g. Sepeko in Komolonik and Oloirobi and Mokilal in Korongoro, the kraal configuration is linear with the village residential area extending for at least ten kilometres without being fitted into the requirements of any rotational or other grazing pattern. It is important to recall that haphazard establishment of settlements in the case of ujamaa agricultural villages created numerous problems when attempts were later made to plan production and settlement patterns.

In short Operation Imparnati had the potential of being a transformation programme but without remedying the pitfalls outlined above that potential was bound to remain a dream. The courage to dare to admit mistakes and be constantly eager to learn from failures as much as from successes is a cardinal principle of development. This quality, the recognition of the importance of self-criticism and a continuous re-evaluation of one's deeds, is unfortunately too often lacking among, if not actively abhored by, the bureaucracy of the ruling party and Government in our country.

In addition to the frontal attempt to 'organise' the Maasai into ranching villages the government is creating what it has chosen to call ujamaa ranches. One of the eight sub-projects in the national Livestock Development Project (Phase II), financed by the World Bank, is the Ujamaa Corporate Ranch Livestock Credit Project. This sub-project was designed to use ujamaa groups to mobilise the indigenous sub-sistence cattle herd for the market, by injecting capital and extension advice. It stipulated the creation of 100 such ranches in all Tanzania, of which 90 were to be set up among traditional livestock producers formed into ujamaa ranches.

The functional model for the ujamaa ranches is one of a breeding and fattening operation designed to benefit existing cattle owners with significant herds. The choice for such ranches was, according to the World Bank, to create credit-worthy ujamaa villages out of members who own livestock grazed on an individual basis and have inadequate ranching facilities. This was to be done by forming groups of individual livestock owners into *simple* co-operative ujamaa groups. Under this scheme Maasailand, being one of the main ranching areas in the country, was assigned a quota of eight ranches. These ujamaa ranches are being pushed onto the people by the Project and the Regional and District Development Directorates, which in turn are being pressured by the Ministry of Agriculture, which has accepted the loan and now has to ensure that it is used. Talamai Ranching Association, for instance, had applied in 1972 to the Tanzania Rural Development Bank for a loan of Shs. 100,000/- to be used in clearing bush and constructing a dam. But it was later directed to apply for a loan of Shs. 1.54 million for the establishment of an ujamaa ranch.

These ranches could be seen as yet another form of pilot and demonstration ranch, but one which is a great deal more intensive of capital and skilled labour than the pilot ranching associations. They can also be considered as a modified application of Mwalimu Nyerere's proposed method of advance towards ujamaa in the animal husbandry areas:

> Another method of advance is for a number of cattle owners to each contribute one or two head of cattle so as to make a community herd, which is then cared for by modern methods and which perhaps has a reserved grazing area . . . Gradually the improvement of the community herd, and the visible experience of the communal benefits from it, will probably lead them to build up the community herd and reduce the size of their separate cattle ownership.

Quite apart from the problems of poor implementation, there is a basic inherent pitfall in the approach being taken: the fact that livestock ownership among the Maasai is very uneven. This factor alone has two over-bearing implications. One is that a flat rate contribution of stock to the communal herd is unrealistic as it ignores the uneven property distribution. The other is that, given the strength of private property feelings among the people, to let private and communal herds coexist hoping that the latter will outbid the former reveals the utopian basis of the ujamaa brand of socialism. So long as there is herd size differentiation, there is no basis for assuming that the big stock owners will voluntarily opt for ujamaa herds and give up possession of private herds.

The weakness of the whole approach implied by the proposal becomes even more obvious when full consideration is given to the present endeavours to put livestock production in those areas on a cash basis, for once that goal is achieved within the framework of the prevailing social formation, it goes without saying that differentiation of a social class nature will begin to materialise immediately. The most obvious immediate consequences of the ujamaa ranches of that type are thus to distract attention away from the *main herds* and the *uneven distribution* of livestock, and to absorb a large portion of the financial and manpower resources earmarked for investment in the sphere of livestock production. In these respects the ujamaa ranches represent a serious drawback rather than a stimulus to further development.

CONCLUSION

In sum, the riddle of Maasai development has not found the right solution yet. These people have been accused of failing to make use of the opportunites and to respond positively to well-intentioned efforts to put them on a developmental footage. Consequently the situation has appeared to many minds as hopeless and the blame is put on 'pastoral conservatism'.

But rarely have the supreme national agencies of change questioned the relevance of their policies, the nature of the change required, and the appropriateness of the methods of implementation to the specific Maasai situation and its real needs. Indeed the nature of development taking place and its tempo leaves much to be desired. However, despite the shortcomings of the Tanzanian policy, the predicament of the Maasai in this country is far more promising than that of their kin across the border in Kenya. At least in Tanzania differentiation based on social class stratification has not been promoted and the loss of their means of production is less of a real danger.

To be certain, I strongly believe that, though it is not simple arithmetic, the development of the Maasai is far easier than most people imagine. But it rests on certain conditions. Without identifying and observing these conditions Maasai development will remain an elusive problem. The task has been given an image of extraordinary difficulty by irrational and reactionary attitudes, and policies based on the failure to understand these people and to grasp the key threads of development in their specific kind of social order.

Livestock production can be the basis for a thriving economy. But this requires a change in the rationale of production away from subsistence to a wider exchange entity: to a *livestock based economy* rather than pastoralism. Livestock raising by the broad mass of the people need not be automatically associated with pastoralism. It is possible to have a sedentary population whose economic mainstay is livestock production. The crucial condition for this is development of the productive forces in the interest of, and by, the broad mass of the producers themselves. It is a misconception to regard the masses as capable of participation in political power only through the ballot box. The people should not be made to sit back and let the government do whatever it wants. Since the well-being of the people must be the purpose of development, they must take control of the situation by creating their own socialist institutions for local management of the process of production, without being overpowered by the centre's requirements of uniformity. To serve the interests of the people what is necessary is the transformation of the totality of human and production relations, the release of the creativity and consciousness of the masses, and the realisation of the full capacity of each individual member of the society in the interest of social betterment.

CHAPTER 11

The Role of Agencies for Rural Development in Tanzania: A Case Study of the Lushoto Integrated Development Project*

Reuben R. Matango

This paper is an attempt to show the extent to which agencies can promote (or inhibit) the development of rural areas along socialist lines, taking the Lushoto Integrated Development Project (LIDEP) as a case study, and in particular its vegetable production and central marketing.

LUSHOTO DISTRICT

Lushoto District covers the Usambara Mountains in Tanga Region. The district has reached a development crisis. The population density in 1974 was estimated at 77 people per square kilometre, while the population growth rate between 1957 and 1967 was 3.2%. Closer examination of the land situation indicates that the highland areas have an extremely high concentration of population — 123.0 per sq. km. — while the lowlands have only 6.8 per sq. km. There is a shortage of land in the highlands, but the lowlands have too little rain to provide an alternative home. The topsoil in the highlands is easily eroded away. For example, 30,000 acres of forest reserve given to the peasants in 1964 quickly showed a rapid rate of soil erosion and a declining production per acre. Good soils in the area produce 3-4 bags of maize (150-200 kg.) per acre. Mechanisation in the highlands is limited and even the available labour force is underemployed. There are about three men to one hectare of cultivated land, and many men have to go out to seek wage employment in Tanga and Mombasa to earn a living and meet family needs. Malnutrition cases among children are many. Surveys in Bumbuli Division indicated that 77% of the children fell below 90% of standard weight.

This deteriorating situation had been noted long before independence, and the colonial government had introduced some control measures — the Mlalo Rehabilitation Scheme restricting cultivation on mountain slopes, 'forced' terraces on the slopes of the highlands under cultivation, and the planting of wattle trees. These measures were not accepted by the peasants because of the way in which they were introduced to the people. The wattle trees took more than eight years before the peasants could extract the bark for sale; coercion was used in terracing, and there was a move to shift peasants from the highlands to the lowlands leaving more room for white settlers and missionaries in the fertile highlands. The destructive process has continued to the present.

THE BIRTH OF LIDEP

In 1964 a Nutrition Research Unit was set up in Bumbuli, in the compound of a mission hospital. The Max Planck Institute, from West Germany, sponsored and largely financed the unit. A number of nutrition surveys were carried out, and the survey findings prompted the establishment of a school-feeding programme and

*A shortened version of Paper 76.3, Economic Research Bureau, University of Dar es Salaam, 1976.

mobile under-fives clinics in Lushoto. Between August 1967 and August 1968 622 children visited the clinics in Mayo and Funta villages. The school-feeding programme was introduced in the primary school at Mayo, with food supplies from the Catholic Relief Services, and in 1968 this school started a small vegetable garden and poulty raising to supplement the Catholic Relief supplies.

By 1969 the Unit had established further mobile clinics at Soni and Magamba. These activities were making an impact both at the village level and on the international scene, especially in West Germany where Mayo village won a prize of 35,000 Deutschmarks through a propaganda film shot in the village. Meanwhile the project had expanded and needed another financial sponsor if it was to continue the various operations already established in the district.

Kubel Stiftung, a non-profit making company in West Germany, volunteered to sponsor the project, and finance came from other agencies: Bread for the World, the Thysen Foundation, Freedom from Hunger, and the (German) Ministry of Economic Co-operation. On 16 October 1969 an agreement was signed between Kubel Stiftung and the Community Development Trust Fund of Tanzania (CDTF) for a project to embrace a wide range of activities: applied nutritional research, village development through agricultural techniques, vocational and technical training for school leavers, home economics, self-help projects, rural health centres, under-fives clinics for the whole district, pilot projects in marketing, conservation of agricultural produce, cottage industries, and co-operation with other research centres in the country.

The birth of LIDEP must be seen as a result of the success of the research unit, but also of the fact that Lushoto district was posing a serious development challenge. An integrated approach was felt to be necessary, and LIDEP set out to demonstrate it.

THE PROBLEM OF EXPATRIATES

The project proposal clearly pointed out that:

> **for the development of rural areas, technical assistance is of only instrumental value. Progress is achieved only by the mobilisation of the people themselves ... It is aimed to create close co-operation with political local bodies (TANU, UWT, etc.) so that the German assisted projects are understood as Tanzanian undertakings.**

In fact much of what follows here will indicate that there was a problem of acceptance of the project at various stages by the villagers and by government officials at the district level. It took time for the project to be understood as a real Tanzanian undertaking, especially when it came to planning, priority setting, control of financial spending, accountability, and ultimately project policies.

It has to be mentioned too that the various project departments were all manned by expatriates. Hardly any steps were taken, either by the Tanzania government, or CDTF, or the project management, to recruit senior Tanzanians into the project. Between 1964 and 1969 two medical assistants were the most senior Tanzanian personnel, and even when LIDEP came into being no steps were taken to recruit for other departments until 1972. By 1970 the project had 13 departments and 16 different operations going on. It had an internal on-the-job training programme for counterparts, but most of these were primary school leavers. This programme was criticised, on the grounds that when the expatriates left at the end of the agreement, the various sections of LIDEP would collapse because the counterparts lacked the necessary training in management, administration and other relevant disciplines.

This reality did not become clear till 1972 when most of these counterparts were rejected for further training by various institutions (Nairobi Polytechnic, Dar es Salaam Technical College, the College of Business Education in Dar es Salaam and some overseas institutions) on the grounds that they did not have the necessary qualifications. Having been given the hope that they were going to take over from the expatriates and then being told that they did not qualify, all of them resigned from LIDEP.

LIDEP AND THE DISTRICT OFFICIALS

Despite the fact that LIDEP had a Board of Governors appointed by Kubel Stiftung and CDTF and charged with all aspects of policy determination and co-ordination, there were mounting criticisms and hatred directed to LIDEP by district officials and villagers. Twice in 1968 and 1969 the members of the Lushoto District Development and Planning Committee expressed concern over the activities of LIDEP, and complained that they did not know what LIDEP was doing. The LIDEP vegetable groups operating in ujamaa villages were attacked as being anti-socialist, especially in Mayo where vegetable growing was confined to a few individuals in the ujamaa village who chose to do some of their vegetable work on days that were allocated for ujamaa activities and did not contribute to the ujamaa work. The Director for Regional Administration (a senior Dar es Salaam official) had visited Mayo and made comments in the visitors' book to the effect that LIDEP was encouraging individualism rather than promoting socialism. At a Regional Development and Planning Committee meeting held in Mlalo, Lushoto, in September 1970 LIDEP was accused of using ujamaa village trainees as sources of cheap labour in building and other construction works instead of training them. Some of the regional officials saw LIDEP as political dynamite. The Regional Commissioner, when opening the Soni Farmers' Co-operative building, declared that Tanga Region would not tolerate another Ruvuma Development Association,* in the guise of LIDEP.

At the village level there was acceptance in some but not in others. In areas such as Baga, Lwandai, Kongoi, Gare, Malibwi and Msale rumours spread that LIDEP were 'blood-suckers' *(mumiani).* The attendance at under-fives clinics in those areas declined, and the project had to close down four of the clinics.

All these problems were said to have come about because the project was imposed on the district. The government officials there were not consulted about what was being done by LIDEP, and LIDEP's plans were not incorporated in the district's development plans. The leading personnel of LIDEP were expatriates who needed guidance on national policy from local officials. However, the Board of Governors drew most of its members from Dar es Salaam or Tanga, rather than Lushoto, and LIDEP was financially stronger than the district authority with a fleet of 19 vehicles (many more than the district government) and finances to the tune of shs.2,000,000 a year, which led to some of its operations being implemented with capital intensive techniques. In addition, the expatriates in charge — including the Director — found it time-saving to get their plans cleared in Dar es Salaam or Tanga rather than going through all the red tape at the district level (from which most issues would have to be referred to Tanga or Dar es Salaam anyway, because there was no established machinery to co-ordinate LIDEP and district activities).

LIDEP was operating in a district in which there were government ministries carrying out similar tasks. Under these circumstances it was necessary to have all

*An umbrella organisation for several ujamaa villages in the southern region of Ruvuma that was independent of TANU control and was banned in 1969.

LIDEP activities co-ordinated with those run by Government. For instance, LIDEP was involved in horticultural work, as was the Ministry of Agriculture. Water supply for the rural population was also provided by the Water Ministry, by mobile units of the Rural Development Ministry, and by the District Council. Nutrition work was done by the Ministry of Health. Rural training was done by the Rural Development Division, and so on.

The role of LIDEP in this situation could have been to remove the bottlenecks — in particular the financial constraints facing the ministries. But this could be done smoothly only if there was close consultation between the relevant ministries and LIDEP. LIDEP could have responded more actively to the village problems because it did not suffer from red tape as much as the Government.

Some cases will illustrate what co-operation could achieve. The District Medical Officer became a member of the Board of Governors. This was after a series of criticisms levelled against LIDEP's approach to nutrition work. First, powdered milk was being given out indiscriminately, so that mothers were induced to bring the children to the clinics just in order to get the milk. Secondly, LIDEP used to offer annual presents to mothers who had attended the clinics throughout the year. Usually the presents were second-hand clothes donated in Europe for the poor in Africa, popularly known in Lushoto as *kafa Ulaya* (meaning, the clothing distributed is the property of the dead in Europe). Thirdly, the habit of sending children from their homes to nutrition education centres and back every day by land-rover was defeating the whole purpose of educating the parents, as most of them did not feel the need to take their children to the clinics ('it is not our business — the land-rovers can do it'). It was an expensive method which the Government could not afford for the whole district, let alone the whole country. Moreover the re-habilitated children were found malnourished again six months after they were discharged, because their mothers never had the chance to learn what they should do to avoid this abnormality.

When the District Medical Officer was allowed to attend the Board of Governors, and the planning of nutrition activities was co-ordinated, there was increasing co-operation between LIDEP and Health Ministry staff. In some cases they exchanged transport, and were able to exchange staff in some areas. Even when the nutrition activities were taken over by the District in 1974 there were no major problems.

The Rural Development Division was the second to initiate this kind of co-operation when in 1971 the training of primary school leavers was done jointly. Also about 8 water supply projects were done jointly by the mobile construction unit. This co-operation facilitated the rationalisation of resources, since the Rural Development Division had one tipper, one land-rover and three technicians, while LIDEP had one land-rover, one technician and one artisan.

These cases indicate that by planning activities together friction could be reduced and economy exercised. But there were still problems over the spending of funds and over accounting for what had been spent. Thus in 1971 a committee of Government and LIDEP was formed in order to facilitate the flow of information between government ministries and LIDEP and to rationalise the use of expertise through co-operation. This structure also brought the Board of Governors of LIDEP and the District Development and Planning Committee much closer than before, because the Project Director of LIDEP was made a member of the District Development and Planning Committee, while some members of the new committee were members both of the Board of Governors and of the District Development and Planning Committee.

THE NEW FACE OF LIDEP

From 1972 onwards LIDEP experienced a number of changes. Counterparts were appointed: for the Project Director, the Project Administrator, and for the heads of many other departments. A section for Research and Development was headed by a Tanzanian economist, and a training programme was started for all these counterparts.

Political education seminars were conducted for the project workers, following which a TANU sub-branch was opened at LIDEP headquarters. The various committees appointed by the Project Director were dissolved and replaced by Representative Committees whose members were elected. Power was delegated to the Tanzanian personnel to a limited extent. The Staff Assembly became vocal and some of the expatriates' powers were reduced (some expatriates protested because 'you cannot argue with messengers who cannot speak English'). As time went on a number of regulations were amended to bring German and Tanzanian conditions into line.

The project also received a new, German, Project Director who was an economist and who felt that it was time to consolidate the project operations. Systematic planning of every operation, and execution and progress reports in phases were stressed in order to step up efficiency. Duties and responsibilities were distributed between the expatriates and their counterparts, though expatriates still held on to the economic and more technical operations. Then this system was scrapped and the Board introduced a 'partnership system' in which there were Project Co-Directors, Project Co-Administrators, Project Co-Accountants, etc., and it was assumed that each would trust the other and that decisions would be made jointly at each level. While this scheme appeared more reasonable and workable, the sole financier of the project was Kubel Stiftung, and this had implications for the kind of decisions that were made.

The partnership scheme operated for more than a year. But in August 1973 it was abandoned and the Board decided that the German expatriates should now assume an advisory role in all the operations of LIDEP, and the Government of Tanzania contributed a subvention of shs. 2,000,000/-, part of which was used to merge the health section of LIDEP with that of the Ministry of Health. The German Project Director was replaced by a Project Adviser, and a Tanzanian Project Director assumed full responsibility for running the project. The foreign financing of the project was extended up to 1976.

THE SUB-PROJECTS OF LIDEP

Despite the many problems facing LIDEP, much was accomplished. In 1972 the 24 operations of the project were consolidated into 7 major departments with a total budget of shs. 2,400,000/-. These were:

1. **FIELD ACTIVITIES**
   a. the Farmers' Supply Shop selling watering cans, seeds, fertilizers, etc. with a turnover of shs. 30,000/- in 1972.
   b. agricultural extension services — horticultural staff stationed in the villages and advising the peasants on vegetable production.
   c. the Central Marketing Services, with branches in Soni and Dar es Salaam. The Soni branch collected and graded vegetables from the peasants, kept records of their accounts and paid them for vegetables sold. It owned some lorries for transporting the vegetables to Dar es Salaam. The Dar es Salaam branch owned a store and a retail shop and supplied hotels, institutions, and markets with vegetables.

2. SMALL-SCALE INDUSTRIES

a. the garage, where motor vehicles were serviced and repaired, and petrol was sold.
b. the metal workshop, producing buckets, watering cans, water tanks, door hinges, bolts, etc. for local sale.
c. the carpentry section, making doors, windows, chairs, and other furniture.
d. the brickworks, which could produce 50,000 bricks per month.
e. the women's textile shop, which began making knitted sweaters for sale in Lushoto and later changed to making tie-dye materials for sale in Dar es Salaam. Both these activities made losses until in May 1975 the Management of LIDEP decided to send most of the girls back to the villages to train village women, leaving only three people in the shop.

3. RURAL TRAINING

a. the building section — which did most of the construction work for the project.
b. Mabughai Training Centre — which took about 300 peasants a year for short courses in horticulture, animal husbandry, book-keeping, political education, masonry, carpentry, metal-work, etc.
c. 'micro-workshops' set up in 4 ujamaa villages. Students were selected by the villages and after 6-9 months training they were provided with tools valued between shs. 1,000/- and shs. 2,000/-. This was a co-operative effort between LIDEP and the Rural Development Division.

4. MOTHER AND CHILD SERVICES

a. Under-fives clinics. Up to 1 January 1974 when the whole department was taken over, LIDEP had established 24 clinics, out of which 9 were closed down because of rumours of blood-sucking, low attendance, or because they were too close to other clinics.
b. Nutrition Education Centres. There were two of these. As pointed out above, this section had to change its policy. Instead of dealing with malnourished children alone, the mothers too were confined at the centres for 3-6 weeks, learning how to feed their children and prepare cheap but nutritious food.
c. Research Laboratory. This did various tests connected with nutrition, including testing the water supply schemes in the area for contamination.

5. COMMUNITY DEVELOPMENT SERVICES

a. village water supplies
b. improved rural housing
c. women's clubs, where mothers could learn about child-care, sewing and knitting.

6. RESEARCH SERVICES

The research and evaluation unit, headed by a Tanzanian economist, produced piecemeal evaluation reports on the project's components, and on other projects in Lushoto District. There was also a study centre, which was effectively a lodging house for visiting researchers.

7. MANAGEMENT

This section comprised: Administration, Personnel, Finance, Planning, Supplies and Transport, and remained the back-bone of the Project. Besides managing the project sections it co-ordinated the project activities with the outside world.

Despite the problems facing the project, a number of these operations registered successes, and made considerable impact in the district. The penetration to the grass roots level was real. Moreover the constitution of the Board of Governors changed so that now the majority of its membership came from the district.

However, the control question, which the remaining part of this paper will deal with, is neither about whether or not LIDEP has made any impact in the district, nor about whether it has solved its many problems, but about whether LIDEP as an agency for rural development will live up to the aims for which it was started. Will it bring about socialist rural development in the areas where it operations, and can it serve as a model agency so that Tanzania can rely on such agencies to promote socialist goals?

THE VEGETABLE CASE STUDY

The vegetable production and marketing components of LIDEP directly affected a considerable number of peasants. Production was under the guidance of LIDEP extension staff stationed in the villages. 12 of these extension men were trained in horticulture at Marangu YMCA Farm School. In addition there were 6 Japanese volunteers, and a number of peasants who had been selected from LIDEP's production groups and given the necessary training at Mabughai. These later returned to their villages where they were paid wages by LIDEP for their services to the various groups — but they were also leading producers of vegetables, and for a time some of them employed labourers for this work.

The idea was that production should be organised in groups. This simplified record keeping at Soni, because the group rather than the individual was paid for what was sold. It was also felt to be easier to supervise groups rather than scattered individuals. The extension men were the intermediaries between LIDEP and the production groups. Usually the seeds, fertilisers, insecticides and other inputs were channelled through the extension men. Later on as the groups increased in number and the early groups accumulated experience in vegetable production, some of the responsibilities, such as spraying and distribution of seeds, were given to the leaders of the groups. This freed the extension workers to concentrate on new groups which needed more attention. The extension workers were also supposed to show the peasants how to grade their vegetables, but the peasants were reluctant to downgrade their crops, so that much of the grading had to be done at the Central Marketing Section in Soni.

Mabughai Rural Training Centre was planned to train peasants who were brought to the centre for short courses lasting about a week. In a year about 300 peasants went through the centre. However a critical analysis of the centre reveals a number of problems. The centre was electrified, and in the hatchery electric incubators were used. But frequent power cuts resulted in losses as many eggs were spoilt. Peasants interested in poultry keeping would not risk their funds on such a business, and in any case there was no electricity in the villages of Lushoto District. A more appropriate technology would have been to use kerosene incubators. These could have been constructed by LIDEP technicians and kerosene was easily obtainable in almost all village shops.

The Centre had a tractor which cultivated an area less than 90 acres. Again tractor mechanisation was equally inappropriate except in the lowlands where there were large fields. The physical conditions in the highlands do not allow extensive use of tractors, and so most of the vegetable groups or even ujamaa villages in the highlands could not use tractors. But the centre also had cattle, and one would have expected that ox-ploughs be used at the centre, because quite a number of peasants kept cattle. Again, Guatemala grass should have been used as animal feed, since it was grown locally to protect the soil from erosion, instead of processed feed being used at the centre.

The capital intensive techniques used at the Rural Training Centre extended into the field — to the vegetable producing groups. The use of chemical fertilizers was introduced to the groups despite the complications of using them and the expense of the fertilisers. For instance, Joseph Angwazi, in a paper that was highly critical of the impact of Mabughai Rural Training Centre on its trainees, observed that 'one seedling of cauliflower at Lukozi area requires 1kg. of fertilizers' and that this meant that each vegetable producing group in the area would require 4 tons of such fertilizers for its 4,000 seedlings.

In the neighbourhood of Mabughai there were five kulaks engaged in poultry keeping and vegetable production. One could understandably expect the kulaks to use the capital intensive techniques, but they did not. Most of them used cow-dung and chicken droppings to enrich the soils, and Guatemala grass for mulching. Some of them produced tomatoes throughout the year. In fact, beginning in 1975, LIDEP embraced them, to supply her with tomatoes and other vegetables which were needed to meet the tenders obtained in Lushoto, Tanga and Dar es Salaam.

CENTRAL MARKETING

The Central Marketing Section grew from a small unit in 1970 to a large department with branches and offices in Soni, Dar es Salaam and Tanga in 1975. The number of vegetable groups and participants was also increasing. The growth of the business can be clearly seen in Tables 1 and 2. Table 1 also shows how the overheads increased. In 1970 the unit consisted of 7 people and two vehicles, and there were 7 production groups with about 200 participants. In 1974 there were 68 groups with more than 2,460 participants, but the overheads and operational costs had risen from a mere shs. 41,285/50 to shs. 1,675,855/95. Producer prices continued to fall (Table 1). Wastage rose from 5% to 15% (Table 2). Price fluctuations caused some concern too, falling dramatically in every period of over-supply. If LIDEP sold to private traders in the markets, then wastage rose in periods of over-supply. If LIDEP was to stick to its main objective in vegetable extension and marketing services — to socialize vegetable production and ensure fair returns to the peasants — then the only way was for LIDEP to do its own retailing and to win as many tenders to supply vegetables to hotels and institutions as possible. Research by the author in 1972 showed that by far the greatest profit could be made by selling to hotels. But once these contracts were won, LIDEP failed to deliver the vegetables early enough in the morning, and so some of the hotels had to purchase the vegetables elsewhere. In 1974 LIDEP won so many tenders that at times of shortage it could not supply all the vegetables, and so it had to start buying from individual kulak farmers outside its schemes, and in the open markets in Soni and Dar es Salaam, to supply all the standing orders. In the first half of 1975 LIDEP brought from individuals, kulaks and open markets more than 60% of its total requirements. Finally there was the question of mismanagement and corruption. The recording of vegetables sent to Dar es Salaam often did not tally with what actually arrived in Dar es Salaam. It was no wonder that one of the staff members of LIDEP managed to swindle a lot of money, although he was just dismissed from work without being prosecuted. In 1973 four others were sacked for swindling and losing project money.

There were also problems with vehicles. From the second half of 1972 the garage repair work of LIDEP deteriorated. There were also more accidents. Poor repair services meant that vehicles were out of action for long periods waiting for repairs, and meanwhile the Central Marketing Section resorted to hiring private transport which was very costly. The overall result was financial loss, and subsidies rising from shs. 27,000/- in 1970 to shs. 519,500/- in 1974. The basic problem was that overheads rose much faster than peasant production of vegetables.

Why were the peasants not able to produce the required tonnages? This is a question that will be examined later. But we can note that as they increased their vegetable deliveries to LIDEP, their producer prices continued to fall. At the same time the prices of industrial products, fertilisers, consumer items, etc. more than doubled within the period.

TABLE 1

Year	Groups	Participants	LIDEP Personnel		Motor Vehicles		Overheads and Operational Costs (Shs.)
1970	7	200	1	Japanese volunteer supervisor	1	7 ton lorry	41,285.50
			1	part-time book-keeper	1	land-rover	
			3	drivers			
			2	turnboys			
			7	TOTAL	2	TOTAL	
1971	20	1,500	1	supervisor (expatriate)	2	7 ton lorries	18,604
			3	market masters	1	land-rover	(data
			3	drivers		(hired transport)	incomplete)
			2	turnboys			
			1	book-keeper			
			10	TOTAL	3	TOTAL	
1972	64	2,200	5	market masters	2	7 ton lorries	185,129.93
			1	adviser	1	3 ton lorry	
			1	business manager	2	VW Combi	
			7	drivers	1	land-rover pickup	
			13	assistants (textiles)	4	motor cycles	
			27	TOTAL	10	TOTAL	
1973	68	2,436	4	market masters	2	7 ton lorries	878,315.65
			2	market inspectors	1	land-rover	
			2	salesmen	2	VW Combi	
			1	accountant	1	Honda motor cycle.	
			1	training officer			
			7	drivers			
			4	turnboys			
			21	TOTAL	6	TOTAL	
1974	68	2,463	2	market inspectors	3	VW Vans	1,675,855.95
			1	accounts clerk	1	9 ton lorry	
			4	market masters	2	7 ton lorries	
			1	training officer	2	3 ton lorries	
			1	foreman	1	land-rover pickup	
			1	salesman	1	Honda motor cycle.	
			21	TOTAL	10	TOTAL	
1975	63	over 2,500 plus some kulaks	1	business administrator	1	9 ton lorry	1,392,074.10
			1	senior market inspector	2	7 ton lorries	
			2	market inspectors	2	3 ton lorries	
			1	assistant market inspector	3	Combi (VW)	
			6	market masters (1 senior)	1	land-rover	
			1	accountant	1	saloon car	
			1	accounts clerk	1	Honda motor	
			11	drivers		cycle	
			7	turnboys			
			4	labourers			
			35	TOTAL	11	TOTAL	

Source: Compiled from LIDEP reports 1970-1975.

THE USAMBARA AGRICULTURAL CORPORATION

It was the plan to turn the Central Marketing Section of LIDEP into a peasants' vegetable co-operative. But the Co-operative Division of the Ministry was reluctant to allow the formation of such a co-operative because of the history of losses and the 'highly risky' nature of trading in perishables.

The LIDEP Board of Governors therefore decided to transform the Central Marketing Section into a Corporation (the Usambara Agricultural Corporation — UAC) from 1 April 1973. This decision had far-reaching consequences. The Corporation became an independent profit-making organisation, which was not involved in production, but depended on the peasant to produce, and made profits on the peasants' production.

It appeared that the new set-up of U.A.C. provided no room for the peasants to be directly involved in the process of decision-making or planning. The Vegetable Production Group meetings, which used to rotate among the villages, where LIDEP planners and villagers exchanged their ideas, ceased. Another practice which ceased was that whereby the peasants sent one person with the vegetable lorry to Dar es Salaam to be the watchdog when vegetables were en route to the market and to learn more about vegetable marketing. In the past the peasants had been educated and persuaded to take certain decisions, such as an increase in the deductions to pay for the overheads. But now they were not involved. Instead the Board of. Governors sitting in Dar es Salaam decided to increase the charges from 30 cents to 40 cents per kilo delivered, and in December 1974 the charges were increased to 55 cents. A committee consisting of the Area Commissioner, Members of Parliament, the District TANU Chairman, the Marketing Inspector, and the two LIDEP Project Directors was directed to help in implementing the Board's decision by informing the peasants accordingly. And in the second week of December 1974 the Area Commissioner (TANU District Secretary) and the TANU District Chairman declared in a public meeting that all vegetables produced in the district should be marketed through LIDEP.

This announcement came as a surprise, because in August 1973 the same Area Commissioner had issued orders to LIDEP and vegetable groups that LIDEP should only market vegetables produced in ujamaa villages and co-operative vegetable groups. The first announcement was probably aimed at encouraging communal production, one of the first stages towards socialism. The December 1974 directive contradicted the former. The implication was that LIDEP would buy and market everyone's vegetables. That being the case there would be no need for group production because individuals would be equally well served. That would lead to a further development: people with bigger plots of land on which groups worked might decide to do away with the groups and employ people directly to produce more vegetables. In fact the kulaks of Mukuzi and Gare were soon doing so, and LIDEP bought great quantities of vegetables from them.

It is now clear that all these steps were taken to serve the institution's interest in its new set-up, the U.A.C., no longer a tool for socialist construction but a capitalist profit-making body — anti-socialist. Peasants could have no value in such an institution, but the value was in the vegetable products on which U.A.C. had to draw profits to pay for its increasing running costs and the salaries of the ever increasing bureaucracy. LIDEP's vegetable Central Marketing was but one of many institutions started with good intentions, but in the course of development the means to reach the ends became the ends themselves.

Any development depends on the participation of the people, their level of

168

AFRICAN SOCIALISM IN PRACTICE

TABLE 2
Summary of Central Marketing Developments May 1970 to June 1975

Year	Vegetables Delivered (Kg.)	% increase over past	Vegetables Sold (kg.)	Vegetable Proceeds (Shs.)	Selling Price (Shs.)	Producer Price (Shs.)	Total Receipts (Shs.)	Total Deductions (Shs.)	Subsidies (Shs.)	Payments to farmers (Shs.)	Losses (Shs.)	% of Waste
May 1970	Estimated 161,749	–	N.D.A.	163,324	1.0	(75%) 0.75	163,326	41,285	27,000	122,040	–	10
June-Dec. 1971	439,355	171	374,432	372,939	0.99	(63.3%) 0.63	372,939	Data incomplete	83,000	354,335	39,500	15
1972	882,382	100.8	740,520	841,043	1.13	(65.4%) 0.74	841,043	185,043		655,913	64,773	16
1973	978,893	10.9	794,363	985,237	1.24	(57.2%) 0.71	1,021,747	878,316		215,326	April-June 42,174	19
1974	1,544,822	57.8	1,364,473	1,883,062	1.38	(74.6%) 1.03	2,086,317	1,675,856	519,000	1,588,112	388,078	11
Up to June 1975	821,289		699,300	1,428,191	2.04	(60.7%) 1.24	1,511,911	1,392,074		1,020,674		15

Source: LIDEP Vegetable Office, Dar es Salaam.
N.D.A. = No Data Available.

understanding of the issues at stake, the level of technology, resource endowments, and the benefits that the participants get. It was important that peasants discussed the work distribution in ujamaa or co-operative vegetable schemes in order to ensure that vegetables were produced around the year, as well as sufficient food crops. It was education and persuasion that would enable the peasants to increase the sizes of the co-operative plots, and it would be possible to provide this education without much strain by using the Rural Training Centre and the extension men. Education was needed so that the peasants themselves could eliminate the middle-men by refusing their occasional high offers. The peasants were required to be involved in the actual planning and implementation — in short, they should have had a share in the decision-making of U.A.C. The assumption that U.A.C. would represent the peasants might have seemed justified. But it is a profit making institution, and has to make profits in order to survive. The peasants want higher returns for the same produce that U.A.C. wants to makes profits on. Should the peasants discover that they are exploited by an institution created to promote their welfare, they will abandon it.

THE ROLE OF AGENCIES IN SOCIALIST RURAL DEVELOPMENT

The role to be played by agencies for socialist rural development in Tanzania must be seen against the background of the history of Tanzania's underdevelopment. From the historical processes of underdevelopment we can learn the kind of institutions that were purposely created to further the exploiters' interests against those of the underdeveloped people. The structures of those institutions of necessity conformed to the requirements of the exploiters. Thus 'changing their role' can be interpreted either to mean a break-down in promoting the exploiters' interests, or as manifestations of inefficiency which can be remedied through administrative or management techniques within the framework of an exploitative system.

Agencies for socialist rural development would thus be required to have structures that counteract those designed essentially for exploiting. They must of necessity be for promoting socialist social relations of production, mass ownership of the means of production, and equality in the distribution of their socially produced wealth. These agencies cannot be imposed on the people in the rural areas, but must grow among them. In other words the peasants will have to start their own co-operatives or ujamaa enterprises whose organisations should remain peasant based. Then the peasants can command and direct development in the way they feel fit and use the agency as a tool in their own hands. Any inefficiencies in their day-to-day operations can be improved by using socialist-oriented administrative and managerial techniques that stem not from exploiting class institutions but from the exploited mass seeking to liberate itself. We can talk of a peasant development agency, if it is under the control of the peasants. What has been characteristic of most of the institutions in this country, especially those geared for developing the rural areas, is their imposition from above, with their form based on the decadent exploitative systems. At the same time attempts have been made merely to improve their efficiency in performance. But whatever improvements have been made were to make the agencies stand on their own and perform their duties within the old structures, not for the improvement of the masses.

A number of changes have taken place in LIDEP to try and improve the situation. They started after a campaign to increase production on the part of peasants. In turn the increased production called for better marketing facilities and so an increased bureaucracy which as usual increased running costs and salaries even at a time of crop failures. A solution to the question of wastage was not to be found in establishing retail shops, and in fact retail shops raised prices. Thus overall they did not lead to an increase in peasant revenue. These and other problems pose questions of who actually should handle LIDEP affairs? The peasants cannot possibly produce their produce and market it in Dar es Salaam without necessarily creating another unproductive bureaucracy. What kind of institutions can overcome these problems, and, if there is need for any assistance, when should such assistance come in?

What we are attempting to put across here is the fact that Tanzania's problems can neither be analysed and solved through the initiative and goodwill of individuals in positions of power, nor through the actions of a handful of institutions like LIDEP under 'good leadership'. The issue has to be tackled through an analysis of the social formations concerned: the structure of the classes, their economic and political power, and the forces that determine the class struggle.

If LIDEP was a peasant organisation operating under the present economy it would face problems at the national level. At the grassroots, the peasants could manage, given the necessary education of the correct type (for their own liberation), to handle many activities and so reduce some of the unnecessary costs which the LIDEP bureaucracy has spawned. Collection and grading of vegetables, transportation, recording and even delivering vegetables to Dar es Salaam or Tanga could be done through a peasant organisation. The organisation could pay allowances more than those paid at present, when the peasants' surplus is used to pay for the allowances and salaries of many personnel of LIDEP.

However, if the economic system remains as it is, then the problem of inflation imported from capitalist economies would hit the peasants, as they need consumer items, plus agricultural inputs and other capital goods which would have to be paid for at exploitative prices.

An overhauling of the entire economic system and disengagement from the monopoly capitalist economies would bring the final solution. Some discussions have tended to suggest that the destruction of the entire bureaucracy in this country can automatically end the prevailing system. This view can be misleading if other factors are not taken into consideration. The present bureaucracy is the product of the social formation in this country and so the destruction of the bureaucracy would have to go along with the destruction of the dominant class with its ideology. Another class in its place is needed — call it the proletariat and peasants — who must create another bureaucracy. But what type of bureaucracy?

Certainly the new leadership must have a proletarian ideology, and the base of the new structure must be made up of workers in alliance with peasants. The new leadership then would work consciously to create new social relations of production. In this situation it is highly likely (though not automatic) that the class struggle against the exploiters and the agents of monopoly capitalism or imperialism would be waged by the workers and peasants rather than by the petty bourgeoisie. The latter certainly fought for and won independence, but they do not see anything wrong with capitalism, and so now they fight to get rid of foreigners in order to give room to themselves to exploit their own people by becoming the agents of international monopoly capital. These agents cannot fight for a national democratic development since this would involve a class struggle. Instead they use an ideology that calls for national unity between all conflicting classes, and the mode of production remains that which the colonialists created. Thus all the existing institutions and the entire bureaucracy conform to capitalist institutions — for it is to them they turn for the capital, technology, management skills, and much else. It is from there that the present bureaucracy gets its base, and not from the peasants and workers at home.

Thus LIDEP was started by a German foundation. While one can safely say that the German institution was not making profits through LIDEP directly, we should not underestimate the political influence the project has had in both Tanzania and West Germany. Several German-aided projects have mushroomed in Tanga Region and it cannot be disputed that LIDEP's influence is great. Some of these projects are profit making, such as the Tanga Fertilizer Company which has continually made losses on the Tanzanian side while the Germans profit from the venture. Other German-aided projects in the region include: the Handeni Trunk Main (a water supply scheme for Chanika), the honey and beeswax project in Handeni, construction of new classrooms and teachers' quarters in the region, construction and repair of feeder roads in Handeni, and the expansion of a jetty at Tanga port. All these are financed by the West German Government, or foundations, companies, and religious organisations in West Germany.

Thus LIDEP's organisation and structures did not conform to the peasants' needs. Right from its inception the peasant's rejection of the institution was regis- tered in various forms: in the clinics, vegetable marketing, and even in the rural water supply where in Funta village the water scheme 'proved abortive because of lack of communication between the water expert, who was a German . . . and because he ignored the advice of the people and chose a source which did not yield enough water'. In expressing their anger the peasants 'dismantled and destroyed part of it in protest against the high-handedness of the German expert'.

On the other hand, water projects, schools and dispensaries are among the important services that people need most, and there should be no dispute over their construction. The peasants would volunteer to contribute their labour freely once they felt the projects contributed directly to their well-being. Only when the role of the people is ignored can protests be expected.

From the start LIDEP experienced a rejection not only from the village level, but from district officials. In the end the bureaucrats were won over and incorporated into the project. For the peasants, only some operations have made a real contri- bution, while others have been marginal, and the U.A.C. has turned out to be an exploiter. The district bureaucracy then resorted to coercive measures. They conditioned the Lushoto vegetable producers to either accept exploitation through their agency or to go back to the middlemen.

This action of the bureaucracy against the peasantry is not new. The bureaucrats believe that they have the best solutions to the problems of the poverty stricken peasants. But at the same time one fails to see how the bureaucracy can reconcile 'the strain between the organisation's needs (which are bureaucratic) and the participant's needs (mass needs)'. This reconciliation is not easy in these exploi- tative organisations. An easy way out is for the bureaucracy to insist on increased production and productivity first, and then to promise participation and equality later on. Then the bureaucrats do not have to wait until that later time when equality is to come.

Reconciliation between opposing class interests is not possible. It would there- fore be the responsibility of socialist-oriented governments to create new systems in which the people themselves can create their own agencies for development. As President Nyerere puts it:

Development depends primarily on the efforts and hard work of our own people and their

enthusiasm and belief that they and their country will benefit from whatever they do. How could anyone expect this enthusiasm and hard work to be forthcoming if the masses see that a few individuals in the society get very rich and live in great comfort, while the majority continue apparently forever in abject poverty?

The central question in present-day Tanzania is whether the required increase in output should overshadow the aim of socialist equality.

CONCLUSION

Some of LIDEP's activities in Lushoto District have made an impact. Others have not. It might be possible to reorganise the various economic units so that they make profits and so justify their existence and continuity in receiving government subsidies. It might be possible for LIDEP to be fully accepted at the district level, especially with a Tanzanian face to its leadership. But one thing remains clear. LIDEP, wherever it has been, or will be, able to bring changes in the rural areas, they are directed by the institution. The peasants will not in any way, under the present structure, use LIDEP (or U.A.C.) as a tool for their own development. Finally, it is not LIDEP alone; most of the other institutions in rural Tanzania also imply that in one way or another the rural population is the loser.

The only truly socialist development agency, that was for the peasants' interests, was the Ruvuma Development Association. It was not imposed but was started in 1959 by the people themselves and slowly grew, establishing branches and an administration that was peasant based. The association had grown from a single village to 18 villages at the time when it was destroyed by TANU in 1969. For the brief period that it existed, it managed to establish its own schools, cottage industries, grinding mills, flour mill, brick-making unit, saw mill, spinning and weaving workshops, soap factory and many other activities all geared to an integrated rural development approach, based on self-reliance. But members of the bureaucracy felt that the R.D.A. was political dynamite which had to be defused before it exploded.

Part III

PARASTATALS AND ECONOMIC MANAGEMENT

CHAPTER 12

The Silo Project*

Andrew Coulson

HISTORY OF THE PROJECT

In 1965 SIDA (the Swedish International Development Agency) at the request of the Tanzania Government sent an agronomist, Mr Sven Gesslein, to 'examine the storage and pest problem on the ground, and to advise us on our requirements'.[1] His report was dated May 19th 1966, and when discussing grain storage and handling it noted that 'very little *labour saving* had been introduced and that even in the Moshi/Arusha area bulk handling was seen only as a possibility for the very distant future'. (emphasis added).

SIDA suggested to the Tanzanian Government that it would be prepared to pay for a more detailed investigation. The result was the Agriconsult Report[2] presented in early 1967 which stated at the outset that the purpose of the proposals put forward was *to introduce modern techniques of grain handling into the country.* The report recommended 'modern silos' for Arusha, Dodoma, Iringa and Dar es Salaam, and after a brief discussion of local storage concluded that there was no major problem locally and that, for the short periods before the grain was taken to central stores, tarpaulin covers and fences could serve as well as godowns, and at much lower cost.

After some pressure from SIDA the Tanzanian Government in September 1967 submitted a formal request for SIDA to finance two of the four silos in accordance with the consultant's specifications. SIDA, however, unexpectedly announced that the Agriconsult Report was not a satisfactory document on which to base a project, and offered Swedish money for another consultancy.

The new consultants, K-Konsult, reported in December 1968.[3] Their terms of reference in 1968 specifically mentioned that modern silos should form part of the project, and thus they were not required to consider whether silos were or were not the best form of grain storage for Tanzania.

K-Konsult returned in February 1969 and produced another report[4] which recommended additional facilities and yet more mechanisation at the silo sites. A project agreement was signed in July 1969 with the following items:

4 silos, total capacity 47,000 tons	T.Shs. 22m/-
40 small godowns, total capacity 16,000 tons	T.Shs. 4m/-
11 grade 'A' houses	T.Shs. 2m/-
Consultancies and Technical Assistance	T.Shs. 5m/-
Unallocated balance	T.Shs. 6m/-
Total	T.Shs. 39m/-

In March 1970 it was strongly opposed by the National Agricultural Products

*An extended version is in the *IDS Bulletin,* Vol.X, No.1, (1978).

Board (NAPB), the body responsible for implementing the project, in the following terms:

In spite of the whole project being considered not viable by both the Management and the Executive Committee of the Board the possibilities of stopping its execution are at present negligible and what remains is for the Board to put its reservations on record.[5]

NAPB's main objections were:

1. From their point of view the project was very costly. In particular since the Treasury intended to charge the NAPB a semi-commercial rate of interest on the whole loan, NAPB's storage costs would rise sharply and they warned that this would mean lower prices of maize for the farmers. (Note: In view of what is said below about the rate of return of the project, this prediction must be regarded as correct).

2. It would require many highly trained experts and mechanics to run the equipment, and there could be problems with spares and maintenance even then. The project would be a break in NAPB's tradition of self-reliance.

3. It would imply too much centralisation of storage facilities, thereby increasing transport costs.

4. NAPB disagreed with some of the figures of wastage used by the consultants, and drew attention to the improvements that could easily be made to the present system.

These objections by the parastatal supposedly in charge of the project were never answered.

Detailed planning and design work started. However when in late 1970 tenders were called for, it was found that they were far in excess of the consultants' figures, 100% in excess in the case of the machinery. K-Konsult had based their figures on European prices plus transport costs. The firms involved wanted much more than this. In conventional terms K-Konsult failed to predict the prices correctly — but objectively it might be fairer to blame the whole system of foreign aid tendering. When K-Konsult were called back by SIDA, in January 1971, to justify their 'mistake', they explained that they had not realised that some prices were different from the Swedish prices![6] They then proposed to increase the size of their silos to bring down the unit costs!

After some uncertainty (by this time very determined lobbies in both the Swedish and the Tanzanian camps were questioning the whole project), it was decided to remove one silo and increase the sizes of the other three.

More design work followed, but when more tenders were called in November 1971 no local contractor tendered on time, but one local (non-citizen Asian) contractor tendered late. In order to allow him to be considered, SIDA insisted on a retendering, which took place in March 1972. The contract was then awarded to this contractor.

ECONOMIC ANALYSIS

As described above, the choice of technique (i.e. silos, and within the many types of silos that could have been chosen, concrete silos) was made in 1967. The 1967 Agriconsult Report was rejected by SIDA but its conclusions that silos were economic was built into the terms of reference of all succeeding reports.

The cost/benefit analysis of the 1967 report was, however, attacked (demolished might be a better word) by an economist who worked on the SIDA files in Stockholm. It was also queried by economists in the relevant Tanzanian Ministries.

The most careful analysis was made by the Swedish economist, who managed to divide the benefits of the project into those resulting from the silos and those from the local godowns. He concluded:

1. That using the consultants' own assumptions, the rate of return on the local godowns was 22%, while the rate of return on the silos was only 5%.
2. That if the technical assistance programme and the senior staff housing (mostly for expatriates) was included in the cash flow then the rates of return fell to 14% for the godowns and 1% for the silos.
3. That making some improvements to the consultants' assumptions about the silos, the rate of return can be put at 'somewhere less than 5%'.
4. The SIDA economist then argued that since K-Konsult had themselves assumed that the silos would be used for short-term storage and that godowns would continue to be used for long-term storage, there would be few gains from using silos for long-term storage. This view was confirmed by K-Konsult's study of long-term storage costs in 1971.[7]
5. He then considered the side-effects of the project, and showed that they were all negative. In particular he calculated that 400 jobs would be lost through having bulk handling rather than sacks and godowns. He recalculated the rate of return using a shadow wage, and found that it was just below zero.

These calculations were worked out with K-Konsult's figures from before the cost escalations were known. If the cost escalations are included the rates of return from the silos fall even more.

From these figures the conclusion is inescapable. The silos should not have been built, and if more storage facilities were needed they should have been built in the form of godowns, whose technology was simple and well-known. This would have been both self-reliant and economic.

WHY WAS THE PROJECT NOT REJECTED?

One wonders how the project came to be implemented when the case against it was so strong. The following might shed some light on this:

1. In the early consultancies SIDA regarded itself as providing a service to Tanzania in recruiting consultants, but it regarded these consultants as Tanzanian consultants and not Swedish ones. Tanzania, on the other hand, regarded the consultants as Swedish consultants whose advice could only be questioned at the risk of upsetting the Swedes. The consultants were consequently left with almost complete freedom of action.
2. In Tanzania there was no one with professional knowledge of silos. At the time of the 1968 report the economists in the Ministry of Agriculture were busy and did not have time to study the K-Konsult report in detail before it was accepted. When the weaknesses in the economic analysis were discovered in January 1971 they were disbelieved by the senior civil servants who argued that the economics must have been approved earlier.
3. The various Swedish consultants and experts failed to produce usable documents. The Agriconsult Report was simply rejected, and the K-Konsult report

was so far out with its figures that it became discredited. The consultants never managed to adapt to Tanzanian conditions. Admittedly Sweden had little previous experience in tropical storage. Her 'experts' therefore prescribed the kind of storage that were accumstomed to build in Sweden (at about the same time Swedish architects designed and built in Tanzania, houses that would have been more appropriate in Sweden). They forgot that the rationale for the only techniques they knew was the shortage of labour in Sweden and the high wages. When K-Konsult's engineers realised their freedom they increased the amount of machinery.

4. On the Tanzanian side the project was dominated by a philosophy of *modernisation.* It was thought that the silos were the latest and most modern form of storage, and therefore would be appropriate for Tanzania in its efforts to catch up in the technological race. This led to a feeling on the part of the Minister of Agriculture that 'silos were right'. Since silos were 'modern' it was very hard for anyone to oppose them and all sorts of specious arguments were used to defend what was really an emotive attitude: 'the consultants had recommended it, it must be right'; 'there have already been more than enough feasibility studies'; 'now is the time for action, no more delays'; 'the silos might not be economic now, but surely one day they would become so'; and — decisively — 'the Swedes will be upset if it was cancelled now'. These arguments were used by people who had not considered the counter-arguments, or who had themselves been involved in the initial negotiations with the Swedes. Many were simply too busy to welcome another complicated problem.

5. The opposition to the project from the NAPB was ignored throughout. It was largely neutralised by support from another parastatal, the National Milling Corporation. (NMC stood to gain from the silos since they would ease the problems of feeding their mills. This saving in transport from godown to mill is one of the few benefits of the project and under the existing cost structure it would have accrued to the NMC rather than NAPB). NAPB eventually came to take a fatalistic attitude from which they argued that the Government had forced this project on them, and who were they to dispute it? In a four page NAPB supplement in the Dar es Salaam *Standard* of 23 February 1972 there is not one reference to the silos, but the following sad comment on storage:

> **To date the Board's total storage capacity of 175,300 tons has been created with finances solely from its own domestic saving without having to resort to any external financial help. This is in line with our policy of self-reliance.**

NOTES

1. S. Gesslein, *Some facts about the Cultivation and Storage of Grain and Oil Plants in Tanzania,* (SIDA, May 1966).
2. Agriconsult, *Survey of Storage and Handling of Foodgrains and Other Crops in Tanzania,* January 1967.
3. K-Konsult, *Foodgrain Storage in Tanzania,* December 1968.
4. K-Konsult, *Appendix to Appraisal Report,* 1969.
5. NAPB Executive Committee Paper No.374/70, 1970.
6. *Result of a Mission to Tanzania,* 18th-27th February 1971.
7. *Op.cit.*

CHAPTER 13

The Automated Bread Factory

Andrew Coulson

The major grain milling companies in Tanzania were nationalised in 1967, and early in 1968 the National Milling Corporation was set up to manage them. President Nyerere appointed J.K. Chande as General Manager. Chande was a Tanzanian Asian, linked by marriage to the Madhvani family, who had built up the second largest grain milling company in the country (the largest company, Tanganyika Millers, was a subsidiary of a Nairobi company). His appointment was one of the few occasions in which the Government used Asian business experience to run a nationalised industry.

The suggestion that NMC should extend its operations from milling wheat to baking that same wheat into bread was formally proposed to the NMC Board in February 1969. The project was not included in the list of National Milling Corporation projects in the Second Five Year Plan, but in the Annual Report of the Corporation for 1968/69 Chande reported that the Corporation was planning 'a fully automatic bakery to cost around 5,000,000/- . . .which, when completed by the middle of 1971 will take the Corporation a step further in its decision to make further inroads into the food processing industry'. Preliminary estimates for a bakery to produce 100,000 loaves a day (or its equivalent in cakes, rolls, etc.) had been made by a Nairobi consultant, and by August 1969 the Tanzanian Government was approaching the Government of the Netherlands to get aid for it.

The Netherlands Government was not sympathetic, and the next donor to be approached was the Canadian International Development Agency (CIDA). A condition of Canadian Aid was that a Canadian consultant should be appointed, and so Angus Butler Engineering Co. of Alberta, Canada, was appointed 'prime consultant' for 'all technical and engineering aspects of the design and construction' and 'to supervise implementation and act as agents in obtaining machinery and equipment'. By September 1970 Angus Butler engineers had spent a few days in Nairobi and Dar es Salaam and produced a feasibility study under which machinery for the bakery would cost shs. 5.5m/- and the bakery as a whole shs. 11m/-.

It was not till August 1971 that a loan agreement was signed in which the Canadian Government lent the Tanzanian Government $1 million (about shs. 7m/-) to cover foreign exchange costs of the bakery. The local costs were to be paid by Tanzania. In the same month, August 1971, Mr Zacharia of NMC and a Mr Warner (a Nairobi baker who acted as consultant for NMC) visited Canada and discussed the project with the only manufacturer of large-scale bakery equipment in Canada. Under the conditions of Canadian aid it was necessary for a Canadian company to supply the equipment. It became clear that $1m would be insufficient for the foreign exchange costs of the project, and this was confirmed when the formal tender from this company, Baker Perkins Ltd., was opened in November 1971 and came to $1,046,421. Since the loan was also supposed to cover the consultants' fees ($170,000), the figure of $1,000,000 agreed only three months previously was already insufficient.

The financial arrangements, involving an extra $350,000 Canadian loan, were completed by the middle of 1972, and it was expected that the bakery would start production before the end of 1974, with capital costs as follows:

Buildings	T/Shs. 4,267,000/-
Furniture and fittings	60,000/-
Machinery and equipment (including freight and insurance)	7,848,000/-
Erection costs	540,000/-
Flour silos	250,000/-
Vehicles	500,000/-
Design costs	
Local (15% of 4,267,000/-)	640,000/-
Canadian ($170,000/-)	1,275,000/-
Contingencies	420,000/-
Total:	T/Shs. 15,800,000/-

Thus the July 1969 figure of shs. 5m/- had multiplied more than three times within 24 months.

The project was already being criticised. A feature article in the *Nationalist* of 31 January 1972 accused it of reducing employment and undermining other national goals, and the Tanzania Investment Bank feasibility study, produced in late 1972, confirmed many details of the *Nationalist* report. By April 1975 the bakery was still not operational, its cost had reached at least shs. 17,000,000/-, and the project was being quoted in Dar es Salaam as an example of inappropriate technology.

WHAT IS WRONG WITH THIS BAKERY?
Firstly, a grossly disproportionate amount was spent on the machinery. Quotations obtained by Indcentre (a United Nations project in Dar es Salaam which carried out industrial feasibility studies) showed that semi-automatic bakery equipment with an equivalent capacity from West Germany or from Japan could have been obtained for between shs. 4m/- and 5m/- for about half the Baker Perkins' price.

Secondly, the bakery buildings were designed more for conditions in Alberta, Canada, than for Dar es Salaam, Tanzania. The roof, a reinforced concrete structure, is supported by concrete beams, sixteen across from side to side of the building and three running along its length. A complicated system of fans and vents is needed to remove excess heat from the oven and other parts of the process. In contrast to this, other bakeries in Dar es Salaam have simply a sturdy concrete foundation, and a high roof over the ovens in which the air can circulate. Such a structure would have cost a small fraction of the cost of the present building.

Thirdly, the design costs were exorbitant. The inappropriateness of both the buildings and the equipment is partly a consequence of the choice by Tanzania of Canadian aid for this project. In fact if costs of such projects as this are to be controlled, this can only be done by keeping close control over the design and consultancy. In this case control was lacking. The Tanzania Investment Bank report comments on the cost increases: 'the situation was one where the consultants (Angus Butler) were in another continent with easier access to information from the manufacturer/supplier (Baker Perkins) than from the client (NMC)'. Angus Butler received $120,000 fees, plus $50,000 travelling expenses, and the TIB report commented that, 'this adds up to 7.5% of the project total — a very high relation taking into account that most of the building design work was done through a local design team under Messrs. French and Hastings of Dar es Salaam'. This local design team was paid 14% of the cost of the buildings (15% if out of pocket expenses are included), and yet their drawings were based on plans and directives from Angus Butler in Canada. The TIB commented on the 15% that 'this figure is unusually high, and is a reflection of insufficient cost control in the planning of the project'.

WAS THERE AN ALTERNATIVE?

Much simpler machinery could have been used. In 1972 Indcentre produced a study of a small bakery designed for Tanzanian conditions. It was mechanised rather than semi-automatic, but it would still produce a high quality bread (the *best* quality bread in Europe is to this day produced by small mechanised units, and even with European wage rates many of these still compete successfully with the products of the large automated factories). In the Indcentre design each plant would have produced 10,000 units a day, and cost just over half a million shillings. Ten units of this sort would have had the same production as the Canadian bakery. Some of the advantages of ten small bakeries over one large one would have been as follows:

1. Less capital investment — shs. 5.5m/- instead of shs. 15.8m/- and the new bakeries could have been built as demand rose, so that not all the shs. 5.5m/- would have been needed at the start.

2. 320 people would have been employed in 10 places scattered around Dar es Salaam instead of only 60 people in one place, but the 10 small bakeries would have been as profitable as the one larger one.

3. The small bakeries would not have been vulnerable to breakdowns. The large bakery has only one oven, and a complicated electronic control system. Many spare parts can only be made in Canada. If there is a breakdown Dar es Salaam's bread supply will be totally disrupted; while a breakdown in one of many small bakeries would simply have meant increased production by the others.

4. The large bakery makes Tanzania dependent on a Canadian machinery supplier to provide spare parts and the expertise to maintain the machinery. It thus continues the colonial process, and further *integrates* Tanzania into the world capitalist system. Since small-scale bakery equipment could in principle have been manufactured in Tanzania, the project takes Tanzania further away from self-reliance.

SHOULD THERE HAVE BEEN ANY NEW BAKERY?

The criticisms discussed above all assume that Tanzania needed some sort of new bakery. But that assumption has been questioned.

A study by Indcentre showed that in 1967 the six largest bakeries in Dar es Salaam produced about 40,000 units of bread a day with a total fixed investment of less than shs. 2.5m/- and employment of just over 200 people. Between 1967 and 1972 these bakeries more than doubled their output at no cost to the Government and at very limited cost to themselves. There was no reason to think that they could not have maintained this expansion if the demand for bread had continued to rise. The investment in the automated bread factory was therefore inessential, to say the least.

Another alternative would have been for the Government to have taken steps to limit the expansion of bread consumption by raising the price of bread. Since wheat flour is much more expensive than maize flour, bread is (despite its obvious convenience value) a luxury food. Even worse, while Tanzania will very shortly again be self-sufficient in maize production, there is little likelihood of her being self-sufficient in wheat production within the next ten years. At present about half Tanzania's wheat is imported, and the TIB experts who studied the agricultural projections concluded that local wheat production *might* grow as fast as wheat consumption — in which case about half Tanzania's wheat consumption would continue to be imported. Since about 80% of the cost of a loaf of bread is the cost of the wheat, the foreign exchange implications of continuing consumption of bread are considerable.

WHO HAS BENEFITED?

The project had such obvious objections, and it was publicly attacked so early, that it is necessary to find an explanation of why it still went ahead.

The Canadian interests involved clearly gained. Baker Perkins sold machinery that could have been purchased elsewhere for half the price. Angus Butler received a large fee for their consultancy. Canadian Aid have been criticised for supporting the project, but Canada has been one of the world's largest exporters of wheat and could be expected to support a project that would enlarge the world demand for wheat.

It is also not difficult to see why Chande and the National Milling Corporation were enthusiastic about the project. Integration forward from milling into baking has been common in capitalist countries — because it gives milling firms control over their main users of flour, who otherwise might decide to buy their flour from some other miller. This would have been logical in Dar es Salaam before nationalisation. After nationalisation, NMC was making money, and under pressure to find new investments in food processing. Bread baking was obviously highly profitable, so it is hardly surprising that the idea was revived.

Once the project was chosen it is not hard to see why the most modern (and most automated) technique was chosen. Chande is a businessman who believes in modern methods. He chose an equally automated technique for the NMC animal feeds plant when foreign aid was not even involved. But if foreign aid was available he could argue that the most modern technique was bound to be profitable — and he would probably put more weight on this intuitive argument than on the actual profitability calculations. Profitability calculations would depend very much on prices, and at the time the studies were done the prices were such that bread baking was inherently profitable. But Chande could argue that whatever happened to prices his bakery would be efficient, and therefore able to produce as cheaply or more cheaply than other bakeries, and if need be undersell them. (This was actually asserted in some of the earlier studies which talked of a bread production cost of only 60 cents a loaf). If foreign aid was available it would hardly matter what the capital cost was, since the capital repayment could be spread out over the life of the project. From a businessman's point of view there is some logic in all this.

But what of the Tanzanian Government and its various institutions? Surely these would argue against such a project? The Ministry of Agriculture was aware of the high relative cost of Canadian machinery from an early stage. The Ministry of Commerce and Industry might have been expected to protest against the loss of jobs, the Treasury and the banks to argue against the mis-use of Canadian Aid, and the Ministry of Planning to oppose yet another industrial project in Dar es Salaam and one that would involve greater dependence and make self-reliance in the baking industry impossible for years to come. None of these bodies ever effectively opposed the project. And when for a time the Canadian Government itself raised questions about the project, they supported it, and so made sure that it still went ahead.

To understand this the first thing to note is that the power to decide what to do about the project was in the hands of a small group of busy people. These were the members of the National Milling Corporation Board of Directors. At the time of the final decision to go ahead they were joined by the Tanzania Investment Bank Board of Directors, because staff of that Bank wrote a feasibility study which raised most of the criticisms discussed in this paper, and the Bank had to consider this feasibility study in order to approve the arranagements for on-lending the Canadian money.

The NMC Board of Directors consisted of 8 people only. It included the Principal Secretaries of the Ministries of Agriculture, Commerce and Industry, and Planning. J.K. Chande as General Manager was in attendance. At least three members of the TIB Board were members or ex-members of the NMC Board, with J.K. Chande a member of the TIB Board in his own right.

When initially the Principal Secretaries (in their capacity as NMC Board members) had approved the project, they had effectively committed their ministries, since it would prove difficult for civil servants within the ministries to take action without the approval of their Principal Secretaries. When, too late, the project was criticised by the TIB study, the decision taken was not to cancel the project. By then, the problems of cancelling probably seemed greater than the problems of going on.

It is unlikely that either of these Boards would have particularly welcomed the idea of ten small bakeries instead of one large one. Ten units scattered around Dar es Salaam would have been much more difficult to control than one large factory. (Similar logic has favoured a few very large sugar plantations instead of many small ones, large-scale factory production of shoes and clothes instead of small workshops, and large-scale production of wheat using tractors instead of small-scale production using oxen — a few of the many examples of this tendency that could have been mentioned). Perhaps the bakery is just the almost inevitable product of a system of state capitalism in which a ruling bureaucratic bourgeoisie has more interest in securing control over production than in efficient production, and more interest in attracting foreign aid than in developing grass-roots self-reliance.

CHAPTER 14

Tanzania's Fertilizer Factory[1]

Andrew Coulson

An underdeveloped country wishing to establish a fertiliser industry ought surely to begin by examining the locally available raw materials. In Tanzania, for example, a report in 1961 drew attention to an anhydrite depost at Kilwa which could have been used to produce cement, gypsum, and sulphuric acid.[2] The latter if combined with ammonia from the oil refinery would have given ammonium sulphate, the fertiliser most commonly used in Tanzania. The report also noted three deposits from which phosphatic fertiliser could have been made. However, the development of these local resources was rejected on the ground that for plants of an efficient size the local market would not be able to absorb all the fertilisers.

After independence, the strategy of the first five-year plan, published in 1964, was import substitution. So the National Development Corporation (NDC) began to think in terms of a factory with a variety of chemical processes that would produce the relatively small quantities of several of the most commonly used fertilisers which were then being imported into Tanzania.

Specifically the proposed plant would make sulphuric acid from sulphur — which would be used to make phosphoric acid and hence super-phosphates from phosphate rock — and ammonium sulphate when combined with liquid ammonia. Potassium salts and nitric acid would not be manufactured, although the plant would contain facilities to produce NPK compound fertilisers. All the raw materials would be imported: sulphur, phosphate rock, liquid ammonia, nitric acid, and potassium sulphate. But the plant would produce and sell to the local market, and was therefore presented as an import substitution project.

It was argued that the minimum efficient size of such a plant would be such that it could produce 100,000 tons of fertilisers per annum, although in 1966 a total of only 30,000 tons was imported. However, the following year the NDC carried out a study which concluded — on the basis of research station data and discussions with individuals — that the consumption of fertilisers would rise at an exponential rate of more than 20 per cent per annum compound interest to reach 80,000 tons in 1971, the earliest date at which a factory could be opened, and 105,000 tons in 1972.

These projections were questionable. Peasant farmers in Tanzania have been reluctant to use fertilisers, often for good reasons. On fertile land, with low standards of husbandry, they often do not give an economic response since sufficient nutrients are already present, while in very dry seasons or areas the fertilisers are unable to stimulate plant growth due to lack of moisture in the soil. Moreover, the use of these purchased inputs increases the element of risk: if farmers borrow money to buy fertilisers and the harvest fails, then they remain in debt. It is also important to note that local varieties of seeds (especially of food crops) have been bred over centuries to resist drought, and not to take up fertilisers. Thus, in most areas of Tanzania, the economic use of fertilisers requires new seeds, such as hybrid or composite maize. It also demands higher standards of husbandry — planting at the right time, regular removal of the weeds which are also stimulated by the fertilisers, sufficient density of plants per acre, etc.

The proposal was sent to 22 international chemical companies and to the Dar es Salaam embassies of several socialist countries. Only two firms — one French, one German — were willing to produce compound fertilisers, including Kloeckner Industries Anlagen GmbH, a member of the Kloeckner-Humbold-Deutz group, which had already proposed an ammonium sulphate plant in May 1967. This German company now offered to make a small equity investment and to establish the required factory, as well as to organise a medium-term supplier's credit to cover most of the capital cost, and to sign a management agreement to operate the plant for at least five years. As the NDC had requested, the project was a 'turn-key' offer, and was quickly accepted.

Kloeckner was a large company, producing a wide range of chemicals and chemical machinery, and was well qualified to be the technical partner for the NDC. It was argued in Dar es Salaam that if anything went wrong the reputation of a world-famous firm would suffer, and that this would provide an incentive to design and run the plant well. The contract contained the clause that 'Kloeckner will select the most modern processes corresponding with the latest technical development in the chemical industry, taking into consideration the objective conditions prevailing in Tanzania', and it has been argued that this gave the firm the power to supply virtually any equipment they liked.[3] Certainly the turn-key offer put a lot of power into the hands of the German company. It meant that there was no competition in the normal sense of the word for items of equipment, and that no outside technical advice would be taken on the details of the plant.

The Kloeckner proposal was valued at 78 million Deutschmarks, and was to be financed as follows in Tanzanian Shillings:

Equity:	NDC	60%	15 million
	Kloeckner	40%	10 million
Suppliers' credit:	Kloeckner		93 million
			118 million
	add Bank overdraft		20 million
			138 million

Since the 93 million shs. loan was guaranteed, and because the profit on the sale of the machinery would presumably be more than 10 million shs., the company did not risk anything in the investment. If, on the other hand, the project succeeded, it would own 40 per cent of the equity, and so be entitled to 40 per cent of the profits.

Perhaps this explains why Kloeckner was content with a 30-page 'feasibility study' and 20 pages of tables to evaluate a project worth 138 million shs. The NDC's own study was about the same length, and considered the project entirely from the Corporation's point of view, rather than the nation as a whole. Thus, for example, since it was assumed that the government would provide, and not charge for, certain infrastructure, notably housing and water supplies, the cost of this was not included in the analysis. The interest on the external loan was included *less* the tax that the NDC could claim back on it, a procedure which did not reflect the real cost to the country.

This cash flow of private costs and returns were discounted and found to yield an internal rate of return of 9 per cent. No allowance was made for risk, and there was no discussion of the sensitivity of this rate of return to possible changes in any of the variables, several of which were inevitably very uncertain, particularly the prices of raw materials and the estimates of the demand for fertilisers.[4]

No serious economist could have approced these procedures, and no business-man would have invested on the strength of the figures and projections shown. But the National Development Corporation went ahead. The project agreement was signed by the Chairman, Paul Bomani, and the General Manager, George Kahama, in February 1968, before it had been considered by the Board, which was presented with the document in April, and given less than a week to decide whether or not to ratify it.[5]

The Kloeckner proposal was for a factory to produce annually 45,000 tons of compound fertilisers, 25,000 tons of triple super-phosphate, 20,000 tons of ammonium sulphate, and 15,000 tons of di-ammonium phosphate, thereby making a total of 105,000 tons. But to do so required 167,000 tons of imported raw materials per annum, namely: rock phosphate, 110,000 tons; sulphur, 30,000 tons; sulphate of potash, 15,000 tons; and liquid ammonia, 12,000 tons. According to the 1968 feasibility study these would cost 54 per cent of the value of the output. In addition, packing materials and small quantities of boron, oil, sodium hydroxide, and vanadium catalyst would have to be imported, and these raised the figure to no less than 64 per cent. The only inputs to be produced locally were water, electricity, and the sand used to slightly dilute some of the products.

The automatic continuous flow processes were the same as those that would be found in a similar-sized plant in Europe, which meant that operating the factory was largely reduced to watching dials and carrying out maintenance procedures. However, it is not clear that there would have been any appreciable advantage in less automation, at least as far as the production of sulphuric acid and phosphoric acid was concerned, although there might have been a case for simpler technology in some of the ancillary processes, such as grinding and compounding.

Problems became apparent remarkably quickly. The rate of interest on the 93 million shs. long-term loan was fixed at 3 per cent above the discount rate of the *Deutsche Bundesbank* which in 1968 was also 3 per cent, so that an overall figure of 6 per cent was used in the appraisal. But in 1969 the discount rate started to rise, and eventually stabilised around 7 per cent, which meant that Tanzania had to pay 10 per cent. This was hardly a 'soft' loan, and indeed if the extra interest had been included in the feasibility study it would have reduced the rate of return almost to zero. Moreover, the loan was to be repaid in the German currency, so that every time the D.M. increased in valued against the dollar, more shillings were needed to repay a given sum. Since one D.M. changed for 1.76 Tanzanian shs. in 1968, and for 3.08 shs. in May 1975, the extra cost was in the order of more than US$8 million.

More fundamental difficulties were created when the government unexpectedly decided in August 1968 that the proposed site next to the oil refinery in Dar es Salaam harbour would not be available. The fertiliser factory needed 50 acres to allow for expansion into ammonia and sulphur from refinery gases, gypsum recovery, and the eventual production of nitric acid, as well as other parts of a chemical industry — for example, plastics. Several of these developments also demanded a site next to the oil refinery, which could have supplied steam to start-up the sulphuric acid process and to operate the phosphoric acid plant in the event of a stoppage.[6] Moreover, the jetty and pipeline for the oil refinery could have been adapted to off-load the raw materials for the fertiliser factory, and to pick up cooling water from the sea. The harbour area was also most convenient as regards communications, with connections to the Chinese-financed Tazara railway, as well as to the central line.[7]

Eventually a new site was found in Tanga, although it was not until September 1969 that the NDC obtained the right of occupancy. The move necessitated facilities being built to land raw materials (including liquid ammonia at -33°C) and to take up sea water for cooling. The East African Harbours Corporation showed no interest in any new construction while Tanga port remained under-utilised, and the government eventually allowed the NDC to commission its own consultant. The design for a new jetty cost 1.8 million shs., and when the tenders were opened in April 1970 the lowest was for just over 40 million shs. No financing for this had been arranged; in fact the Treasury had not even seen the feasibility study before the NDC went to tender. This was serious, since it was arguable that if more use had been made of the existing Tanga port, then a much simpler jetty (or just a pipeline on piles) would have been sufficient. But to re-design would have meant another delay, so the jetty was approved. Eventually about three-quarters of the cost was paid for with loans from the governments of West Germany and the Netherlands.

The construction and installation of the fertiliser plant was substantially complete by May 1971, but the jetty was not ready until December. When the plant was 'run' the cement pipeline bringing the cooling water from the jetty burst — in the rush to build, this had not been designed for the correct pressure. So the damaged pipes were replaced, the operating pressure was reduced, and a safety valve installed. The factory began to function in April 1972, but due to the time it had stood idle after completion there were several leaking connections, and corrosion in the phosphoric acid plant had to be rectified.

For much of the period of delay an expensive staff had been maintained at Tanga able to do little or no productive work. Also the first instalment on the machinery loan had had to be repaid. For these reasons, additional costs of 32 million shs. were incurred before the plant started earning income. At 31 December 1972 the total NDC investment in the company was 201 million shs. — compared with 138 million shs. in the feasibility study — and in addition the government had spent nearly 42 million shs. on the jetty.

The feasibility study had expected that less than 200 would be employed initially, at a cost of about 1 million shs. per annum. By 1972 there were some 400 workers, of whom 40 were expatriates, costing about 6 million shs. By March the following year 637 were employed, of which 44 were expatriates, and in 1974 the annual salary bill for the total staff of 733 was nearly 12 million shs. — 12 times the original estimate.

There were many other difficulties. The Tanga town water-supply was increasingly unreliable — for example, 56 days of production were lost from this cause when the plant was shut down on three occasions in 1973 — and the water problem was not solved until the factory drilled its own borehole the following year. The Middle East war interrupted phosphate supplies, forcing the factory to close down completely for a period, and leading to rapid price rises. Moreover, along with the oil crisis the price of liquid ammonia increased astronomically.[8]

Finally, the factory had the greatest difficulty in distributing its products. The intention had been to use the railway, but the problem was to get return loads for the wagons which otherwise tended to pile up at distant places, waiting to be sent back empty to Tanga. It was also hard to supply Southern Tanzania, since this meant using lorries from Mikumi at a cost per mile which was approximately three times as expensive as rail transport.

The result of all these problems was that the factory operated well below its designed capacity which ranged from 90,000 to 105,000 metric tons of fertilisers, according to the mix. The actual production was only 13,500 tons in 1972, 33,000 tons in 1973, and 66,500 tons in 1974. With its overheads too high, and with the prices of raw materials rising, the company was bound to lose money unless it could pass its costs on to the farmers. But the fertiliser prices were set by the Economic Committee of the Cabinet only once a year and often with delays, so it was a slow and difficult process to get an increase approved. Moreover, the Ministry of Agriculture and the Tanzania Rural Development Bank, who were the main purchasers, naturally tried to prevent or delay any climb in prices.

Although prices did rise fast, they were unable to stop the company reporting losses of 21 million shs. in 1972 and 29.9 million shs. in 1973. By 1974 the Government had conceded that prices would be a mark-up over costs — much higher prices were approved, and the management began to talk about 'breaking even'. The following figures show the rise in ex-factory prices by the Tanzanian Fertiliser Company:

T.shs. per metric ton

Product	Feasibility Study, 1968	1972	1973	1974	1975	1976
NPK	700	850	990	1,859	2,754	2,754
TSP	683	830	967	2,154	3,018	3,018
DAP	870	1,075	1,243	2,835	n.a.	n.a.
AS	329	425	512	1,394	2,041	2,041

Source: Tanzania Fertiliser Company records and statements.

Between 1969 and 1971, fertilisers were purchased by international tender for less than the cost of production at the Tanga plant. However, by 1972 the TFC had been given a monopoly which enabled the company to undercut the imported prices, albeit at a reported loss of 21 million shs. that year. By 1975, imports could be made more cheaply than the fertilisers produced at Tanga: NPK could be imported for 1,750 shs. per metric ton, TSP for 1,600 shs., and AS for 650 shs.

A better indication of the financial problems of the TFC is probably the size of its overdraft at the National Bank of Commerce which was 64.8 million shs. at the end of 1972, and no less than 178 million shs. in May 1975. So the Bank and the purchasers of the fertilisers were paying for the factory. The situation was full of paradox. Fertilisers had always been a questionable investment as regards maize — except for improved varieties — and rice, and the price now became so high that they were hardly economic on tea or cotton. At this point the government stepped in with a support programme costing 122 million shs. per annum to enable the fertilisers to be used by farmers with the help of a large subsidy. The demand for the 1975-6 season was then put as high as 150,000 tons (*Daily News,* 12 January 1975), partly to be financed from World Bank loans and the rest from parastatal surpluses and taxation.

There is evidence that both the NDC and the government are today more careful about the small print in the agreements they sign with foreign companies. But there are some further important implications for Tanzania and other African countries that can be learnt from this study. The first is that a factory producing for a local market cannot be allowed to depend on imported inputs, especially if these form a high proportion of the total costs. The people's needs must be met, as far as possible, from local resources. In the case of fertilisers, this might mean making more use of natural manure, and local raw materials, as outlined in the 1961 report.

More broadly, every country must have an industrial strategy, and the following are just some of the factors which would have been clear if the production of fertilisers had been part of such an overall plan in Tanzania:

— The factory would have been put near the oil refinery so that it could use the waste gases and steam.

— The production of cement would have been developed at Kilwa so that sulphuric acid could have been produced there too.

— The manufacture of sulphuric acid would have been on a sufficient scale to supply all other uses of this basic industrial chemical, including — for example — the tanneries and paper-making mills.

— The mining of local phosphate would have been recognised as essential.

— The importance of transport would have been realised, and the siting of the petro-chemical complex would have taken this into account.

— The development of industry and agriculture would have been planned *together* so that local available natural fertilisers would have been used where possible. Artificial products to meet real (and not imagined) local needs should have been identified by the farmers themselves, rather than by research stations.

In short, industrial projects have to fit together so that the sum is more than the parts, and without an overall plan this cannot happen. The fertiliser factory in Tanzania illustrates what can go wrong.

NOTES

1. This is an up-dated version of a case-study which appeared in *Maji Maji* (Dar es Salaam), XII, 1972, the first published account of a partnership venture between the National Development Corporation and a multinational company in Tanzania. It is reprinted, with permission, from *Journal of Modern African Studies*, Vol.XX, No.X, 1977.
2. Arthur D. Little, Inc., *Tanganyika Industrial Development*, (Boston and Dar es Salaam, 1961).
3. Kloeckner has replied to this criticism that the technological choices were explicit in the equipment list which was part of the contract. But the fact remains that no one in Tanzania queried this list, so that in practice the decision on what technology to use was passed to the company.
4. This point was made as early as 1968 by Z. Dobrska, 'Criteria for Public Investment in Manufacturing: five Tanzanian case studies', Economic Research Bureau, University of Dar es Salaam, Paper 68.25, pp.53-65.
5. Knud Erik Svendsen, 'Decision-Making in the National Development Corporation', in Lionel Cliffe and John S. Saul (eds.), *Socialism in Tanzania: an interdisciplinary reader*, Vol.II, *Policies* (Nairobi, 1973), p.95.

   In November 1968 a separate contract for operating and managing the factory was signed between the NDC and a subsidiary of the main German firm, namely Kloeckner-Humbold-Deutz-Chemie-Anlagenbau GmbH. A lump sum of D.M. 225,000 was paid before the factory started, and thereafter annually 4 per cent of the profits after depreciation but before tax was deducted, up to a maximum of D.M. 600,000. But even if the factory lost money, the Kloeckner expatriates would get their salaries and allowances, and the subsidiary firm would get D.M. 300,000.
6. The failure to install a supplementary boiler to provide steam was one of several technical weaknesses at the plant identified by the National Industrial Development Corporation consultants from India early in 1975. It was made even more necessary by the fact that

only 1,400 tons of sulphuric acid could be stored, so that if the plant for phosphoric acid stopped, then the production of sulphuric acid also had to halt once its tanks were filled.

7. The original site became a naval base which could have been placed elsewhere. Retrospectively, it is clear that the NDC should have cancelled the whole project if they had really tried hard and failed to get the Cabinet to agree to the harbour location. It is obvious that, at least initially, there could only be one petro-chemical complex in Tanzania, and that logically the fertiliser factory should have been built next to the already constructed refinery in Dar es Salaam.

8. In 1974 the c.i.f. prices at Tanga in US$ per metric ton were as follows: rock phosphate, 86; sulphur, 100; sulphate of potash, 197; and liquid ammonia, 450. The feasibility study of 1968 had been based on the figures of 19, 27, 57, and 50 US$ respectively.

CHAPTER 15

Transfer Pricing: The Issue for Tanzania

L. LeVan Hall*

A 'transfer price' is defined in a standard accountancy text-book as:

The price charged by one segment of an organisation for a product or service which it supplies to another segment of the same organisation.

This definition and much of the discussion related to transfer prices emphasises the importance of such prices in evaluating separately two or more of the branches, divisions or subsidiaries of a company within which goods can be transferred at arbitrarily set or managed prices.

While it is a real concern for evaluating companies in developed countries, it becomes impelling for developing countries to see how transfer pricing applies to goods purchased and/or sold between countries in which subsidiaries of a single parent operate. A gross loss to one country can in fact result from managed transfer prices. In addition we must consider not only the possibility of a gross loss in absolute terms but also the possibility of the loss of a country's foreign exchange. The use of managed prices can virtually obviate any country's attempt to conserve scarce foreign reserves.

Were an enterprise to purchase all goods or services (particularly raw materials) from independent suppliers (independent in the sense that there were no owner-ship or management linkages of any sort) then it would be expected that, with the buyer and seller each striving to maximise his advantage, the price paid (or received) for goods or services would be the optimum that each participant could obtain. In such a case only the skill of the negotiators would have a bearing on the result. The issue of transfer prices, even narrowly stated as in the first definition, would be irrelevant, since both parties to the transaction would be assumed to be independent and attempting to maximise the benefit to their individual firms.

However where the two parties are not independent and where the overall purchasing (flow of materials) is centralised for the maximum benefit of a specific corporate group, the issue of the price at which goods should be transferred from one subsidiary to another becomes very relevant.

THE RATIONALE FOR PRICE MANAGEMENT

A decision to manage prices, and thereby profits, by a firm depends upon a number of factors:

a. the degree of control over subsidiaries exercised by central management;
b. the differing taxation structures in various countries of operation;
c. laws or restrictions applicable to the repatriation of profits in different countries;
d. the actual percentage of ownership held by the parent company in each subsidiary;

*Formerly of the Institute of Finance Management, Dar es Salaam.

e. future political/economic changes expected in different environments in which subsidiaries are located;

f. the degree and sophistication of surveillance practised in differing countries;

g. differing exchange control restrictions.

a. **Control.** Control can mean either legal control (ownership of more than 50% of the shares) or effective control, through management by individuals with loyalties to a parent company. Where effective and legal control of both ends of the seller-purchaser transaction rests with one parent the ability to manage prices is greatest. Management control is the most crucial here and, in practice, usually held by the parent. Decisions at a policy and senior operating level are inevitably made by senior management, not shareholders, if only because the information and knowledge bias rests with the former group. Thus senior management control of a firm allows for the maximum opportunity to manage prices between firms in differing countries.

b. **Taxation.** Since the objective of any group of firms under one parent is to maximise the group's profit, this must imply the minimization of the sum of each individual subsidiary company's corporate taxation, charges, levies, etc. Thus there is an obvious reward in minimising taxable income in a country where the definition of taxable income is less liberal, and/or the rates of taxation are higher, and transferring these profits to another less stringent environment (a 'tax haven'). One method of accomplishing this goal is to simply transfer raw materials from a low taxation environment at high sales prices to the manufacturer (or next processing stage) in the higher taxation environment. Since this transaction, between subsidiaries of the same parent, is, by definition, not independent, market prices or competitive prices would not apply and actual prices could be substantially lower. The effect is to reduce income, and so taxation, in the higher taxation environment and increase income in the lower taxation environment.

c. **Repatriation of Profits.** A factor that complements taxation rates is the ability of the parent company to repatriate, i.e. withdraw to the parent, funds from a particular environment, through dividends.

In a period of dwindling foreign exchange reserves many countries so affected have enacted legislation to limit both the amount of dividend declarations and the timing of withdrawals by foreign owners or partners. While in the short term such limitations often can be accommodated (see the case of Lonhro, in *African Development,* March 1974), in the longer term the necessity of parent global investment policies, especially the need for growth, demands tangible returns, in the form of cash dividends from existing subsidiaries for investment in other projects. Where two companies or divisions operating in different countries have a purchaser-supplier relationship and are controlled by the same parent through either management or part or whole ownership, the objective would be to maximise profit in the country where the fewest restrictions on repatriation exist. The company might even choose to forego a slight benefit from lower corporate taxes if it could transfer its funds to an environment where the size of legally allowable dividend repatriation was greater.

d. **Ownership.** The percentage of ownership held by the parent company in subsidiaries or associated firms in different countries, or even in the same country, is another factor to be taken into account. Where the parent owns a larger percentage in one of two equally profitable firms, the emphasis would be to manage transfer prices to benefit that firm in which the larger percentage ownership exists. This factor would, of course, be balanced against other factors such as the effective taxation rate and ease of repatriation of profits. Here the gap in ownership — that is, the percentage difference of ownership between the two or more subsidiaries — would often be the most critical factor.

e. **Political/Economic Environment.** Since the intention of any business firm is to maximise profits, in the short or long term, the degree of political/economic stability ('stability' used here to denote favourable treatment of non-resident business firms) is a major influence on parent company plans for utilising pricing policies to manage profits. Where the long term prospects for continued majority or substantial minority ownership and, more important, for management continuity and control, are judged poor, in Tanzania for instance, the incentive to emphasise short-term profit transfers, by managing prices, is very real. The justification for this behaviour by management is the need in a limited time span to recover the original capital invested and to make a return on it in the form of profits. Conversely, where the long term prospects of its subsidiaries are more promising from the parent firm's point of view, for example in Kenya, a more leisurely pace in profit stripping can be undertaken. Obviously this area is a matter of judgement on the part of management and is open to serious mistakes in judgement or timing (as in Cuba, Chile (temporarily), Mozambique, etc).

f. **Evasion of Exchange Restrictions.** Although not normally included in transfer pricing discussions, exchange restrictions often serve as a major impetus for manipulation of prices of goods entering the country. Here collusion is essential, for prior agreement must have been reached between the supplier outside Tanzania and purchaser in the country. Basically these two parties to a contract agree to 'over-invoice' goods (usually capital goods). Thus a larger sum of foreign exchange is expended than is necessary, the additional sum over the normal price being divided among the participants *in a previously agreed upon manner.* An example of this type of price manipulation arose in 1974 where machinery ordered by a parastatal was inspected for price and quantity by the General Superintendence Company and found to be of inadequate quality, given its previously stated purpose, and in addition was invoiced to Tanzania at Shs. 9.0 million, which was Shs. 5.5 million greater than the price of comparable equipment available elsewhere. In this particular case the explanation could have been ignorance as much as deliberate manipulation. However the loss to Tanzania, should this type of transaction go undiscovered, is the same.

Summary. All of the previously outlined factors are considered by parent company managements when deciding whether to manipulate profits through transfer prices between subsidiaries in different countries. No one factor, in itself, is necessarily conclusive. The significance and importance attached by management to these related but different factors will depend upon the company structure, its management, the objectives of the parent, the products or services involved, host environment, etc.

Certainly price and profit management is a fact of life and is practised by most if not all multinational firms to varying degrees. This price management is largely justified on the basis of 'effective international financial management'. Consequently the efforts of host countries must be concentrated so as to minimise the negative effect of this form of profit management. Later on we review some possibilities in that direction.

THE IMPACT

Developing countries have great difficulty in assessing a valid net cost/benefit of multinational company operations, or for that matter any foreign investment. More specifically the host country seeks to ensure that the long term fund outflows, in the form of repatriated profits, etc., do not exceed the actual initial fund inflows and/or the value of technical and mangerial skills received. However, their concerns are often with the net outflow in terms of dividend remittances, product royalties and management/technical fees, while largely ignoring the more insidious and less visible form of fund outflows, namely the manipulation of sales and raw material prices. The United Nations in their booklet entitled *Multinational Corporations in World Development* discuss in some depth the *cost* of foreign investment in developing countries. While determination of the extent of fund transfer through pricing is difficult to ascertain, it is certainly significant. The few studies available suggest that company transfers abroad in the form of transfer pricing far exceed all other forms of benefits — dividends, remittances, royalties, product/service and management or technical fees — accruing to multinationals in developing countries.

If such a situation does exist, then it follows that where significant economic activity is carried on by multinationals the costs of such activities to the countries concerned may very well exceed the benefits received from such participation.

THE TANZANIAN SITUATION

Tanzania has professed to be developing a socialist political and economic system. Since the Arusha Declaration in 1967, significant steps have been taken to bring previously privately owned companies under the ownership control of government or government created agencies, in particular, under the National Development Corporation. In addition, heavy government equity participation in industrial enterprises formed in Tanzania has been the practice since 1967. Despite this encouraging first step towards control of the industrial sector, *effective* control remains with the management of the firms, and localisation has done little to change this.

The majority of large industrial concerns in Tanzania (in 1975) remain with expatriate management, and in many cases expatriate management seconded or employed by a minority, private, shareholder. The result has been to leave effective managerial control in the hands of the foreign parent corporations despite the surface appearance of control by the government. Companies in this group would include:

Williamson Diamonds (De Beers)
General Tyre E.A. Ltd. (General Tyre International Ltd., USA).
Tanganyika Extract Co. (Mitchell-Cotts)
Tanganyika Instant Coffee Co. (Nestle)
National Radio Co. (Hitachi)
Philips Electronics Co.
B.A.T. (Tanzania) Ltd. (British American Tobacco)
Tanzania Breweries Ltd. (East African Breweries Ltd.)
Metal Box (T) Ltd. (Metal Box UK)
Tanzania Fertilizer Co. Ltd. (Kloeckner Industries Analagen, West Germany)
Mwanza Textiles Ltd. (Sodefra, France)
Sunguratex (Local)

Coca-Cola Ltd. (Coca-Cola International)
Agip (Agip International, Italy)
Tanzania Tanneries Ltd. (Ehrnberg, Sweden)
Tanzania Portland Cement (Cementia Holding A.G., Switzerland)
Blanket Manufacturers Ltd. (Maruki & Co.)
Kilimanjaro Textile Corp. Ltd. (Miscellaneous small shareholdings)
Tanzania Distilleries Ltd. (Gilbeys, UK)
Tanita Co. Ltd. (Oltremare, Italy)
Tanzania Diamond Cutting Co. Ltd. (N. Zallman, Belgium)
Mwananchi Tractor and Vehicle Assemblers Ltd. (Lonhro, UK)
National Bicycle Co. (Atlas, India)

The foregoing represent only a partial list of companies where either the management has been directly seconded from a minority or majority shareholder, or conditions exist where the company management's major allegiance is to the minority shareholders external to Tanzania (e.g. Tanzania Portland Cement).

Although some of these companies did not import raw materials they did export a finished or semi-finished product on which export price management could in fact take place. Local examples of suspected or actual manipulation of prices were numerous; however, three examples will illustrate the issues. These examples cover a range of price or price related activities and include:

i. raw material import price adjustments;
ii. maintenance of foreign exchange outside the control of the country;
iii. primary product transfer to an external firm for obtaining the majority of value added.

1. **Metal Box Co. (T) Ltd.** This was jointly owned (50% each) by Metal Box, UK and the Tanzanian Government (NDC). Utilising the raw material, tin plate, imported through the parent company (Metal Box, UK), this company manufactures tin cans etc. for various firms in Tanzania such as the National Cashew Co. Ltd., Tanganyika Meat Packers Ltd., etc. At various times in the past, sources of tin plate have been scarce, and as the volume consumed by Metal Box Co (T) Ltd. is small by world standards, the purchasing of this raw material has been channelled through Metal Box, UK. Due to their participation in, and ownership of, plants worldwide, Metal Box, UK is able to secure adequate supplies and also obtain quantity discounts. For this service, Metal Box Co. (T) Ltd. pays the parent 5% of the f.o.b. price. However, when General Superintendence Company, a worldwide import/export inspection firm, was employed by the Bank of Tanzania in November 1972 for import inspection, they ascertained that, whereas Metal Box, UK received a 10% quantity discount on price from their Japanese suppliers, neither this discount, nor any part thereof was remitted to Metal Box Co. (T) Ltd. The net result was that Metal Box, UK were receiving an effective commission of 15% of the value of raw materials purchased on behalf of Metal Box Co. (T) Ltd., approximately shs. 25 million in any one year. At existing levels of production, the commission would be shs. 3.7m. This amount could be compared to the amount of dividends declared in the same year of shs. 2m, of which Metal Box UK's share after withholding tax would be approximately shs. 0.9m.

2. **Tanganyika Extract Co. Ltd. (TECO).** TECO was jointly owned by Mitchell Cotts International (51%) and the Tanzania Government (49% NDC). This company owned a plant at Arusha, which extracted liquid pyrethrum (used as an insecticide) from pyrethrum flowers for sale to overseas markets. In fact, the majority was sold

to Mitchell Cotts, UK for further processing in the UK. Mitchell Cotts operated worldwide with a large percentage of the pyrethrum extract they procured coming from their plants in South America. Since Mitchell Cotts International controlled an estimated 60% of the world market for pyrethrum, their ability to affect the world price was substantial. The plant at Arusha has operated at between 40% and 70% of capacity during its existence owing primarily to lack of flowers produced in Tanzania.

During the period 1970 to 1973 the price of pyrethrum on the world market dropped perceptibly as a result of the introduction of synthetics. However, it was also true that significant capital in the form of deposits and debtor balances were due to TECO by non-residents of Tanzania. According to Mitchell Cotts, this was because of lack of payment by overseas (UK) purchasers. During this period Kenya had opted for their own marketing board as a result of dissatisfaction with the prices being obtained by Mitchell Cotts. A possible conclusion here is that these significant balances (approximately shs. 8m in 1973) were being held pending possible changes in Tanzania's policy with regard to the export of pyrethrum and the ownership of TECO — economic blackmail!

3. **Tanzania Tanneries Co. Ltd.** This company was jointly owned by Erhnberg, Sweden (25%) and the Tanzania Government (75%). Originally started in 1968, the intention of the company was to process hides and skins, a significant Tanzanian natural resource, to finished or semi-finished state. It is essential to understand that the value added in this industry rises very rapidly as the hide or skin becomes leather and then, of course, shoes, bags, etc. It would seem that Tanzania, with an existing shoe industry, could in fact process many of its hides to the leather stage and, with effective marketing, perhaps seek overseas markets for leather not used locally. It is interesting, therefore, to note that in excess of 60% of all hides sold by Tanzania Tanneries Ltd. up to 1973 were in the wet-blue stage (basic raw material) and in turn, a large proportion of these hides or skins were sold to Erhnberg, Sweden, the minority shareholder, for further processing to finished goods for sale in the European market. Here the question raised must be how much effort was made by the local management, seconded from Erhnberg, to finish processing in Tanzania and/or to locate European or other markets for the product? It is also worth mentioning that Tanzania Tanneries Ltd. made no profit during its first three years of operation, a result which contrasts with one's expectations for this type of industrial firm.

Summary. These are only three of the instances where questionable practices have surfaced with respect to companies in which the effective control rested with a shareholder or their appointed management from outside Tanzania. In all these instances, senior management (either general, financial or marketing) rested with parent company appointees. It should be noted here that an often utilised method of avoiding the close surveillance of actual prices of goods being transferred was to build into the price exaggerated freight and handling charges. An example was the case of fertilizer arriving c.i.f. Dar es Salaam from the UK with a freight cost of 99 US dollars per ton (on charter), whereas fertilizer could be shipped from Dar es Salaam to the UK at $25 per ton.

SURVEILLANCE
A control system or surveillance on a preventive basis is both difficult and expensive for developing countries.

Initially, Tanzania lacks sufficient management skills, both technical and financial, to avoid the reliance on expatriate staff in the management area. The result has been continued reliance on expatriate management both in the operational aspect, i.e. the firms, and in the control aspect, i.e. the holding parastatals like NDC. In the meantime, until 1974, the training of managers was largely left to the existing parastatals, in an on-the-job form, with the result that little progress in this area was evidenced. However, it is important here to realise that the appointment of Tanzanian nominal managers (nominal, often, as they are under-trained and inexperienced), is unlikely to materially alter the situation. In most instances, the significant skills and experience necessary in international bargaining are still an essential ingredient to avoid exploitation, and Tanzania is in short supply presently of these skills.

A second method chosen by the Tanzania Government and one which initially appears to have met with some success, was the appointment of the General Superintendence Co., a firm whose function it has been to inspect imports and exports world-wide for reasonableness of price and quality. This firm, not obviously connected to any suppliers, operates in many countries and depends for its success, to a large extent, on the known integrity of its operations. Although primarily initiated by the Tanzanian Government in late 1972 as a preventive measure to check what was, at that time, evidence of foreign exchange manipulation, it is interesting to note that upon the introduction of the import inspection procedure, over 400 import orders at specific prices were cancelled by the respective importers during the first three months of its operation. In addition, significant irregularities — mistakes, lack of knowledge and possible fraud — were noted during the scheme's two years of operation in firms such as :

Mtwara Cashew Company
Tanzania Fertilizer Company
National Textile Company
Metal Box, Tanzania
Electric Supplies Company
Kibo Paper Products
Tanzania Elimu Supplies

This service, however, is costly (1% of the f.o.b. price of goods inspected, including administration by the Bank of Tanzania) and the system is not foolproof nor necessarily the most desirable control system in the longer term.

CONCLUSIONS

Theoretically, inter-country price management represents a potentially lucrative profit area for those firms in a position to practise such pricing. The rewards for any multinational corporation are significant and the ethical questions have been avoided by referring to 'effective international financial management'. Potentially, Tanzania represents a rich ground for such practices, given the significant participation by foreign corporations both in ownership and (more importantly) management together with the existing lack of experienced Tanzanian managers.

While the impact and extent of this practice in Tanzania is not easily ascertained, the foregoing examples and the experience of the Bank of Tanzania with the General Superintendence Company would indicate a rather wide scope.

The challenge here is to minimise such practices since the cost to the country in efficiency and loss of foreign exchange reserves is likely to be significant. Moreover, if Tanzania is to control its wealth, then steps must be taken to eliminate or significantly reduce the opportunities for profit management detrimental to its economy.

Tanzania, like most other developing countries, needs at least partial industrialisation if it is ever to increase its population's living standards significantly above subsistence level. However, this very process of industrialisation creates sophisticated firms where the skills and training necessary for operation are primarily those with which these countries are inevitably in short supply: namely financial and general management skills. Tanzania has resorted to expatriate general and financial managers on a large scale and only recently initiated the types of programmes which could localise these positions in the future.

Accepting this situation as it is at present and accepting the fact that the most effective control is informed and honest management and workers, the following steps would appear to be justified, if effective and not just the present nominal control is to be exerted over present and future industrial enterprises:

1. Managing Agent Agreements should be avoided, if at all possible, as the characteristics of these agreements include:
   premium prices for the personnel included;
   personnel included are invariably seconded from the parent company and it would be unusual if their loyalty did not remain with the parent;
   they are an effective means by which a minority shareholder can maintain effective operational control.

2. Until such time as Tanzanians are adequately trained in sufficient numbers in the two critical management areas, i.e. general and financial, the utilisation of individually hired (or aid supported) skilled expatriates should be substituted for those on managing agent agreements. While the skills may not be perceptably different, and in some cases may even be slightly less, their loyalty is much more likely to be allied to the Tanzanian firm.

3. The Tanzanian Audit Corporation should as a priority assume all audits for companies with managing agent agreements. In addition, these audits should be expanded to include purchase and sale price testing by utilising the existing services of the General Superintendence Company (Tanzania).

4. The Government should strengthen the general and financial management areas of the existing holding companies — NDC, State Trading, Tanzania Export etc. — so that these organisations can properly perform their monitoring function instead of, as in the past, acting primarily as public relations and divident deposit points.

5. Existing companies should avoid purchasing through parent companies except where international tenders are in effect. In any case, all large scale purchases should be made by independent tender at all times.

6. The Government should continue its presently concerted effort of supporting local training of Tanzanians as general and financial managers. This should not imply that Tanzanians are any more able or honest than existing expatriates, but it is probable that their loyalty in most instances is more likely to rest in the country rather than in a foreign company or country.

7. Tanzania should continue to utilise the services of the General Superintendence

Company for pre-inspection and in addition, perhaps, consider using their services in the international tendering area. In addition, it is essential that, in the future, prosecution of companies and/or individuals involved in foreign exchange manipulation be instigated and actions made public. Here it should be emphasised that, to date, little activity is discernable in this area. (With the exception of one instance of an expatriate chief accountant being deported, there is no visible sign that prosecution is being undertaken.)

While some of the foregoing recommendations may not be either feasible or desirable at this time, it is essential that a start be made now if the desire of the Tanzanian Government is to protect the wealth of the country for all of its citizens.

CHAPTER 16

Corporate Structure in Agriculture and Socialist Development in Tanzania: A Study of the National Agricultural and Food Corporation*

Philip C. Packard[1]

This paper is concerned with a principal problem confronting any country embarking upon a socialist road to development: how to control the public sector in such a way that national objectives are realised. The paper attempts to illustrate this problem by drawing upon a case study of the major agricultural parastatal organisation in Tanzania. It goes on to suggest that certain measures are needed if Tanzanian objectives are to be achieved. It is therefore a paper on 'policy', and takes Tanzanian socialist objectives as its point of departure and is concerned with how they can be promoted and strengthened.

The concept of 'control' is of course complex. In the Tanzanian context control should not mean coercion, as a wide number of national statements and pronouncements on socialism preclude it. Control must therefore connote a willingness by individuals and organisations to carry out tasks, plus some mechanism — or organised system — through which tasks are carried out. Further, control should carry the additional meaning that actions must be fully consistent with objectives. In short, control means: clear objectives, actions to carry out objectives, deviations from objectives leading to 'feedback' and corrective actions.

This mechanical, or technocratic way of looking at control may beg the main question: are objectives clearly defined and widely understood and *accepted?* The answer is that 'control' as defined above does rest on political and social arrangements in the society at large, so that one can expect a public sector's behaviour and performance to be affected continually by shifting social and political forces. However, ignoring these broader problems, it is still possible to point to defects in structure and organisation within the public sector, in cases where the objectives are widely understood and accepted. This paper will dwell on this latter situation, but it does not exclude the wider problem of national objectives which are not translated into meaningful policies and actions within the public sector. Indeed the wider problem is implicit in socialist development itself, and will be taken up in the concluding portions of the paper.

THE PUBLIC CORPORATIONS ACT, 1969

The watershed for announced socialist policies and actions dates from the Arusha Declaration of 1967, after which Tanzania began to develop practical ways of dealing with the large numbers of industries which were nationalised at that time.[2] Nationalisation obviously increased the responsibilities of the National Development Corporation (NDC) and other parastatal organisations which had to deal with the former capitalist enterprises. By 1969, it was felt in government that not only must planning be articulated with greater consistency but that responsibilities for industry within the public sector needed to be clarified as well. Accordingly the President,

*An earlier version of this paper is in the *East African Journal of Rural Development,* Vol.V, No.1/2, (1972).

through Presidential Circular No.2 of 1969, laid down the principles upon which the planning system was to be responsible for public industry.[3]

The planning system was now to be such that, 'each parastatal organisation should be responsible to one ministry', and there was to be '. . . a three level structure: parastatal organisation, the sectoral ministry and the President through the central co-ordinating Ministries'. Under the Public Corporations Act (Act No.17 of 1969), the President issued an 'Order of the President' setting up the Tanzania Tourist Corporation (TTC) and the National Agricultural and Food Corporation (NAFCO). These two parastatal organisations took over some of the subsidiary enterprises of the NDC. As the names imply, the former was to be responsible for tourism, and the latter (partially) for agriculture. NDC was left responsible for industry so that sectoral overlaps were to be minimised.

For the Agricultural sector, 'Kilimo' (the Ministry of Agriculture) now had the National Milling Corporation, the Tanzania Sisal Corporation and the various marketing boards, in addition to NAFCO, reporting to it.[4] 'Government' (i.e. the executive arm of government) was empowered to add to, remove or transfer activities among parastatals *and to create or abolish any parastatal organisation.* NAFCO was to '. . . be responsible for agricultural development and food processing'.

NAFCO came into existence and began to operate during fiscal year 1969 (beginning 1 July 1969). The distinctive character of NAFCO, as of TTC and the 'old' and 'new' NDC, was that it constituted a *holding company* of operating companies. NAFCO itself was not to produce goods and services directly, but, through its organisational efforts, oversee production and encourage 'development' in the agricultural sector.

Eight enterprises were transferred to NAFCO in 1969. Table 1 lists the subsidiaries of NAFCO, (the first seven transferred from NDC, the Basotu Wheat Scheme was transferred from Kilimo). The value of these subsidiaries as measured by fixed investment constituted about T.shs 45,000,000[5] with the National Agricultural Company[6] comprising more than half of this aggregate (shs. 26,653,937). Table 1 also sets forth various kinds of information on the subsidiaries which illustrate their character.

The significance of the various magnitudes can best be seen simply by analysing the return on net assets[7] for each subsidiary. With the exception of Northern Dairies Ltd. and Arusha Plantations Ltd., all enterprises transferred in 1969 suffered losses on operations during the accounting period set forth for each in Table 1. It is true of course, that these losses are 'book values', including as costs depreciation allowances which reduced accounting profits. However, it is clear from Table 1 that most of these subsidiaries of NAFCO cannot be considered 'successes' in the normal meaning attached to commerical operations in Tanzania and elsewhere.

The great majority of these eight subsidiaries were engaged in commodity production for the export trade. The exceptions were Northern Dairies Ltd. for dairy processing and the Basotu Wheat Scheme for wheat production. NACO sold its beef to domestic butchers and to Tanganyika Packers Ltd., the latter canning this beef for export to the UK market.

Each subsidiary corporation had share capital issued as its equity. The ownership of this equity carried (via appointment of members of the Board of Directors) the authority to direct the broad policies of the corporation and to make such important decisions as allocation of any profits that arose during the course of operations. In other words, share capital, ownership and decision-making in cor-

TABLE 1
Enterprises Transferred to NAFCO, 1969-1971

Subsidiary	Ownership NAFCO %	Fixed Investment (shs.)	Profit (+) or Loss (−)	Net Assets (shs.)	Return on Net Assets	Commodities (major)	Destination	Management Agreement
National Agricultural Co.	100	23,653,937	− 359,130	21,171,809	LOSS	BEEF	Domestic (Fresh) Export (Canned)	None
Northern Dairies	80	1,434,704	+ 61,907	789,964	8.0%	MILK	Domestic	Kenya Creameries
Bukoba Tea Co.	90	6,459,643	− 183,449	3,914,848	LOSS	MADE TEA	Export	George Williamson
Arusha Plantations	100	91,827a (1968/69)	+ 22,242 (1968/69)	137,022a (1968/69)	16.2%a	COFFEE	Export	None
Kwamtili Estates	49	3,308,444 (1969/70)	− 118,721 (1969/70)	2,055,187 (1969/70)	LOSS	COCOA	Export	Expatriate Manager
Lime Products Development Ltd.	70	503,856	− 82,437	454,124	LOSS	LIME JUICE	Export	None
Mafia Coconuts	35	2,090,141	− 144,181	2,410,226	LOSS	COCONUT & FIBRE	Export	Minority ownerb
Basotu Wheat Scheme	100	4,491,127 (1970)	− 260,168 (1970)	1,899,071 (1970)	LOSS	WHEAT	Domestic	Expatriate Manager
Coastal Dairies	100	4,928,812	+ 51,862	2,051,862	2.5%c	MILK	Domestic	Kenya Creameries
Kiru Valley Development	50	1,500,000 (1970)	n.a.	n.a.		BEEF; BEANS	Domestic; Export	ADICT (UK)
Mwananchi Ocean Products (1970)	50	2,000,000 (1970)	n.a.	n.a.		PRAWNS	Export	Japanese
Kilombero Sugar Co.	100	55,451,291 (1969/70)	+ 2,364,194 (1969/70)	77,509,996 (1969/70)	3.0%	REFINED SUGAR	Domestic	HVA (Dutch)
Mtibwa Sugar Estates	50	13,047,995 (1970/71)	− 1,823,573 (1970/71)	881,093 (1970/71)	LOSS	REFINED SUGAR	Domestic	Madhvani
Total		118,961,777	− 471,454	113,275,202				

a. Fixed Assets are understated in accounts thereby showing a return on assets which is too high.
b. Management under one of owners having 25% of total equity.
c. Product period *only* 15.12.1969 to 31.12.1969.

All figures are for 1969 unless stated.
n.a. = not available.

porate matters were all looked on in the Tanzanian setting as one would look on these matters elsewhere. Differences could arise on the substance of the issues to be raised and over government policy as this was introduced via ministerial directive and conveyed through members of boards of directors who held influential, and, in many cases, key positions in government.

This is not to say that ownership carried with it *control* over management of subsidiaries in the sense that enterprise activities were substantively influenced through equity ownership (i.e. through board members representing majority ownership). There is a distinction between ownership and control of enterprises and this distinction could be of fundamental importance to the effectiveness of the planning system in Tanzania. What is important is to distinguish the 'announced' system of parastatal organisation and control from the actual system.

It can be seen from Table 1 that NAFCO had majority control in eleven of its thirteen subsidiaries.[8] The exceptions were Mafia Coconuts Ltd. and Kwamtili Estates Ltd., though for the latter 49% equity ownership constituted the major shareholders' interest among the shareholders in the enterprise.

Set against this ownership pattern was the character of management in the subsidiaries. Seven out of the thirteen had management agreement contracts with foreign organisations that in the majority of cases had non-equity interest in the enterprise. In the cases of Mwananchi Ocean Products, Mtibwa Sugar and Kiru Valley, the managing agent also participated in ownership.[9]

Management agreements were drawn up between foreign interests and the Tanzanian Government to meet the obvious need for skilled management in various parastatals. One can of course argue about the effectiveness of these agreements but the point to note here is the lack of control exercised by NAFCO over these subsidiaries.

A management agreement is a contract based on the premise that, for a fee, the managing agent will produce the proper results. In other words the management agent is similar in its origin to the institution of the board of directors: it is a form of corporate practice borrowed from elsewhere, outside Tanzania. If one is to accept the obvious fact that skilled management is lacking, and that, through contracting for management services one can expect effective results, it does follow that it is *not* in one's interest to interfere with the management of the enterprise. The likely result of this approach is that review of management actions by the board of directors will be perfunctory, so that the board in effect abdicates responsibility for shaping the operations and development of the enterprise.

These observations rest on the attitudes or preconceptions that members of the boards of directors had about managers and the functions of managements in the parastatal organisations. These attitudes and preconceptions were reinforced by the fact that, for the most part, the members of boards were civil servants. Their experience, together with their attitudes, militated against too detailed questioning or understanding of management. As civil servants, it was of importance that they were recognised to have *authority* — i.e. that they had the prerogatives as board members to direct the broad policies of the enterprises. As a corollary, it was of importance that management of corporate enterprises showed respect for the administrative system in which civil servants conducted *their* business. The 'rules of the game' within the civil service were different from those of corporate enterprise. Put another way, the sanctions a civil servant faced had very little to do with corporate 'efficiency' or profit making. Therefore, civil servants as board members, ignorant of the substance of corporate enterprise and its management, were likely to apply their own standards of performance to managers. It was, therefore, very difficult to find sanctions which would operate against managements of those enterprises which were not, in commercial terms, successful.

With respect to the managements of enterprises in which no management agreements existed (six in number), three expatriates and three Tanzanian managers were employed. The tendency existed for these managements to be more sensitive to board members *as civil servants.* This was especially pronounced in the case of Tanzanians. Expatriate managers on direct employment avoided the conflicts of interest which could be present when foreign interests entered into management agreements. In one sense, then, the professionalism of managers had a better chance to flourish within the framework of the management agreement, as compared to direct exposure of individual managers to the influence of the civil service. In another sense managers working under management agreements could at times act in the foreign company's interest and against Tanzania's. One could not assume, therefore, that management agreements were 'better' than other contracts for management. Rather, what was at issue was the *system* in which the manager of a corporate enterprise was to operate.

This can be characterised, in a slightly different way, as a confusion of roles. On the one hand, civil servants as board members supported strongly the view that they were to direct the broad policies of the enterprises. On the other hand, they accepted management and its actions uncritically, thereby abdicating any substantive control over the enterprises. In the process, 'policy' took on meanings to be found within the civil service. Sanctions could be applied for cases where corporate enterprises ran afoul of civil service practices and regulations. Concern for commercial success was still important for these civil servants but the diagnosis of the enterprise operations and suggestions for improvements in the future as well as the long term planning of the enterprise, were left to the management. It was therefore unlikely that civil service 'action' would lead to commercial 'success' in future. An enterprise which was sustaining a loss on operations could argue, for example (i.e. its management could argue) that 'expansion' was necessary to bring about future profits. The decision by the board of directors to call upon government (Treasury or financial institutions) for funds was considered a *substantive* decision. In reality it was merely an administrative decision which avoided economic analysis of why the enterprise was losing money.

We have identified 'decision-making' with respect to NAFCO subsidiaries as taking place within the enterprise (i.e. by management) and within the board of directors. The latter, of course, is also the vehicle for transmitting government policy to management. It is important to recognise that, even though government had articulated policies for the parastatal enterprise, no meaningful *control* was in fact exercised over management in the sense of translating government policy into programmes of action for the enterprise, nor was parastatal activity evaluated to determine whether government policy had been carried out effectively. For the latter, we would expect that the *raison d'etre* of NAFCO as a holding company would have been to develop programmes for action and to evaluate enterprise performance.

THE OPERATIONS DEPARTMENT: LIME PRODUCTS AND BASOTU WHEAT SCHEME

NAFCO was considered important by its subsidiaries as an agent of government.

The subsidiary had to conform to NAFCO regulations: salary scales and definitions of employment grades, cash disbursement procedures and submission of reports, for example. Also, the enterprise was dependent upon NAFCO and its procedures for acquiring funds from financial institutions and for dealings with the Treasury. All these were very similar and in most cases equivalent to civil service procedures.

The substantive problems of policy and control were another matter. The holding company was divided into separate departments which reported to the general manager.[10] The Operations Department had the broad and diffuse responsibility of following the activities of the subsidiaries. It was not clear whether this responsibility extended to evaluation of subsidiaries' activities and to the development of plans and programmes for the subsidiaries. No clear terms of reference existed in this regard; the actual structure and operations of the Operations Department tended to resemble a division of a government ministry. The Development Department did have clear responsibility for 'initiating' new 'projects' (i.e. new corporate enterprises which would become subsidiaries in NAFCO). The actual workings of this Department also tended to resemble activities within a ministry.[11]

The role of the Operations Department can be illustrated with two examples. Continued losses by Lime Products Development Ltd. led to discussion in the board meeting of solutions to this problem. Cash flow reports indicated that the processing factory was operating much below rated capacity, so that revenues were falling short of operating costs. The board, after much discussion, 'decided' that the price of lime juice paid by the foreign buyer should be raised. The proposal was rejected by the foreign buyer. Subsequently, the matter was reconsidered within NAFCO (not by the board of Lime Products), and the operations officer began a study of how to increase the supply of the raw material (limes) to the factory, to raise its production and revenues and so bring about profits on operations. The point to be emphasised, however, is that the initial approach was *administrative*, which, when rejected by the foreign buyer, led to reconsideration of the problem.

During the planting season for the Basotu Wheat Scheme, planting was delayed by bad weather, and when the weather cleared, tractors were not available in sufficient quantity to carry out the full planting programme. The matter was referred to NAFCO headquarters. It was decided that extra tractors should be hired to meet the original production target. No analysis was made of the costs of planting with extra equipment at a later date when expected future yields of wheat could be expected to be lower as compared to earlier more favourable planting dates. No analysis was made of the probable costs and returns from hiring extra tractors. It might be argued that to meet a production target is fully in accordance with socialist objectives. There is nothing in the record to suggest that government made the production target the overriding objective for BWS. The decision was an administrative one, and taken without any consideration of costs and their effects on the performance of the enterprise.

In each of these cases, operations officers had little or no role in the decision. For Lime Products, no analysis had been made of the implications of under-utilisation of capacity and the possible effects of increasing production on the profits of the enterprise. No system within NAFCO Headquarters existed for analysis of the cash flows of enterprises by operations officers.and the presentation of this analysis to the board. For the case of Basotu Wheat Scheme, no reasonably reliable information existed upon which any sensible decision could be based, but by planting late BWS jeopardised the possibility of covering the costs of planting.[12] These examples illustrate that, on the one hand, decisions about the subsidiaries involved no independent analysis of the subsidiaries by the Operations Department, and that, on the other hand, the decisions taken by NAFCO were essentially administrative and without sufficient content upon which to base commercial decisions.

THE DEVELOPMENT DEPARTMENT: SUGAR AND DAIRY EXPANSIONS

Five subsidiaries had been added to NAFCO since the break-up of the 'old' NDC and the transfer of subsidiaries in 1969. Three of these companies were in existence prior to their transfer to NAFCO. Mwananchi Ocean Products and Kiru Valley were both joint ventures subsequently entered into by NAFCO.

The two new corporations were established (i.e. incorporated) with little substantive work being done by the Development Department of NAFCO. No cash flow projections were drawn up for either intended enterprise, nor were any appraisals made of their commercial prospects. Both in effect were 'projects' which were funded by government with the management and scheme of operations supplied by the foreign interests.

NAFCO proposed to government for the fiscal years 1970-71 and 1971-72 a diverse and ambitious set of development projects.[13] It was difficult to see where these projects (including expansion of existing enterprises) fitted into any overall socialist strategy for the country, or where they could be expected, in the words of Presidential Circular No. 2 of 1969 '(to) not only pay their own way but also (to) take part in capital creation'.[14]

Two sectors, in which NAFCO was likely to participate to an increasing extent in future, were sugar refining and dairying, which can be taken as illustrative of the problems facing NAFCO.

The Five Year Plan for 1969-74 listed within the 'tentative investment programme' for NAFCO shs. 94,000,000 for 'sugar expansion Kagera-Mtibwa'[15] and the Annual Plan, 1970-71, estimated shs. 7,500,000 for the Mtibwe Sugar Estate.[16] (This latter figure was to be government's, i.e. NAFCO's, contribution to equity. Table 1 lists *total* equity at shs. 13,047,995 in the 1970-71 accounting period.) A technical and economic feasibility study was carried out by Madhvani on the Mtibwa project. There was no consultation with the Development Department of NAFCO, and the arrangements for the joint venture were conducted between Madhvani and the Treasury. There is no evidence that this study was weighted in terms of its enormous cost (over shs. 50,000,000 for fixed investment). The proposal put forward was very similar in outline to the factory for refining sugar at Kilombero: highly capital intensive and having a high import content. It should be emphasised that Tanzania was pursuing a policy of self-sufficiency in sugar production, and that the high level of production (despite the internal tax on sugar) could be expected to guarantee profits for enterprises engaged in sugar refining. The point is, however, that commercial profits from highly protected capital intensive factories beg the question: can alternative ways of producing sugar be found which are most consistent with overall development? This question was never asked, yet alone answered! To answer this question one must first ask what group is to be responsible for critically assessing feasibility studies (such as the Madhvani report), and on what basis development expenditures are to be judged acceptable or unacceptable. This takes us back once again to the socialist objectives of Tanzania and the necessary programmes to carry out these objectives.

The plans at Kilombero called for an eventual division of sugar cane growing on a fifty-fifty basis: half of the cane for the refinery to come from 'outgrowers', and half from the estate of the company. Kilombero Sugar Co. had made a concerted effort to encourage outgrowers of cane. One man from the company worked full time with the outgrowers developing liaison with the refinery. But this policy was considered a concession to the development aspirations of Tanzania; a shift towards further dependence on outgrowers was not contemplated or welcomed. The feeling of management was that cane supplies from outgrowers were 'too irregular' to base too much of the factory intake on these supplies. Implicit in this was the view that the risks of increased dependence on outgrowers were too high in terms of possible (even probable, in management's view) greater operating costs of the factory and interruptions in production schedules. It is, of course, true that higher operating costs cut into company profits and reduced the management fee paid to the managing agent. But whatever the calculations the significant point is that it was the management of Kilombero Sugar that made the decision to limit the intake of outgrowers' cane to fifty per cent of the total factory intake. This was a decision which had not been reviewed within the government, and certainly not within NAFCO. Madhvani also contemplated that a fifty-fifty split between outgrowers' and estate cane would be reached 'eventually' in the new joint venture with NAFCO.[17]

The third subsidiary to produce sugar was planned to be at Kagera, and it could have been expected that, unless policy was articulated on the character of the refinery and such matters as cane growing, similar proposals would be put forward to NAFCO by foreign interests.

The issues which surrounded this sector of sugar refining were difficult to cope with in the absence of any guidelines over the relative importance to Tanzania of foreign exchange, profits to be generated by enterprises, and the distribution of income between parastatal enterprises and out-grower producers of sugar cane. If capital-intensive, high-import-content sugar refineries were to be built and operated, difficulties still remained over the relations between outgrowers and the management of the enterprise.

Sugar refineries, like other processing plants, are built to 'standards' and men trained in engineering standards tend to concentrate on practices which are in conformity to the standards laid down. Thus, cane below 'standard' sucrose content, and in 'irregular' supply (irregular in relation to 'usual' practices) was to be avoided, by providing adequate supplies of cane for the refinery from *estate* production. Moreover, engineering standards call for a certain degree of refinement in the final commodity. These practices are not necessarily the best *economic* practices. The character of the product is after all an economic question, decided as it is for sugar in Tanzania, by the market. Higher costs of production which arise from deviations from engineering standards should be looked at carefully. Costs of outgrowers' cane to the factory are at the same time income to these outgrowers. Moreover, it is not necessarily the case that the costs of sugar from outgrowers need remain high or that supplies need be irregular. These are organisational questions, and when put into the context of the interests of both outgrowers and parastatal enterprises need to be looked at as a problem in planning. To repeat, it was the absence of articulated objectives (or guidelines) to develop and carry out programmes to realise objectives that constituted the problem.

In 1972 NAFCO had two dairies.[18] The serious long-term problem which faced these dairies was the supply of raw material. The market for processed milk exceeded the supplies of raw milk supplies. The question was whether there was to be a long run solution to raw material shortage.

In its 1971-72 estimates, NAFCO proposed development expenditure for three dairy farms, amounting to almost shs. 10,000,000.[19] At the same time, the existing dairies would be altered and expanded to take imported milk powder as raw material input. Raw milk would still be purchased from smallholders (co-operatives in some areas), but the proposed expenditures would reduce the relative importance of this latter raw material for the dairies. It was not clear what the future shape of the dairy industry, including milk processing and raw material inputs, would be. Two issues arose from the investment proposals for dairy farms and the imports of milk powder. Dairy farms would fall under NAFCO, and therefore profits from vertically integrated production of milk and its processing would accrue to NAFCO (i.e. to its subsidiaries). The whole question of income distribution, the relative profits to go to parastatal enterprises versus the incomes to be earned by agricultural raw material producers, had not been faced squarely. It was easier, of course, to invest in dairy farms rather than to try to cope with the admittedly complex problems of small-holder milk production for the market, but this did not obviate the fact that there was no overall policy on raw material supplies either by NAFCO or by the Ministry of Agriculture.[20]

Imports of milk powder eased the difficulties that managements of dairies faced in assuring supplies of raw material in the proper amount and quality. In this latter respect, dairy 'standards' were similar to standards which existed in sugar refining; and it was desirable from the industrial (processing) point of view, to reply upon standardised raw materials such as milk powder. The question could be raised, as it was raised for sugar refining: were there alternative ways of processing milk which would be less capital intensive and have less import content? Moreover, it might have been the case that 'high quality' standards for processed milk were not economic, in that the price for the commodity would be higher than it ought to be for wide-spread consumption. But wide distribution and 'lower quality' commodities are not questions resolved by resorting to engineering standards. The point of relevance for NAFCO was that these questions **were not being asked** by its Development or Operations Departments. Development expenditures for the industry were deter-mined by the 'needs' of the dairies, as these needs were seen and interpreted by the managements of those enterprises.

SOCIALIST OBJECTIVES

The terms *socialism* and *socialist objectives* have been used as the policy norms by which the planning system is to be judged. The problems with these terms can best be appreciated by quoting briefly from the main statement on Tanzanian ideology, The Arusha Declaration:[21]

> To build and maintain socialism, it is essential that all the major means of production and exchange are controlled by the peasants *through the machinery of their government and their co-operatives* (author's italics, pp.233-4).

This is followed by a list of 'industries' sufficiently comprehensive to embrace all of NAFCO's activities.

> In a really socialist country no person exploits another; and . . . the incomes derived from different types of work are not grossly divergent (p.233).

> TANU is involved in a war against poverty and oppression in our country; this struggle is aimed at moving the people of Tanzania (and people of Africa as a whole) from a state of poverty to a state of prosperity (p.235).

These are not pious statements, devoid of political and therefore economic significance. On the other hand, they are not devoid of ambiguity in their future articulation and application within the planning system.

If we speak of government as constituting the operating and control of ministries, then for NAFCO objectives are *not* articulated by government, nor is government 'control' consistent with achieving announced objectives. For if we take the broad objectives contained in the statements quoted from the Arusha Declaration above, then it is evident that it is impossible to build a programme of action which deals adequately with prohibitions against 'exploitation', against 'grossly divergent' incomes, and which speaks in the most general terms of 'poverty' and 'oppression' in Tanzania. For a parastatal such as NAFCO these objectives can well be in conflict — as they are likely to be in relation to parastatal directives to 'not only pay their own way but take part in capital creation'. Furthermore, the presumption that ownership of property by the parastatal organisation constitutes control proves misleading, in that objectives are not articulated sufficiently at the parastatal level, and the parastatal carries out no substantive evaluation of its subsidiaries.

From NAFCO's point of view, what was needed were statements from government on the requirements and restraints expected of and placed upon the parastatal organisation. To take the broad objectives of the Arusha Declaration once again, it was necessary that confusion over objectives be removed by giving 'weights' or 'priorities' to the potentially conflicting objectives (in the short run) of announced socialism. The role of administration should be to convey requirements for, and express constraints on, objectives assigned by government to the parastatal organisation. Implicit in this role of government is the *delegation* of responsibility to the parastatal for meeting the objectives. The planning system as it related to government and parastatal organisation, therefore, needs to be *decentralised* so that the parastatal organisation could be responsible for developing programmes for actions to meet stated and clear objectives laid down by government. It was clear, of course, that government could, administratively, *sanction* and therefore constrain, actions of the parastatal organisation. However, it could not easily bring forth parastatal results which were in accord with socialist objectives.

NAFCO as a holding company stood as an intermediary between its subsidiaries and government. Clear statements of objectives by government with assigned weights or priorities would have allowed NAFCO to function as the parastatal organisation was intended: to develop programmes for action to implement government policy. These programmes, to be effective, would have had to extend the concept and practice of the parastatal sector to include the subsidiaries of the holding companies: in other words, another 'tier' needed to be added to the planning system, as that system was conceived in 1969. *Delegation* of responsibility was once again needed for NAFCO to allow these subsidiaries sufficient latitude to carry out assigned objectives. As in the case of the relations between government and NAFCO, *decentralisation* was necessary in the formulation and implementation of programmes for action. Both delegation and decentralisation called for the internal reorganisation within NAFCO headquarters that we referred to earlier. Considerably more responsibility would then fall to the Operations and Development Departments in conveying policy, helping to formulate programmes for the subsidiaries and *evaluating the subsidiaries.* For the latter, evaluation was a necessary ingredient in any attempt by NAFCO to control its subsidiaries.

The most difficult problem for the public sector centred around the actual production units which were the holdings companies' subsidiaries. It was at this level of the planning system — the fourth tier — that the ambiguities and conflicts of government policy were acutely manifest. The role of management in the socialist system was most *unclear*. The socialist prohibitions which are embodied in the statements from the Arusha Declaration on exploitation — no grossly divergent incomes, and increasing reliance on local resources — all set limits to management *conceived in the conventional way*. Moreover, the directive to establish Workers' Development Councils in all parastatal organisations (Presidential Circular of 1970) further emphasised *participation* in decision-making. This was a further redefinition of the 'orthodox' management concept. It was the case that management, as a positive concept in a socialist participatory context, *had not been adequately defined*. It was necessary that concrete rules and practices be articulated at the subsidiaries' level to which workers, management and other interests, including government, could refer, and if necessary appeal. Within this framework of rules and practices, management could have followed quantitative and commercial — i.e. corporate — approaches to defining immediate goals and means to effect goals. Management would adhere to efficient methods of production within the constraints of the framework of rules and practices laid down. A problem of great importance for achieving effective management performance had to be with sanctions which could be applied (by NAFCO and government) to 'bad' management. Management re-definition called for effective but different sanctions, as compared to those which exist within a commercial milieu. This is a problem to which we return below.

The assigning of weights or priorities to government policy, and conveying and articulating policy through the 'tiers' of the planning system, would not eliminate ambiguities and conflict. At the production level of the subsidiaries, we have seen that 'interests' existed and were likely to conflict. The relation between management, workers, government and raw material suppliers (as in the case of NAFCO) were such that all had potentially divergent 'interests'. Thus, for example, higher wages might conflict with earning surpluses, or the use of locally produced raw materials might interfere with 'efficiency' as the latter was conceived and practised by management. To put it another way, weights and priorities need sufficient content to enable NAFCO to convey government policies to its subsidiaries, but it is also necessary that sufficient latitude exist for delegation and decentralisation. Thus further articulation at the subsidiary level of weights and priorities would raise the question of how potentially conflicting 'interests' could be contained *in the interests of overall socialist development.*

Workers' Development Councils were conceived in Tanzania as institutions for participation in decision-making. Therefore, within these institutions further articulation of weights and priorities must take place. It was in the nature of the ideology of Tanzanian socialism to assume that participation in decision-making could *minimise* conflicts among 'interests'. The responsibility of a holding company such as NAFCO was clear in this regard. It was to participate in decision-making by conveying government policy and helping to formulate programmes for action which would minimise conflicts among 'interests'. Moreover, conflicts which impeded efficient production ('efficiency' within the constraints of the framework of rules and practices laid down) would have to be dealt with by a NAFCO discharging its responsibility to government to see that *overall* socialist objectives were achieved as effectively as possible. Therefore, NAFCO would have, in certain cases, to *sanction* (i.e. constrain) actions inimical to the broader objectives of Tanzania.

We have pointed to the role of the administration in the present institutional structure of ownership and control at the parastatal level. At present the administration stands as proxy for those 'interests' which can be expected to conflict at the level of production. It is therefore necessary that the institutionalisation of participatory decision-making (as in the Workers' Development Councils) reflect directly the various 'interests'. The role of the administration must be therefore relegated to conveying government policy to parastatal organisations such as NAFCO and standing ready to *sanction* actions inimical to overall socialist objectives of the country.[22]

CONCLUSIONS

At the present time, it is difficult to foresee a speedy end to the conflicts and ambiguities in the planning system we have described and analysed. The parastatal organisations[23] in the agricultural sector, for example, all suffer from the difficulties dealt with at length in this paper. The possible exception is the Tea Authority, which has embarked on a programme of small-holder tea production with tea processing factories under the ultimate control of co-operatives or other local groups which will be formed to carry out production in conformity with socialist objectives. Officials of the Tea Authority have apparently grasped the enormously complex task of carrying out commercial production within the public sector.

The most difficult question facing the planning system as a whole has to do with inculcating socialist *values* in such a way that delegation and decentralisation can be made effective. To put it another way, the ideology of socialism in Tanzania must be made sufficiently concrete that individuals within the planning system can understand socialism at *their* planning level, and carry out tasks with both specific and overall objectives. If values are effectively inculcated, the planning system will be *respected,* and thus as a corollary, sanctions can be applied against 'bad' planning. In particular, it will then be possible to sanction 'bad' management. The tasks of socialist development therefore turn on building a workable planning system which carries broad objectives into realised activities. One must hope that the present corporate structure can be adapted and that corporate activitiy can be made consistent with socialist aspirations in Tanzania.

NOTES

1. Adviser on Parastatal Organisations, Ministry of Economic Affairs and Development Planning, Dar es Salaam, 1970-1972: now Director of the Training Programme, Policy Analysis Division, FAO, Rome. This paper was written while the author was on assignment in NAFCO and is, therefore, based on first-hand experience with the problems raised in this paper. Because certain Tanzanian government documents are available only to government officers, I have referred to administrative decisions, memoranda, official documents and other dicta which cannot be cited formally or quoted from at length.
2. K. Svendsen, 'Problems After the Arusha Declaration', and J.K. Nyerere, 'Public Ownership in Tanzania' in K. Svendsen (ed.) *Self-Reliant Tanzania,* (Tanzania Publishing House, Dar es Salaam, 1969), pp.209-19 and 200-205.
3. A.W. Bradley, 'The Nationalisation of Companies in Tanzania', in D.A. Thomas (ed.), *Private Enterprise and the East African Company,* (Tanzania Publishing House, Dar es Salaam, 1969).
4. Under Presidential Circular No.2 of 1969. The Tea Authority was also formed from within Kilimo, and made responsible to Kilimo.
5. Different dates for the balance sheets (given in parenthesis in Table 1) do not alter significantly the figure given of shs. 45,000,000/-.
6. National Agricultural Company Ltd., a ranching company which had inherited some of the assets and land of the post-war groundnuts scheme.

7. Profit divided by Net Assets for an accounting period.
8. Fifty percent ownership is considered to be majority control, as the Chairman of the Board is appointed by 'government' (i.e. NAFCO).
9. For Mafia Coconuts Ltd. one of the minority owners was the manager who had established the estate. This is not quite the same as a foreign interest undertaking to supply 'management' to the enterprise for a fee.
10. The four departments were Administration, Accounts, Operations and Development. The first two were clearly 'administrative' in character, as they were responsible for seeing that regulations and procedures were conformed to by the subsidiaries. The latter two were ostensibly concerned with policy, evaluation, development and implementation of plans and programmes. The point to be made about the internal organisation of the holding company is that the structure was hierarchical in that each department reported to the general manager. There was little or no horizontal contact among departments which could affect the *content* of decisions emanating from NAFCO to the subsidiaries.
11. This point is taken up below where the role of the Development Division is discussed within the context of the on-going 'development' programme of NAFCO as a holding company.
12. Obviously, costs are incurred in planting which will be returned when the wheat is harvested at the end of the season. It is necessary to estimate the time at which planting should be carried out. But the costs and returns for various estimated planting schedules must also be estimated if one is to know the possible and likely results from carrying out a planting schedule.
13. By mid-1971, the total fixed investment of NAFCO subsidiaries was of the order of shs. 130,000,000. NAFCO's development expenditure requests (for investment) were over shs. 20,000,000 for fiscal year 1970-71. (See the *Economic and Annual Plan, 1970-71*.) The development expenditure requests for 1971-72 were close to shs. 50,000,000 but this was a wholly unrealistic figure, from Treasury's point of view. Shs. 20,000,000 was the order of a fifteen percent increase in fixed investment for NAFCO's subsidiaries.
14. It is the case, of course, that for most projects estimates call for positive 'returns' (or profits) to be earned after some point in future. A project will, therefore eventually 'pay its own way' but it may take a very long time before it begins to 'take part in capital creation'. NAFCO projects, in other words, are not highly 'productive' (in planner's jargon); nor do they have a short 'payback period' (to use the commercial term).
15. *Tanzania Second Five Year Plan for Economic and Social Development, 1 July 1969-30 June 1974, Volume II: The Programmes*, p.54. The following were the estimates in total for the five year period:

Mafia Coconuts	shs.	7,800,000
Kagera-Mtibwa		94,000,000
Basotu Wheat		10,100,000
Mbeya Abattoir		400,000
Total	shs.	112,300,000

16. The estimates approved by the Government for fiscal 1970-71 were the following:

Mafia Coconuts	shs.	1,098,000
Basotu Wheat		2,880,000
Mtibwa		7,500,000
Kiru Valley		1,500,000
Mwananchi Ocean Products		1,000,000
Bukoba Tea		700,000
Lime Products		100,000
NACO		4,787,000
Other 'projects'		1,510,000
Total	shs.	21,075,000

Therefore, about shs. 3,000,000, made up of estimates for Kiru Valley and Mwananchi Ocean Products, together with 'other projects' constituted development expenditure for new projects not listed in the Five Year Plan, or not for the subsidiaries transferred to NAFCO in 1969. This is about fifteen percent of the proposed development expenditure by NAFCO for 1970-71. See Annual Plan 1970-71, p.121.

17. The schedule for increases in outgrowers' cane to be used by the new refinery at Mtibwa was peculiar in that very little outgrower cane was called for in the early years of production, followed by a rapid increase in outgrower cane in a very short time. This seemed a very difficult schedule for outgrowers to meet and was probably unrealistic.

18.   Mara Dairy Project also came under the aegis of NAFCO. It was not as yet an established subsidiary, so that it was not included in Table 1.

19.   By 'dairy' is meant the processing plant, and therefore 'dairy farm' refers to what is usually meant by a commercial farm producing raw milk for processing. In addition, one mixed-farming and ranching scheme would have both dairy cows and beef cattle. This project was also proposed for 1971-72.

20.   There was a kind of 'policy', obviously, and it had to do with what was easiest to do: deal in investment for large scale projects where NAFCO's future responsibilities would be minimal. This is the administrative method of passing along substantive decision-making on policy to the enterprise. The same approach was eventually taken with respect to Lime Products Development Ltd: increased raw material supplies from lime orchards. This avoided the problems of organising smallholder lime producers.

21.   J.K. Nyerere, 'The Arusha Declaration: Socialism and Self Reliance', in J.K. Nyerere, *Freedom and Socialism* (Oxford University Press, Dar es Salaam and London, 1968, pp.231-250).

22.   Therefore, the statement in the Arusha Declaration that control should be exercised 'through machinery of . . . government' is inadequate for effective implementation of socialist development.

23.   National Milling Corporation, Tanzania Sisal Corporation, Tanzania Tea Authority and NAFCO are all holding companies. The marketing boards and credit institutions are different in function and therefore in organisation.

Part IV

EDUCATION AND CULTURE

CHAPTER 17

Contradictions in Tanzanian Education Reform

Marjorie Mbilinyi*

INTRODUCTION

One of the three basic policy statements during the 'Arusha Declaration' period of 1967, *Education for Self Reliance,* called for reform in the form and content of schooling. Specific aspects of the education reform policies identified with *Education for Self Reliance* are given in the second section of this article, and the third section analyses policy practice. The significance and determinancy of education reform under the conditions of existence of the Tanzanian social formation are discussed in this introductory section and re-examined in the concluding section after the reform policy and practice have been discussed in detail.

'Social formation' is defined as 'the concrete articulation of a dominant mode of production with elements from other modes of production, operating at several levels (economic, political and ideological), where under specific conditions any one level (economic or political or ideological) may be predominant at a given moment'. Although the economic level ultimately determines the very conditions of existence which 'allow' for the political or ideological level to be determinant at a given moment, the political and ideological levels are never simple reflections of the economic level. The relationships between the three levels must be examined at the specific level of the given social formation conceived of in a dynamic sense.[1]

Social formations do not automatically reproduce themselves, nor do ruling classes automatically rule and keep on ruling. This is a necessary emphasis given the functionalism which predominates much critical work regarding the role of the state and schooling in particular.[2] Without a doubt, the ruling class struggles to establish and reproduce its hegemony with respect to all levels of the social formation, and these struggles are obviously against the 'opposite' struggles of the exploited classes. Under given historical material conditions, revolutionary transformations of the relations of production and the forces of production occur, based on class struggles in all levels of the social formations, although class struggles may be more determinate in one level at a given moment.

Under non-revolutionary conditions, class struggles still exist at all levels. This is to state the obvious. Its implications for correct investigation with respect to any level is that one analyses the dynamic pattern of class contradictions and class struggles in their specificity, with respect to each level and with respect to the inter-relationships between levels as well. Analysis along these lines aims to explain the way in which class contradictions and class struggles are expressed, and the consequences for the historical development of the social formation, in order to contribute to the production of theory necessary for correct revolutionary action. It is important to conceive of these levels not as self-contained structures, but rather as interrelated aspects of the social formation. This will become clear in the analysis of formal education, which conceivably represents all three levels at once.

*Senior Lecturer in Education, University of Dar es Salaam.

An important assumption of the theoretical framework underlying the analysis is that formal education and education reform are problematic, and not foregone conclusions. To ask: *who owns and controls schools?* and *whose interests do the schools serve?* are genuine questions with potentially contradictory answers. Formal education is contradictory, and the process of class struggle situated at the more specific level of educational institutions may influence if not determine contradictions situated at the level of production. Formal education is one of the fundamental institutional forms of the means of production and transmission of knowledge — and therefore must be considered *both* as an ideological instrument and as one aspect of the productive forces. Hence, analysis of schooling 'cuts across' the ideological and economic levels. At the same time, schooling is increasingly an instrument of the state and must also be posed as an element of the political level.

The 'extent' to which, and the way in which, the form and content of schooling contribute to the reproduction of the conditions of existence of the relations of production and the forces of production within a given social formation are therefore posed as problematic, the object of investigation. Education reforms of the state are of particular importance as efforts to alter the form and/or content of education in order that it *does* contribute to the reproduction of the conditions of existence of the relations of production, and to resolve contradictions which hinder the reproduction process within schooling, the workplace, and between the two.

What of the nature of the Tanzanian social formation? Only brief mention will be made here of certain significant aspects, since other contributions to this volume will have provided thorough analysis of the questions. Post-colonial Tanzania will be loosely described as an underdeveloped capitalist social formation. The capital accumulation process is based upon household peasant production of agricultural commodities and state farms based on wage labour. The surplus produced by peasants, themselves differentiated to varying degrees in different parts of the country,[3] is appropriated by instruments of the state and by foreign capital. Industrialisation has not yet developed to a significant extent, so that the proportion of the producers who exchange their labour power for a wage remains very small. Although limited hiring of labour has developed in agricultural production based on kulak peasant household production or capitalist farming, such developments are mainly restricted to certain parts of the country and remain fluid. The surplus produced on state farms depends proportionately more on mechanisation than on labour power, and has therefore not absorbed a large proportion of wage workers. The villagisation process, particularly since the 1974 drive to settle all peasants in permanent villages, may lead to a transformation of the labour process given its facilitation of direct penetration and management of peasant production. Mass education which is based on manual vocational skills oriented towards agricultural production clearly *may* enhance this penetration process, the penetration of peasant production by capital through the various instruments of the state. The argument underlying this article is that mass education reform is developing in that direction, and at the same time contradictions are developing within education and between education and production which do not allow us to predict absolutely the consequences of the reform process.

EDUCATION REFORM POLICY

In 1967 TANU declared the national policy of socialism and self-reliance, 'The Arusha Declaration', and took immediate steps to implement the policy. The

Leadership Code forbade national leaders from earning more than one salary and engaging in capitalist enterprise. The major means of production were nationalised. In order to make sure that the peasants and workers (productive labour) took full or at least partial control of economic, political and cultural institutions, later policies like *Mwongozo* and *Decentralisation* were issued. The *Education for Self-Reliance* policy was declared in 1967 to see that educational institutions were in line with socialism and self-reliance. The policy had the following objectives: orientation of schooling to the rural areas and specifically to agriculture; the development of co-operative attitudes, creativity, critical thinking and self-confidence; the unity of manual and mental work; loyalty to the party and the government and to the masses, the peasants and workers; the fostering of egalitarian values. The bookish academic education of early post-independence years was attacked as irrelevant to the economic system and conducive to stratification and class formation.

In order to achieve these policy objectives, the entry age was raised to seven years so that primary school leavers would be old enough to be productive after school. Primary school education was to be considered terminal education, 'complete in itself', and not a route to higher education. Schools were to become in totality productive units where both students and teachers produced together, and where students made basic decisions about how to produce, the inputs of production and how to distribute the proceeds of production, and where productive activities were also learning activities, not solely alienated manual labour as in the old colonial days. Both urban and rural schools were to engage in productive activities, though the specific activities they would pursue would depend on the specific location. Manual work such as sweeping, cleaning, cooking, cutting grass, which was done previously by hired labour, was now to be done by the students themselves, in particular at the University where capitalist tendencies with respect to social relationships between student and 'servant' and bookish education had advanced furthest. Examinations were no longer to be relied upon as the sole or most important measure of selection or evaluation. Instead, teacher and pupil assessments of coursework, productive activity and character were to be included. All of these suggestions as to implementation were relevant to all levels of the educational system.

Since 1967, other policy statements and resolutions have followed to clarify and implement *Education for Self-Reliance.* One of these is President Nyerere's speech 'Education for Liberation' (1974) in which he noted that *Education for Self-Reliance* tended to be descriptive and universal, and that Tanzania's education policy needed to be more specific to Africa and to the task of liberation. He noted that attitudinal change is not enough for liberation of the masses; knowledge and skills are also necessary to take control of society: 'The purpose of education is not to turn out technicians who can be used as instruments in the expansion of the economy. It is to turn out men (and women) who have the technical knowledge and ability to expand the economy for the benefit of man in society'. Economic development and increased productivity is not for the sake of 'profit', to be milked by a few members of society, but rather to meet the growing consumption and production needs of the masses, the workers and peasants. In the struggle for liberation, the workers and peasants are no longer tools of the minority, but take command of production.

The Musoma Resolutions of the TANU National Executive Committee in 1974 represent the effort to hasten the implementation of the *Education for Self Reliance* policy. Partly in response to growing peasant demands for more educational opportunity for their children, especially after the national villagisation programme, UPE 1977 (Universal Primary Education) was declared. Standard I places were to be provided for all seven year olds by 1977 all over the country. In order to implement UPE, the resolutions called for mass mobilization and self help, use of local resources for teaching and building materials, the use of older school pupils, school leavers and secondary school students, and local craftsmen, peasants and 'elders' to teach. Rapid expansion of secondary schools was also called for, adopting the same measures of implementation as for UPE 1977.

Education and *work* were to be united in all education institutions, not only to cover costs of schooling, but also to insure that youth developed the correct attitude to manual labour as future peasants and workers, and to break down the petty bourgeois arrogance of students in higher educational institutions who would become the future bureaucrats and experts.

The recruitment process to the University was changed, in order that all Form VI leavers work for two years after National Service before applying to the University. Recommendations of employers and TANU branch executive committees would be necessary as well as academic credentials. The new intake resolution implied that students of the University should be workers and peasants.

PRACTICE

Great advances have been made in the effort to change the educational system in order to serve the Tanzanian masses.[4] Primary school fees were abolished, formerly a major obstacle to equal access for all children to school. The majority of Standard I intake are seven years or older, thus ensuring that primary school leavers will be at least 14 years old.

Students of nearly all primary and secondary schools and colleges of national education engage in productive activities, mainly farming but also poultry keeping, fish keeping, handicrafts and tailoring, brickmaking, etc. In primary and secondary schools, in addition, work like weeding and cleaning is now done by the students. In this way students contribute to cutting down on school costs and also engage directly in manual productive work.

Schools are being built all over the countryside in nearly every village through the energies of the peasants and workers themselves. Initially each regional administration developed its own procedures of implementation, especially in recruiting the new teachers necessary to handle the large numbers of students entering Standards I and II. The challenge involved is immense, especially in those regions and districts where as few as 25% of the seven year olds had been enrolled in school at the time of the Musoma Resolutions. In such places, enrolment must triple or quadruple to achieve UPE. In order to meet this challenge, Standard VII leavers have become 'untrained' teachers, though they are often former 'volunteer' adult education teachers. Zonal coordinators take charge of training student teachers, each one responsible for four wards. They have received instruction in teacher education, and their efforts are also complemented by correspondence coursework in teacher education handled by the Institute of Adult Education Correspondence Section and back-up radio programme.

The Standard VII Examination retains its position as the primary measure for selection to Form I as well as evaluation. Efforts have been made to offset the exam by the use of school recommendations for Form I selection. The first group of Standard VII leavers to be selected are those recommended by schools so long as they fall within a given range of examination results, based on the ranking of all students' results. Nevertheless, the four Standard VII papers (Swahili, English, Maths and General Knowledge) remain the paramount determinant of a child's chances to enter Form I. In 1976, 5% of the Standard VII leavers were placed in Form I — as UPE proceeds the proportion will necessarily drop to less than 1% so long as the present structure is retained.

The Musoma Resolutions have been instrumental in changing the weight of National Form IV Examinations in the selection and evaluation procedure from its former position as, *de facto,* the sole selection device. A system has been devised by the National Examinations Council whereby records will be kept on every secondary school student concerning: coursework assessment based on end of term school tests and classroom work; integrated projects based on group work for sciencies, social studies and languages; and character assessments by teachers. All of these will be combined with the National Form IV and VI examination results in a fifty-fifty combination and used to evaluate and select students for higher education and employment.

Three new intakes into the University of Dar es Salaam have now been observed. Some were selected through the old Mature Age Entry scheme, which depends on performance in the Mature Age examination. Others were selected on the basis of previous academic and professional credentials, many of these being Form VI leavers with diplomas in education, agriculture, etc. In addition, employer and TANU branch executive committee recommendations were also considered. The new intake system did not mean, however, that the doors of the University were opened to peasants and workers, but rather to professionals like teachers, lawyers, technicians, etc. The new intake system is therefore in practice an upgrading programme for bureaucrats and experts.

How have the Form VI leavers been affected by the programme? Certainly many are doing jobs they had never expected nor aspired to do before. In the past a Form V or VI student with good performance could be relatively certain of getting a place at the University or in a diploma course somewhere. Now such students must compete with Form IV leavers for jobs as clerks, secretaries, untrained teachers in private schools etc., i.e. white-collar, non-manual positions.

One of the more fundamental objectives of **Education for Self Reliance** policy was to redefine primary schooling to be an end in itself, terminal, and not a means to higher education and employment. Hence the emphasis was on a relevant rural-oriented curriculum. However, it is impossible to close the eyes of the masses to the fact that, in the material conditions of today, those with steady monthly incomes employed as factory workers or sweepers, if not teachers or managers, are better off than the poorer peasants dependent on the extremities of weather and rain for an annual harvest. On the average, peasants still earn much less per month than the minimum wage, and at the same time do not share the same social facilities like dispensaries, water, electricity, etc. There are of course wealthy peasants who hire labour, use mechanised implements of production, and often branch out into trading and other activities. But the majority of peasants are poor, depending on family and other household labour for agricultural production and forced some-times to work on wealthy peasants' farms. Bureaucrats who tell peasants not to expect employment or higher education for their children are at the same time enjoying social facilities which peasants do not have access to. Their children go to better equipped schools with more highly trained teachers, and they earn incomes ten times or more than that of the peasants, incomes which in the final analysis are drawn from the labour of the peasants. To change the expectations of the masses therefore requires more than changes of school curricula.

The teaching methods and the organisation of school and classroom prevalent in primary and secondary schools are diametrically opposed to the objectives of developing creativity, critical thinking, self-confidence and cooperation. The classroom is run in bureaucratic fashion, one-man rule at the top, students powerless at the bottom. The prevalent use of the cane is symbolic of the authority relations in the school and classroom. Rote memory learning is relied upon: partly because of lack of teaching materials and textbooks; partly because some teachers lack the initiative and/or incentives to create their *own* teaching materials and books; partly because of the effect of examinations on both teachers and students; partly because the syllabus is too 'full', with isolated subtopics rather than well-integrated units related to the core principles of the particular subject matter; partly because there are too many subjects and periods. A human being learns from practice. If placed in a competitive situation, where students are ranked on a weekly and term basis according to who does 'best', if one's rank objectively depends on doing better than others on an individual basis, then it is objectively necessary for that person to behave in a competitive way. Competitive behaviour leads to competitive persons, not cooperative persons. Likewise, if students do not engage in practical problem-solving in which critical thinking is called into play, they can hardly become critical thinkers overnight. In a situation of domination and subordination, where democratic procedures of policy-making and lesson evaluation are not followed, self-confident citizens capable of making their own decisions and unafraid to criticise leadership when it has erred will not be produced. Self-confidence, cooperation, critical thinking and creativity — these attributes do not fall from heaven. They arise from social practice.

Teachers are as alienated as their students. They teach curricula which they do not design; and teach for examinations which they do not set. Teachers and their Heads carry out directives from above, in a pattern of work relationship not unlike that between teacher and student. Genuine teacher complaints about over-stocked, irrelevant syllabi are ignored or else teachers are criticised as being incompetent. Lack of feedback from the classrooms to the curriculum developers not only frustrates teachers, but it also removes the chance for creative curriculum development through practice. The way to create and enrich meaningful school curricula can only be through social practice, involving progressive teachers and students and other progressive forces in its evaluation and redesign. Decentralisation of curriculum development so that all teachers and students, together with party leaders, peasants and workers engaged in the process, linked to decentralised and transformed examinations, would provide for more meaningful curriculum and at the same time allow the full energies of teachers and students to be mobilised.

In most schools, teachers do not themselves join students in productive or manual labour. The most they do is to supervise students' work. Nor do students in most schools have control over major decisions about what to produce and the distribution of proceeds. This is especially true of primary schools but also true of many secondary schools. Students are ordered to grow this or that, in this or that location, to sell at such and such a price. Teachers buy the produce at cut-rate prices if at all and at the same time teachers and Heads are promoted on the basis of the productivity of the students. The contradictory nature of school productive activities has led students and parents in such schools to complain that students are being exploited by teachers.

There have been definite problems in providing learning experience through productive labour. Self-reliance activities are isolated from academic coursework in the timetable, and are not designed to promote meaningful learning. At the University students do not engage in any form of productive manual work. The exceptions are practical work related to agricultural and engineering courses. Here the manual work is related to coursework specialisation and is not the result of the ideological aim of engaging in manual labour *per se.* Hence, education students engage in teaching practice as a practical component of their education coursework, just as the manufacture of *bati* stoves is a practical component of engineering. But manual work in order to shed intellectual arrogance? To 'taste' the drudgery of the peasant or the productive worker? full-time work in a factory or a rural village? This has not yet appeared on the agenda.

Efforts to unite mental with manual work in education are a part of the socialist objective of destroying the contradiction between the two types of work in the division of labour. It is difficult to blame teachers for being unwilling to get their hands dirty in the fields or workshops, if other non-manual 'employees' are also not engaged in manual work of some kind as a regular feature of their work. Why should the teacher do manual work when the clerk, the accountant, the general manager and the director in parastatal and ministry do not? If we are serious about 'uniting' mental and manual labour, implementation should not be restricted to schools alone, but instead be found in all institutions, thus matching the reality of the school with the reality outside the school.

UPE 1977 has been of great significance in opening up the doors of formal education to all children. An inevitable problem will be uneven regional development in that some areas already have achieved high rates of school enrolment, with corresponding resource endowments in the way of trained teachers, teaching materials, permanent school buildings, etc., whereas less developed areas are forced to rely on lesser trained teachers and to do without books and other teaching materials.

Related to uneven development of primary school enrolment is the issue of access to post-primary levels of the education system. Less than half of the children in our public secondary schools are children of peasants, despite the fact that 90% of the population are peasants.[5] A disproportionate number of children are children of the bureaucrats and the experts. Although selection to Form I is based on Standard VII examination results, there are problems and loopholes in the selection procedure. Crude manipulation takes place, such as selling of examination papers which occurs annually. The children of bureaucrats and the intelligentsia repeat Standard VII if they fail, and then pass; or receive private tutoring at home to train for the examinations, something which peasants cannot provide themselves or afford to pay someone else to do. Moreover, urban schools, especially those found in the more wealthy areas of each city, have highly trained teachers, more facilities, more textbooks and teaching materials that are up to date. The rural schools where the majority of peasant children attend lack such resources, as do urban schools in the 'poor' neighbourhoods of the cities. Since the quota system for Form I operates only on a regional and district basis rather than by school or ward, and does not distinguish among the family backgrounds of children, it means children from better endowed schools are *necessarily* at an advantage, as well as children of the bureaucrats and experts.

Public secondary schools have not been expanding but *private* secondary schools have at a very fast rate (14% increase of private school enrolment in 1974, compared to 3% in public schools). Private schools include those run on commercial terms for special communities, those operated under different religious bodies, and those run by TAPA (Tanganyika African Parents Association — formed in the colonial period by TANU). Since private schools charge up to shs. 2,000/- per year for fees (the average is around shs. 1,200/-), only households with access to relatively high incomes can afford to send children to such schools. Recruitment for places in Form V, Colleges of National Education and other training institutions is from both public and private schools, so that those with unequal access to private schools have unequal access to higher education and employment. Large numbers of private secondary school students are 'transferred' to public secondary schools by the end of Form I or in Form II or III. They usually do not take vacant places. Instead classrooms are filled beyond capacity (up to 60 or more students in a classroom) by the 'newcomers', and new streams have even been created for these private secondary school students in public schools. The phenomenon is not restricted to Dar es Salaam, but is found in public day schools in other urban centres as well. The private school transfers are not children of peasants, they are children of the bureaucrats and experts.

Using private schools to get children into public schools is not surprising though it is contradictory to socialist policies. So long as the public secondary school system is so restricted in size, and access to higher education and employment (and therefore a reasonable and certain income) depends on access to secondary education, then some mechanism of getting children into the public school system through the back door if not the front will be found by those able to manipulate the system.

The Musoma Resolutions emphasised the need for incorporation of science and technology into all levels of the school system, and all forms of adult education. Increased skills and knowledge related to science and technology contribute to the raising of the productive forces and also increase the potential power of the producers to control the production process. Acquisiton of fundamental knowledge about the nature of the social formation, about how to investigate relations of production and the productive forces, as well as about science and technology, are essential aspects of the masses' struggles against imperialism and capitalist tendencies. In practice, however, the basic skills curriculum of adult education and primary education does not provide for acquisition of this kind of knowledge as well as the skills of critical and creative thinking. Mass education (primary and adult education) remains basically oriented toward reading, writing, numeracy and vocational manual skills separated from their theoretical content. At the tertiary level like the University, an opposite emphasis is found on bookish education separated from its practical and productive content.

The degree to which foreign capital has penetrated the education system requires careful study. All of the basic education reforms have relied in part if not in entirety on foreign sources of finance situated in advanced capitalist countries. Donors or investors (like the World Bank who *loan* the government money) influence the design, implementation and evaluation of basic education reform policies, inevitably so.[6] Grants and loans have included technical aid 'packages' which include forced importation of machinery and spare parts and other equipment as well as experts and teachers from the donar economy, at prices which are not negotiable. The development of the technical secondary schools programme is essentially revealing.[7] On the one hand, importation of this kind robs the national industrialisation programme of the challenge to develop local industry for such local needs, based on local resources at all levels (small industry as well as big industrial plants). On the other hand, imported technology promotes bourgeois forms of organisation of work. Moreover, direct influence if not control over various aspects of the education system represents a form of political struggle as to whose interests the education system will ultimately serve, those of the peasants and workers or those of foreign capitalists and national forces aligned with them. The heightened interest which the World Bank and other capitalist agencies have shown towards instruments of mass education like UPE, and the form and content of the reforms attributed to such agencies, require critical investigation.

CONCLUSION

Earlier sections have provided a brief description of Tanzanian education reform policies and their implementation. This concluding section asks the following questions: What are the contradictions and struggles which have developed within the education system? How can they be explained?

Struggles have emerged over: the nature of curriculum (including content, instruction and evaluation strategies and the structure of decision-making); school production and distribution of produce; access to post-primary levels of education; the structure of decision-making, power and control in the classroom, school and within the hierarchical education system overall. Underlying these struggles is the fundamental contradiction between capital and peasant labour, which at the level of the social formation itself becomes the contradiction between the state and peasant labour. The capital accumulation process depends upon increasing the labour intensity of peasant production in order to increase the volume of output, but it clearly does not depend on increases in labour productivity. The skills and knowledge necessary for peasant production are acquired at the site of production, the peasant household, whereas the ideological preparation to fit into a state-managed production system organised on a village-basis is being shifted to the school (UPE and adult education).

Both coercive/repressive and ideological apparatuses are relied upon to increase social control over the peasant labour force. Moreover, a high degree of coercion is found within the so-called ideological apparatuses of schooling: for example, caning of students as the predominant mode of control; fining or imprisonment of parents for not enrolling children in the new UPE programme or for withdrawing them from school later; the emphasis on student 'discipline' and punishment of student resistance to the hierarchical authoritarian structure of the school (especially at secondary school level) by expulsion from the national school system.

Other contradictions have emerged which relate to the fundamental one between capital and peasant labour. Schooling has historically raised the parents' and students' expectations of higher education and wage employment. Indeed, the primary extrinsic and material incentive for doing school work is to pass into secondary school and on to a petty bourgeois occupation. At the same time, the economic structure is based on peasant household production with a low rate of industrialisation and even lower expansion of wage employment due to the organic content of capital in the high growth sectors, where machinery and other implements of production are imported and often the raw materials as well. Hence, expectations for wage employment cannot be fulfilled. At the same time, the international terms of trade are such that peasant incomes cannot be expected to rise an appreciable amount so long as peasant production is geared towards capitalist markets.

The degree of dependence on the weather, especially rainfall, also indicates the degree to which nature has not been mastered by man, leading to constant uncertainty about the very means of subsistence. The little income peasants do receive for marketed crops is subject as well to constant struggles with the petty bourgeoisie and the state over surplus appropriation.

Many of the basic problems facing the education system and especially education reform, such as inadequate resources of qualified teachers, textbooks, and other teaching materials, and student and teacher motivation to work, can only be resolved through a reliance on public-oriented incentives leading to 'voluntary' labour power. Public-oriented incentives (often referred to as moral incentives) are entirely opposite to bourgeois incentives which capitalism depends upon: monetary rewards and other extrinsically oriented rewards and punishments based on individual competition. Given the scarce resources, material individual-based incentives cannot be relied upon by the masses nor by any but a very small minority of bureaucrats and experts. Demands therefore that teachers and students should work hard 'for the good of the nation' are contradictory under the present conditions of a highly inegalitarian income structure and hierarchical decision-making, power and control,[8] as well as the bourgeois material incentives which permeate the production system itself.

Tanzanian policy statements are clearly contradictory given the structure of decision-making, power and control developing within the schools and within the production system, and the fundamental relations of production between capital and peasant labour which appear to be strengthened by the implementation of the very same policy statements. The ideas of *Mwongozo,* of *Decentralisation,* of *Musoma* and *Education for Self Reliance* have contributed to the growing struggles by workers and peasants and students for control over state instruments like schools and over production and distribution enterprises, and over a greater share of the surplus produced by themselves.[9] The consequences of such struggles will partly depend upon adequate organisation and direction, which relate struggles in one level to struggles in all levels of the social formation, and correctly situates the social formation conceptually within the context of worldwide capitalism.

NOTES

1. Mustafa, Kemal, 'Notes Towards the Construction of a Materialist Phenomenology for Socialist Development Research on the Jipemoyo Project' in Marja-Liisa Swantz and Helena Jerman (eds), *Jipemoyo* 1/1977, University of Helsinki.
2. Althusser's work on ideological state apparatuses, see especially 'Ideology and Ideological State Apparatuses', in R. Cosin (ed.), *Education Structure and Society,* (Penguin), Harmondsworth, 1972, has suffered from this form of functionalism, as has work based on his formulation including my own (M. Mbilinyi, 'Peasants Education in Tanzania', *African Review,* Vol.6, No.1, 1976). Personal efforts to reformulate a more adequate explanatory framework in which to analyse schooling remain tentative. Criticism from colleagues and students at the University of Dar es Salaam and others has been absolutely necessary in this effort and is gratefully acknowledged here.
3. Marjorie Mbilinyi, 'Transition to Capitalism in Rural Tanzania', Economic Research Bureau Paper, University of Dar es Salaam, 1974.
4. Detailed discussion of Tanzanian education reform is found in Mbilinyi, 'Peasants Education . . .' *op.cit.,* 1976, including a more complete bibliography on the subject.
5. Mbilinyi, Marjorie *et al,* 'Secondary Education in Tanzania: Agent of Cultural Imperialism?' in Marjorie Mbilinyi (ed.), *Who Goes to School in East Africa?,* (East African Literature Bureau, Arusha, forthcoming).
6. For further discussion of the role of international capital, see M. Mbilinyi, 'Basic Education: Tool of Exploitation or Liberation?', *Prospects* (December, 1977).

7. See Christian Council of Tanzania, *Rural Vocational Education Training*, Dar es Salaam, 1977.
8. In this connection see Peter Clecak, 'Moral and Material Incentives', *Socialist Register* 1969, (London, Merlin Press).
9. For evidence of these struggles, see K.F. Hirji, 'School, Education and Underdevelopment in Tanzania', *Maji Maji* No.12, (Dar es Salaam, 1973), and Henry Mapolu, (ed.), *Workers and Management* (Tanzania Publishing House, Dar es Salaam, 1976).

CHAPTER 18

Neo-Colonial Tactics: Macmillans and the Tanzania Publishing House*

Robert Hutchison

2nd August, 1967

Mr. F.K. Burengelo,
Principal Secretary,
Ministry of Education,
P.O. Box 9121,
Dar es Salaam.

Dear Fred,
I thought I would let you know that three Liberians arrived in the office about eight days ago. Their assignment was to prepare books in Primary English, Primary Mathematics and Primary Science.
To date each author has prepared the manuscript of two books in their appropriate subjects. They are staying for six weeks so you can imagine how much work will be accomplished before they leave.
I do hope one of these days some authors will come from Tanzania and allow rapid progress in connection with the preparation of books.
My kindest personal regards,
Yours sincerely,
D.H. KAY

The message of the letter from Britain quoted above, is clear. You Africans can, you Africans should, depend on us. D.H. Kay was the man Macmillan sent out in the 1960s to set up publishing houses in as many ex-British African countries as possible. F.K. Burengelo was the first Chairman of the Tanzania Publishing House (TPH), which had been incorporated as a company on 27 April, 1966.

In the latter half of the 1960s the primary school population in nearly every African country was growing very rapidly. The number of pupils in primary schools in Tanzania almost doubled in the first ten years of Independence. A few old-established London-based publishers fought very hard at this time in competition to exploit the growing need for essential primary school textbooks in independent Africa. The potential pickings were great. A contract for a Primary Mathematics or English course for Tanzania could be worth several million shillings.

What Macmillan did, and what other publishers didn't do, was to go into direct partnership with African governments, partly in order to 'make friends' with the key Ministry of Education officials and partly in order to create the veneer of a national publishing house. The phrase 'national publishing house' has been used again and again by Macmillan-men in the short history of TPH — despite the fact that, as will be shown, for its first five years TPH was dominated and largely controlled by Macmillan and was very little more than a vehicle, albeit at times a very inefficient one, to serve Macmillan's main ends i.e. money-making.

*This is a slightly shortened, but not updated, version of an article that appeared in two parts in the *Daily News* (Dar es Salaam) on 26 and 27 July 1973. The author was for a time Manager of T.P.H. after the management agreement with Macmillans had been ended.

Versions of the TPH story, mostly larger and cruder Macmillan profit-making machines, can be found in more than half-a-dozen African countries. There have been setbacks — in 1968 a Governmental Committee of Inquiry into the Ghana Publishing Corporation reported that 'one or two activities of Macmillan' were 'not in the national interest' and recommended that Macmillan should 'be requested to negotiate the cancellation or at least a review of the Agreement'. And in East Africa Macmillan's influence has declined very markedly. But to this day Macmillan, through its Overseas Education Department, controls a major chunk of school-book publishing in the English-speaking countries of the Third World and 'English as a Foreign Language' book publishing throughout the world.

The initial agreement to set up TPH was quite straightforward. The company was to be a partnership between Macmillan and the National Development Corporation of Tanzania (NDC) which was established in 1965 to spearhead Tanzania's industrial expansion. Each patner would have an equal shareholding. Macmillan provided J.O. Parry as the first Managing Director of the company and it was agreed that Macmillan would receive an annual fee of 10 percent of the invoice value of the books sold in each trading year, in exchange for which Macmillan would:

a. advise the Company on its organisation and the appointment of staff
b. edit and advise on manuscripts and,
c. assist in the processing of all manuscripts with particular regard to format, quality of paper, printing and binding, and costs of production.

But by providing the manager and through the agreement to 'advise' and 'assist' Macmillan effectively controlled the entire operation. At the very first Board Meeting:

It was agreed that by the next Board Meeting Macmillan would have drawn up
a. a schedule of operations for the rest of the year 1966
b. a financial forecast for the rest of the year and for the year 1967. This would include an investment budget and also a cash-flow schedule.

Also, through having the Principal Secretary of the Ministry of Education as Chairman of the Board of Directors of its publishing house, Macmillan could exert much more leverage to try and ensure that the most lucrative primary school courses were given to TPH to publish. However, despite this advantage and despite calling an extraordinary Board Meeting in December 1967 to persuade 'a rather undecided Burengelo to say yes to TPH' (Parry to Kay, 14 December 1967), TPH lost the Primary English Course to Longmans. Everyone at Macmillan was 'very upset indeed' and Parry's contract was not renewed. The reason for the upset emerges from the letter written to Parry by his successor, G.J. Farmer, on 2 April 1968:

Do you remember Burengelo's refusal to discuss the course during your farewell dinner? He had the same afternoon (12 March) signed the letter to NDC which countermanded the Board resolution made in December. Now he says that TPH gave no assistance during 1967 so far as the English Course is concerned, while all the time Longmans were investing money in trial editions and had their experts on the spot. There is little documentary evidence in the file of any activity by us . . .

However, in 1968 'activity' and 'assistance' by TPH increased remarkably. 1968 was Macmillan's golden year in Tanzania with a TPH loss of shs. 371,000/- in 1967 being turned into a profit of shs. 966,000/- in 1968.

It was the combination of the new General Manager's business acumen with a considerable degree of overcharging, but most of all the effect of the new agreement between Macmillan and NDC, which brought money rolling in for Macmillan. The new agreement was not signed until 10 October 1968, but took effect from January 1968. Not only did Macmillan as shareholders receive a sizeable dividend as a result of the 1968 trading, but Macmillan also took a substantial percentage of the nearly six million shillings that comprised the TPH turnover in 1968.

A.C. Mwingira who succeeded Burengelo as Principal Secretary in the Ministry of Education was quick to point out that the new draft agreement was not in the interests of Tanzania. Prior to joining the Board of TPH in September 1968, Mwingira expressed his concern about the draft agreement in a letter to the General Manager of NDC. Several paragraphs of the letter are worth quoting:

1. **The main effect of this Agreement is to secure extortionate potential profits for Macmillan and Co. at virtually no risk to themselves. Macmillan propose to charge 12½% of the manufactured cost of the book for editorial services which are rather ill-defined. These services could be great or negligible but in either case Macmillan would be entitled to charge the full 12½%. My question is why can't most of these editorial services be done in Tanzania?**

2. **For doing normal production services Macmillan should be entitled to claim another 15% of manufactured cost. Again, irrespective of what these services may amount to! Surely, most of these jobs are the work of TPH. Please note that the General Manager will normally decide whether manuscripts be sent to Macmillan or not.**

3. **So far, for ill-defined services, Macmillan are claiming 27½% of the manufactured cost risk-free. This will be later added to the overall cost of the book on which profits will be based; so Macmillan will also get 50% of the profit on that element as well. Again risk-free, on a guaranteed market.**

4. **For advice and comment, professional or legal, Macmillan shall charge 20% of cost. But who will decide on what those costs should be in the first place? Or that they are reasonable? . . .**

5. **I cannot understand the relationship between Clause 8 of the Agreement and Clauses 9, 10 and 11. Whereas under Clause 8 the Company shall use printing facilities within Tanzania in preference to printers outside the country, Clauses 9, 10 and 11 authorise the General Manager to place printing orders where he likes and tell the Board of Directors *afterwards*. What are these printing jobs which are so high powered that they cannot be done adequately in Tanzania? Any experienced publisher could easily produce a technical answer to the questions raised in this paragraph that would sound good to the uninitiated . . . But this would be blinding with science.**

Mwingira concluded his letter with this opinion:

All in all, this agreement binds TPH to Macmillan, but in no ways does it bind Macmillan to TPH. Macmillan only stand to win handsomely. In many matters Macmillan have virtual 'carte blanche' to write their own terms, although admittedly this depends to some extent on the General manager being 'sympathetic'.

Despite Mwingira's protestations, the new agreement was, after strong pressure from Macmillan, signed by both parties virtually unamended, and the new General Manager was very 'sympathetic' to Macmillan interests. Indeed it is curious how many of Mwingira's worst suspicions have been justified. It is hardly surprising that, as Farmer reported to J.F.K. Ashby (who in mid-1968 took over as Macmillan's Overseas General Manager from Kay), Mwingira 'was not too keen to join the Board of TPH'.

The real money-spinners TPH produced for the Ministry in 1967-9 were the Primary Swahili Course Pupils' Books One to Four, the Primary Mathematics Pupils' Books One to Three, and the primary school Atlas. From 150 to 200 thousand of each of these eight books were produced. All of them except one were printed outside Tanzania, all of them involved expensive colour printing; and in the case of five of the titles Macmillan took 27½% of manufactured cost 'risk-free'.

Tanzania is an extremely poor country with a very limited budget for school books. The Ministry of National Education now recognises that these books were much too expensively produced. Indeed a more expressive illustration of the colourful contrast between production for profit and production for need would be hard to find. Ever since the production of these four-colour follies the Ministry has been struggling hard — if somewhat in isolation — to produce many more books for the same money, for since 1970 the Ministry officials have been reluctant to take any publisher's advice about anything, which has meant that such publishing expertise as exists in the country has not been fully utilised.

Three examples will illustrate how Macmillan made easy money. When at the end of 1968, TPH invoiced the Ministry of Education for 160,000 copies of Swahili Book Three *(Kitabu cha Tatu cha Kusoma)* the net price, after royalty and discount, was shs. 2/25 per copy. When, in 1971, the Ministry came to reprint the book, the price per copy to the District Councils (who purchased for the primary schools in their Districts) was shs. 1/08 per copy. Anybody who knows anything about book printing will know that the initiation cost (i.e. editorial and production work, typesetting, proofing and the preparation of film for litho reproduction) of a 30-page book, spread over a six-figure print run, amounts to only a few Tanzanian cents per copy. When one also remembers the considerable inflation in the costs of printing materials (i.e. paper and ink) throughout the world in the intervening years, one can see how well Macmillan was scoring in 1968.

Or to take another example, Macmillan's editorial and production commission for Primary Mathematics Book Four *(Kitabu cha Nne cha Hesabu)* amounted to over £3,000. By 1969 this could and should have been done in Tanzania, but as Mwingira had said, the 1968 Macmillan-NDC agreement did not foster Tanzania's professed aims of self-reliance. To a western reader £3,000 may not seem an excessive commission for one book, but at that time £3,000 represented the total annual oncome of one hundred Tanzanians.

A final example of Macmillan methods is one that lingers on in the minds of Tanzania's education officials. In 1970 TPH published 10,000 copies of each of Parts One and Two of **Secondary Mathematics Book One** for the Ministry (and about 3,000 more of each for sale to private schools and individuals). The cost to the Ministry was shs. 8/50 per copy — a total of shs. 170,000/- for 20,000 books each of about 200 pages. The books were printed in Tanzania, but the editorial work and production up to film stage were done in Basingstoke. Of the shs. 170,000/-, about one-third, £3,056, went direct to Macmillan in commission and preprinting costs. In 1971, tired of being over-charged by publishers, the Ministry of National Education took **Secondary Mathematics Book Two,** Parts One and Two direct to a printer. Book Two had about 12 percent fewer pages that Book One and the quality of illustrations and of cover design and materials were not quite so good. The Ministry paid the printer shs. 50,000/- for 20,000 books. In other words, more money went to what Ashby once called the 'writing and advising machine' in Basingstoke for Book One than was paid by the Ministry for finished copies of Book Two.

In 1970 and 1971 TPH published a few more titles for the Ministry of National Education, but by that time the Tanzanian officials had grown wise to Macmillan's profit-grabbing and the margins on the books that TPH were given to publish in those two years were very small — in some case partly because of increases in the cost of paper and cover board, TPH actually made a loss on these projects. In fact, in both 1970 and 1971 TPH sustained substantial losses. This was during the reign of the third man that Macmillan sent out to manage the company, J.P. O'Hanlon, a former private secretary to the British Ambassador in Warsaw. Indeed, Macmillan's last chance of taking substantial 'revenue' out of Tanzania was in 1971, when the Primary Mathematics and Swahili books came up for reprint.

In the event, and with good reason, the Ministry connived with Tanzania Elimu Supplies (who now have a monopoly in the distribution of books and materials to primary schools in Tanzania) to reprint these books without TPH's permission but, in some cases, using TPH's materials. There was a considerable degree of irony about this setback for Macmillan, for in 1967 Macmillan had been involved in a major scandal when trying to usurp the publishing rights of other publishers in a similar way to that in which TPH had its publishing rights violated in 1971.

While trying — with various degrees of wholeheartedness — to squeeze as much money as possible out of the Ministry of National Education and thereby impress their Macmillan bosses, Parry, Farmer and O'Hanlon were also not averse to splashing quite a lot of that money on themselves and their fringe benefits. They brought their expense account habits with them to Tanzania and set a bad example of conspicuous consumption to all.

Parry had a 'housing problem' that was costly to TPH. For some reason he paid shs. 30,000/- a year's rent in advance — to Chief Dantes-Ngua, the Regional Commissioner for Kilimanjaro Region, yet never moved into what must have been, for that rent, something approaching a palace. The 1967 accounts also show a figure of shs. 25,431/- as 'staff recruitment and accommodation costs' though no staff apart from Parry were accommodated and hardly any were recruited, and a further figure of shs. 9,213/- 'architects fees' written off' — the latter sum being for another house for Parry that was never built.

Parry enjoyed steady relations with the firm called Kanti Printing Works, which was owned and run by four brothers Patel who were all given expulsion orders from Tanzania and declared prohibited immigrants in August 1969 for customs and exchange control evasion. *The Standard,* Tanzania's English-language newspaper, on 13th August 1969, reported an official government statement describing the Patel brothers as 'smuggling gangsters'. In September 1967, Parry wrote to Macmillan that he 'planned to go on a 12-day safari with one of the Kanti partners. We intend calling on District Councils for orders, and armed with a letter of introduction from the Ministry of Education, I am sure we will be very successful'. In April 1968, Farmer sent Parry (who by then had left Tanzania) a list of nineteen invoices received from the Kanti Printing Works and added 'quite a few of these invoices have already been approved by you; but there are a number which now require verification'. Two months later Farmer wroter to Macmillan: 'There are no receipts for the relevant amounts (6 items) which together total shs. 3,542/90. Did Mr Parry think that receipts are unnecessary? We think they are necessary even had the names of the payee "transporters" appeared on the cheques. Surely as all the cheques were drawn personally from TPH No.2 account by J.O.P in cash, receipts from the "transporters" are absolutely indispensable.' Parry also bought from Kanti Printing Works 4,000 sheets of hardboard, for flannelgraphs, at what Farmer described as 'at least double the normal price' and Farmer also reports to Ashby that '£5,000 was remitted to Mr Parry by Macmillans on 19.11.67 and was, I believe, paid into Mr Parry's personal a/c No.2. When I asked him for the paying-in book and cheque book, he was unwilling to show them to me.'

It can be safely asserted that Parry managed TPH extremely badly, so badly, in fact, that Ashby told the ninth Board Meeting of the company that:

due to the mis-management difficulties Macmillan and Co. Limited were prepared to forego the commission due to them with the exception of the sum of £7,000 sterling. This sum would then be given to the company by Macmillan and Co. Limited, in order to meet any liabilities incurred by the company due to the mis-management by the previous General Manager.

Farmer was in Tanzania for two years and two months (from January 1968 to March 1970). During that time he received from TPH in salary, gratuity and allowances a total of shs. 323,336/- (before tax), or approximately shs. 150,000/- per annum. This does not include the free use of a car and an exceptionally good flat at a very low rent. But the entire TPH running costs in 1968 — including salaries and wages, office rent, advertising, postage, vehicle expenses, audit and accountancy fees, depreciation and provision for slow-moving stock, only amounted to shs. 370,936/-. So that it is fair to say that in 1968 40% of the overhead of a growing two-year-old 'national' publishing house went directly to its expatriate General Manager. This didn't satisfy Farmer who, as Ashby once expressed it to NDC, was constantly 'whining about his really quite generous contract terms'.

Macmillan also brought with them an autocratic managerial style and a discernible contempt for African capabilities and culture. 'We all know what a useless language Swahili is', Farmer confided in me when I met him in Dar es Salaam in November, 1971. Though Farmer's relations with staff were good on the whole, he ran the small company in a manner to be expected from a former Adjutant in the Baluchistan Signals. Under O'Hanlon, staff relations deteriorated badly; the senior Tanzanian complained that 'TPH is being run just like a personal enterprise by the General Manager' and that O'Hanlon treated him like 'a puppet on a string'. In 1971, the year O'Hanlon left Tanzania, TANU, Tanzania's ruling party, issued a set of guidelines covering a wide range of political questions and stressing the importance of involving people in solving their problems. They said:

The truth is that we have not only inherited a colonial government structure, but have also adopted colonial working habits and leadership methods. For example, we have inherited . . . the habit in which one man gives the orders and the rest just obey them.

Macmillan's men were part of that inheritance. There were very few staff meetings in the first five-and-a-half years of the company's existence. One man gave the orders and the rest just carried them out. Frustrations and resentment mounted.

But it was in their attempts at creative publishing that the Macmillan managers were perhaps at their most pathetic. Like most publishers, Parry, Farmer and O'Hanlon had creative and intellectual pretensions. Apart from the school textbooks — the projects from which they expected fat profits — and supplementary readers in Swahili for the primary schools, all three publishers were responsible for other books which were expected and costed to make money, but which were in the main publishing disasters.

Parry published a short biography in Swahili of the then First Vice-President, A.A. Karume. The main problem with the book was that the Tanzanian flag appeared upside down on the cover, and when this was discovered the book was withdrawn with thousands of copies unsold.

Farmer produced two lengthy English-language books — *Self-Reliant Tanzania* and *Private Enterprise and the East African Company.* Both projects were started by Parry but Farmer did most of the editorial and production work (under instructions from Basingstoke) and both books were published at the end of 1969. The contents of *Private Enterprise and the East African Company* are much more relevant to

Kenya than they are to Tanzania. Even while it was in preparation, private enterprise was being actively discouraged in Tanzania — in favour of co-operative and state enterprises of various kinds. The book, which consists of a number of essays of uneven quality, lacks unity and coherence. Five thousand copies of it were printed and, more than three years after publication, less than a third of that quantity had been sold. Tens of thousands of shillings had been wasted.

Self-Reliant Tanzania proved to be an even more costly production. It was a very long time in preparation and was out-of-date when it appeared. After being advised from Basingstoke — 'it seems to me that if it is the first book containing some comment on the Arusha Declaration then we will easily sell about 10,000 copies' — Farmer ordered 5,000 paperback copies and 5,000 further copies to be printed but not bound up, plus — and this was his *pièce de resistance* — 100 copies bound in leather with gold lettering on the spine. These latter were for presentation purposes and Farmer sent about 30 copies to a carefully selected list of people who he knew had 'an interest in Tanzania'. These included President Nixon, Bryan Campain (the manager of the Twiga Hotel which Farmer frequented), the Aga Khan, H.C. Farmer (Farmer's brother who lived in Brighton) and J.H. Wilson, then Prime Minister of Great Britain. The latter two received copies personally signed by President Nyerere, the other three had to make do with unsigned copies.

The total printing and binding costs for this book (including goldblocking) came to shs. 84,311/-. The book was presented to President Nyerere at a small ceremony on 8 December 1969. Despite all the publicity and fuss, fewer than 4,000 copies were sold in the first three years after publication and tens of thousands more Tanzanian shillings had gone down the drain.

One reason for the poor performance of both these books was a factor that Mwingira had spotted in 1968. In the 1960s, Macmillan constantly boasted about its world-wide organisation and the advantage that would accrue to African publishing houses in which Macmillan was involved through being able to distribute their new books through this world-wide network. Mwingira's comment on this was:

> **Can't TPH appoint her own distribution agents other than Macmillan? Aren't we narrowing the scope of TPH right from the word go and treating TPH simply as a micro-Macmillan Limited of Tanzania, with no outside connections outside our territorial boundaries, except under the patronage of Macmillan?**

Mwingira was right again. While TPH was managed by Macmillan men there were virtually 'no outside connections . . . except under the patronage of Macmillan', *Self-Reliant Tanzania* could probably have sold at least one thousand copies in Britain had it been reasonably promoted through a fairly conscientious agent. But Farmer largely relied on Macmillan. To the Macmillan organisation in Britain selling a thousand copies of a book from the Third World means nothing. It's hardly worth their effort (as they see it). So Macmillan bought a nominal quantity of copies for sale in the UK (100 in 1969 and a further 75 in 1971) and made scant effort to sell more. Their aim was not selling copies from the Third World, but making quick money by exploiting a glaring need. As Mwingira had said, the agreement 'binds TPH to Macmillan, but in no way does it bind Macmillan to TPH'.

TPH, the micro-Macmillan Limited of Tanzania, was, of course, Macmillan's agent in Tanzania and sold Macmillan books there. But because of the low discounts offered by Macmillan on schoolbooks, and through imposing the postal or freight charges on the African company, TPH continued, as Farmer reported, 'to lose money on nearly all of the transactions undertaken on behalf of Macmillan' at least until the end of 1968. Macmillan also dumped books. In December 1968, tens of thousands of English-language story-books that Macmillan couldn't sell in Zambia were dumped on TPH.

But probably worse in their effects than this kind of manipulation were the content and assumptions of many of the Macmillan Swahili books that TPH were obliged to sell. In 1967, Swahili became the sole medium of instruction in primary schools throughout Tanzania and so the need for Swahili books was enormous. For decades Macmillan had been publishing books in Swahili — many of them were written by colonial officers. It was these very same colonial books, plus a few books that do have literary value, that Macmillan with bland insensitivity was determined to sell in Tanzania even into the 1970s, even after the Arusha Declaration and subsequent policy statements had made it crystal clear that Tanzania had set its face firmly against the assumptions of a colonialist and capitalist society. As late as November 1968, Hudson suggested to Farmer a reprint of a book called *Uraia* (Citizenship) a book first published in 1927 and reprinted a dozen times since. (Sometimes when the book was reprinted the opportunity was taken to substitute new photographs of the Royal Family for old — indeed it would be interesting to compare the edition of 1927 and that of 1964.) TPH, the 'national' publishing house was still selling this book in mid-1971 and thereby provoked a question in the Tanzanian Parliament. Mrs B.N. Kunambi, MP 'wondered amid loud applause' why no step had been taken to withdraw the book 'which had colonial flags and also pledges of allegiance to the British Monarchs', (*Sunday News* 4 July 1971). The Minister of National Education replied that the place for such books was in a museum. This incident caused considerable embarrassment to some of the Tanzanian members of staff of TPH.

Three months earlier, in April 1971, O'Hanlon cabled Basingstoke: PLEASE DESPATCH TO US URGENTLY 35,000 COPIES OF MILANGO YA HISTORIA BOOKS ONE AND TWO 40,000 COPIES MILANGO YA HISTORIA BOOK THREE. Fortunately for Tanzanian school children, despite two reminders from Macmillan, O'Hanlon never confirmed these orders, so the books were never supplied. *Milango ya Historia* means 'Gateways of History' and the three books in this series were written by L.W. Hollingsworth and first published more than forty years ago. Even when writing for African children 'history' to Hollingsworth was almost exclusively the history of Europe, but when he turned to Africa, as he did in one chapter of Book Three, his distortions were of a predictably blimpish kind. On page 87 Book Three we find a paragraph which, translated, would read:

Black people of Africa have not made any contribution towards the progress of the world. For the past centuries, nothing of any significance has come out of Africa (except for Egypt).

Such sentiments, though now recognisable as racist rubbish to any serious historian of Africa, may well have been in accord with the prejudices of Macmillan's experienced publishers, though one wonders whether they and Hollingsworth considered profits from Macmillan and royalties for Macmillan authors to be things 'of any significance'.

The smoother faces of international capitalism often like to mouth the word 'training' when talking about their third world associated and subsidiary companies, and, sure enough, in the revised Macmillan agreement with NDC a clause about training is well to the fore:

Macmillan shall provide training facilities for selected members of the company's staff

at Macmillan's London Office, such training to consist of general refresher courses and specialised courses in editing and book production. Macmillan shall not charge any fee for providing such training facilities but shall be reimbursed by the Company for all its out-of-pocket expenses in connection therewith.

In the five-and-a-half years that TPH was managed by Macmillan men, precisely one Tanzanian was sent for 'such training'. In 1970 the managers of TPH spent more than six times as much money on entertaining (mostly themselves and visiting Macmillan staff) as on training staff.

Though TPH is potentially a very important institution to Tanzania and though Harold Macmillan continues to send a greetings cable to Dar es Salaam every Christmas, TPH is not and never has been an important part of the Macmillan empire. The operation is too small, the political climate too unfavourable and Macmillan did not even bother to mention TPH in the list of 'Companies, Agents and Representatives' in its 1973-74 General Catalogue. This is partly a reflection of the fact, that, though still a shareholder, since October 1971 Macmillan has had virtually no say or influence in the running of TPH. At that time the Tanzania Government replaced the Macmillan management with an individual manager who was appointed directly by, and was thus answerable more directly, to TPH. For the last five years the management staff has been Tanzanian.

Since then TPH has begun to face up to the major challenge of building a strong self-reliant publishing house that combines professional efficiency and financial integrity with a comprehensive and creative editorial programme. It still faces many problems: most importantly a close working relationship with the Ministry of National Education has yet to be established. But it has, in 1972, published one book that is proving very popular and is likely to have a profound impact on the teaching of history in secondary schools in Africa. *How Europe Underdeveloped Africa,* by Walter Rodney, should be compulsory reading for all Macmillan staff.

INDEX

achievements, 6, 46-57.
Agriculture, Ministry of, 141, 142, 182.
agricultural policy, 53-54, 158.
agricultural extension workers, 78-82, 125.
aid from overseas, 1, 7, 9, 11, 14, 70, 98-101, 179-183, 184-189, 225, *see also* Canadian aid, Swedish aid, US aid, West German aid.
Arusha Declaration (1967), 1, 2-3, 43-46, 115. *The Arusha Declaration Ten Years After* (1977), 6, 43-71.

bureaucracy, 5, 9, 11-13, 38, 61, 63-64, 66-67, 154-155.
bureaucratic bourgeoisie, 12-14, 90, 183.
bread factory, 6, 9, 179-183.

Cameron, D., 103.
Canadian aid, 9, 179-183.
capitalism, 14-15, 20-24, 41, 46, 87-88.
cattle, *see* ecological controls, livestock, pastoralism, ranching associations.
Chinese aid, 57.
class interests, 3, 5, 11, 12, 23-24, 44, 46, 77, 82, 93, 170-172, 223-226.
Cliffe, L., 94, 96.
Cliffe, L., and Cunningham, G., 114.
coercion, 4, 8, 66, 117, 119, 130-131.
communal farming, 2-3, 8, 32-34, 78-80, 83-84, 85, 107-109.
construction, 58.
consultants, 100, 175-178, 179-181, 182.
contradictions, 2, 11, 225-226.
cooperatives, 1, 12, 168.
corruption, 2, 147.
crops, cash, 13-14, 87-88.
crops, food, 53, 132, 133 (table), 162.

dairy products, 206-208.
Decentralisation (of the Government administration) (1972), 11, 12, 52, 116-117.
Defence Forces, Tanzania People's, 5, 39-40.

democracy, in local areas or villages, 29-30, 33-34, 40-41, 52-53.
District Development Corporations, 12.
Dodoma Region, 7, 106-112.
Dumont, R., 123.

East African Community (EAC), 39, 56.
economic dependence, 182, 185-187.
ecological controls, 8, 54, 137-141, 142-143, 146-147, 158.
education, 2, 3, 10-11, 13, 27, 48-50, 84, 217-227.
Education for Self-Reliance, 2, 3, 11, 49, 217-226.
Education, Ministry of National, 228-232.
equality, 43-44, 48, 51-52.
"experts", 7, 8, 9, 13, 34, 41, 93-98, 142, 143-144, 148-150, 159-162.

failures, 6, 53, 57-69, 186-188.
famine, 7, 82, 85, 110-111.
fertilizer, 78, 184, 188-189.
fertilizer factory (Tanga), 6, 9, 69, 71, 184-189.
foreign aid, *see* aid from overseas.
foreign policy, 38.
foreign trade, 41.
foreign consultants, 98, 146, 159.
foreign investment, 100.
Freedom and Development (1968), 4-5, 11, 24-35.

General Superintendence Company, 6, 198-199.
government agencies, 158.
government costs, 63.

health, 161.
health policy, 50-51.
Hinton, W., 86, 102, 103.
Hirji, K., 88.
housing, 59, 78, 80.
Hyden, G., *et al*, 99.